Employment Law:
An Introduction for HR and
Business Students

Second Edition

KATHY DANIELS

Kathy Daniels teaches Employment Law and Employee Relations at Aston Business School and is a tutor for ICS Ltd in Employment Law and related topics. She is also a tutor on the Advanced Certificate in Employment Law for the Chartered Institute of Personnel and Development.

She is a lay member of the employment tribunals, sitting in Birmingham. Prior to these appointments she was a senior personnel manager in the manufacturing sector.

She has two other books in print published by the CIPD: *Equality, Diversity and Discrimination: A student text* (2005) and *Employee Relations in an Organisational Context* (2006).

The Chartered Institute of Personnel and Development is the leading publisher of books and reports for personnel and training professionals, students, and all those concerned with the effective management and development of people at work. For details of all our titles, please contact the publishing department:

tel: 020-8612 6204
e-mail publish@cipd.co.uk
The catalogue of all CIPD titles can be viewed on the CIPD website:
www.cipd.co.uk/bookstore

Employment Law:
An Introduction for HR and Business Students

Second Edition

Kathy Daniels

Chartered Institute of Personnel and Development

Published by the Chartered Institute of Personnel and Development,
151, The Broadway, London, SW19 1JQ

First edition published in 2004
This 2nd edition first published 2008

Typeset by Fakenham Photosetting Ltd, Norfolk
Printed in Spain by Graphycems

British Library Cataloguing in Publication Data
A catalogue of this publication is available from the British Library

ISBN 978 1 84398 188 6

The views expressed in this publication are the authors' own and may not necessarily
reflect those of the CIPD.

The CIPD has made every effort to trace and acknowledge copyright holders. If any
source has been overlooked, CIPD Enterprises would be pleased to redress this in
future editions.

Chartered Institute of Personnel and Development, CIPD House,
151, The Broadway, London, SW19 1JQ Tel: 020 8612 6200
E-mail: cipd@cipd.co.uk
Website: www.cipd.co.uk
Incorporated by Royal Charter.
Registered Charity No. 1079797

Contents

LIST OF LEGISLATION REFERRED TO   ix

LIST OF CASES CITED   xi

PREFACE   xix

Chapter 1	THE FORMATION OF EMPLOYMENT LAW	1
	An introduction to employment law	1
	Criminal and civil law	2
	Sources of law	5
	The role of Europe	7
	Key institutions	9
	Explanation of common terms	11
	Key learning points	12
	Useful websites	12
	Examples to work through	13
Chapter 2	THE EMPLOYMENT TRIBUNALS AND THE EMPLOYMENT APPEALS TRIBUNAL	14
	The history of the employment tribunals	14
	The process of the employment tribunals	17
	The operation of the employment tribunals	21
	The role of the Employment Appeals Tribunal	23
	Increasing claims to the employment tribunals	24
	Key learning points	30
	Examples to work through	30
Chapter 3	CONTRACT OF EMPLOYMENT	31
	Who is an employee?	31
	The contract of employment	36
	Implied terms	38
	Implied terms of law	41
	Continuity of employment	46
	Key learning points	47
	Case summaries	48
	Examples to work through	49

Chapter 4	ATYPICAL CONTRACTS AND THE VARIATION OF CONTRACTS	50
	Specific categories of employees	50
	Varying a contract of employment	62
	Employing asylum-seekers, ex-offenders and those requiring work permits	63
	Key learning points	65
	Case summaries	65
	Examples to work through	66

Chapter 5	INDIVIDUAL PROTECTION RIGHTS	67
	The Working Time Regulations 1998	67
	Payment of wages	72
	The National Minimum Wage Act 1998	75
	Payment and sickness	78
	Maternity protection	78
	Statutory paternity leave	82
	Adoption leave	83
	Parental leave	83
	Time off for dependants	84
	Time off for public duties	84
	Key learning points	85
	Case summaries	86
	Examples to work through	86

Chapter 6	DISCRIMINATION (1)	87
	Discrimination	87
	General occupational qualifications (GOQs) and requirements (GORs)	94
	Victimisation	95
	Harassment	96
	Vicarious liability	99
	The Equal Pay Act 1970	100
	Key learning points	106
	Case summaries	106
	Examples to work through	107

Chapter 7	DISCRIMINATION (2)	108
	Issues specific to sex discrimination	108
	Issues specific to race discrimination	109
	Disability discrimination	109
	Gender reassignment	114
	Sexual orientation	115
	Religion	116
	Trade union membership	117
	Age discrimination	119

	Key learning points	123
	Case summaries	124
	Examples to work through	125
Chapter 8	TERMINATION OF EMPLOYMENT (1)	126
	When does a dismissal occur?	126
	Eligibility to make a claim of unfair dismissal	129
	Potentially fair reasons for dismissal	129
	Disciplinary procedure	135
	The right to be accompanied	139
	Constructive dismissal	139
	Automatically unfair reasons for dismissal	141
	Remedies for unfair dismissal	142
	Key learning points	146
	Case summaries	146
	Examples to work through	147
Chapter 9	TERMINATION OF EMPLOYMENT (2)	148
	Wrongful dismissal	148
	The differences between unfair and wrongful dismissal	151
	Termination by summary dismissal	151
	Redundancy	153
	Transfers of undertakings	160
	Key learning points	165
	Case summaries	165
	Examples to work through	166
Chapter 10	TRADE UNION LEGISLATION	167
	Trade unions	167
	Recognition and derecognition	169
	Time off for trade union duties	171
	Collective bargaining: disclosure of information	172
	Industrial conflict	173
	Consultation	179
	Key learning points	181
	Case summaries	182
	Examples to work through	183
Chapter 11	PRIVACY AND CONFIDENTIAL INFORMATION	184
	The Human Rights Act 1988	184
	The Data Protection Act 1998	190
	The Access to Medical Records Act 1998	193
	Patents, inventions and copyright	194
	Restrictive covenants	195
	Confidential information	196

Public interest disclosures 197
    Key learning points 199
    Case summaries 199
    Examples to work through 200

Chapter 12 HEALTH AND SAFETY LEGISLATION 201
Health and safety legislation 201
Duties of the employer 203
Duties of the employee 205
The employer's liability relating to claims of work-related
    stress 206
Penalties for breaches of health and safety 208
Enforcing good standards of health and safety 210
    Key learning points 212
    Case summaries 212
    Examples to work through 213

Chapter 13 STUDY SKILLS IN EMPLOYMENT LAW 214
Finding information 214
Assignments 216
Examinations 219

Index 223

List of legislation referred to

Access to Medical Records Act 1998
Civil Partnership Act 2004
Conduct of Employment Agencies and Employment Businesses Regulations 2003
Control of Substances Hazardous to Health Regulations (Amendment) 2002
Copyright Designs and Patents Act 1988
Corporate Manslaughter and Corporate Homicide Act 2007
Data Protection Act 1998
Disability Discrimination Act 1995
Disability Discrimination Act 1995 (Amendment) Regulations 2003
Disability Discrimination Act 2005
Employment Act 2002
Employment Equality (Age) Regulations 2006
Employment Equality (Religion and Belief) Regulations 2003
Employment Equality (Sexual Orientation) Regulations 2003
Employment Protection Act 1975
Employment Protection (Part-time Employees) Regulations 1995
Employment Relations Act 1999
Employment Relations Act 2004
Employment Rights Act 1996
Employment Rights (Dispute Resolution) Act 1998
Employment Tribunal (Constitution and Rules of Procedure) Regulations 2001
Employment Tribunal (Constitution and Rules of Procedure) Regulations 2004
Equality Act 2006
Equal Pay Act 1970
Equal Pay (Amendment) Regulations 1983
Fixed-Term Employees (Prevention of Less Favourable Treatment) Regulations 2002
Flexible Working (Eligibility, Complaints and Remedies) Regulations 2001
Health Act 2006
Health and Safety at Work Act 1974
Health and Safety (Consultation with Employees) Regulations 1996
Health and Safety (Display Screen Equipment) Regulations 1992
Health and Safety Information for Employees (Modifications and Repeals) Regulations 1995
Human Rights Act 1998
Immigration and Asylum Act 1999
Industrial Training Act 1964
Information and Consultation of Employees Regulations 2004
Law Reform (Contributory Negligence) Act 1945
Management of Health and Safety at Work Regulations 1999
Manual Handling Operations Regulations 1998
Maternity and Parental Leave Regulations 1999
National Minimum Wage Act 1998
Part-time Workers (Prevention of Less Favourable Treatment) Regulations 2000
Patents Act 1977

Personal Protective Equipment Regulations 1992

Protection from Harassment Act 1997

Provision and Use of Work Equipment Regulations 1998

Race Relations Act 1976

Race Relations Act 1976 (Amendment) Regulations 2003

Racial and Religious Hatred Act 2006

Rehabilitation of Offenders Act 1974

Regulation of Investigatory Powers Act 2000

Reporting of Injuries, Diseases and Dangerous Occurrences Regulations 1995

Right to Time Off for Study or Training Regulations 2001

Sex Discrimination Act 1975

Sex Discrimination (Gender Reassignment) Regulations 1999

Sunday Trading Act 1994

Telecommunications (Lawful Business Practice)(Interception of Communications) Regulations 2000

Trade Union and Labour Relations (Consolidation) Act 1992

Transfer of Undertakings (Protection of Employment) Regulations 1981

Transnational Information and Consultation of Employees Regulations 1999

Work and Families Act 2006

Working Time Regulations 1998

Working Time (Amendment) Regulations 2003

Workplace (Health, Safety and Welfare) Regulations 1992

List of cases cited

A v Chief Constable of West Yorkshire Police (2002) EWCA Civ 1584 — 114

Abadeh v British Telecommunications plc (2000) IRLR 23 — 111

Addis v Gramaphone Company Ltd (1909) AC 488 — 150

Ahmad v United Kingdom (1982) EHRR 126 — 187

Airlie and others v City of Edinburgh District Council (1996) IRLR 516 — 65

Alexander and another v Midland Bank plc (2000) ICR 464 — 205

Allied Ironfounders Ltd v Macken (1971) ITR 109 — 160

Amicus and Solent & Pratt (2002) TUR 1/168 — 182

Anderson v Jarvis Hotels (2006) EAT 0500/05 — 86

Archibald v Fife Council (2002) IRLR 651, HL — 113

ASLEF v United Kingdom (2007) ECHR 110022/05 — 8, 189

Aspinall v MSI Mech Forge Ltd (2002) EAT 891/01 — 199

Aspland v Mark Warner Ltd (2005) ET 2200483/05 — 19

Aviation and Airport Services v Bellfield and others (2001) EAT 194/00 — 77

Avon County Council v Haywood-Hicks (1978) ICR 646 — 18

Azmi v Kirklees Metropolitan Council (2007) EAT 0009/07 — 116

Babula v Waltham Forest College (2007) EWCA Civ 174 — 198

BAC Ltd v Austin (1978) IRLR 332 — 203

Baggs v Fudge (2005) ET 1400114/05 — 116

Balamoody v United Kingdom Central Council for Nursing, Midwifery and Health Visiting (2002) IRLR 288, CA — 89

Bamsey and others v Albon Engineering Ltd (2003) EAT 365/02 — 70

Barber and others v RJB Mining (UK) Ltd (1999) IRLR 308 — 71

Barlow v Borough of Broxbourne (2003) EWHC 50 (QB) — 212

Bartholomew v Post Office Telecommunications (1981) EAT 53/81 — 132

Barton v Investec Henderson Crosthwaite Securities Ltd (2003) IRLR 332 — 92

Bass Leisure Ltd v Thomas (1994) IRLR 104 — 154

Beart v HM Prison Service (2003) EWCA Civ 119 — 113

Berg and Busschers v Besselsen (1988) IRLR 447 — 162

Blackpool and the Fylde College v National Association of Teachers in Further and Higher Education (1994) IRLR 227 — 192

Blatchfords Solicitors v Berger and others (2001) EAT 25.4.01 — 157

Blue Circle Staff Association v Certification Officer (1977) ICR 224 — 168

Board of Governors of St Matthias Church of England School v Crizzle (1993) ICR 401 — 124

Bolton School v Evans (2006) IRLR 500 — 198

Booth v United States of America (1999) IRLR 16 — 57

Bouchaala v Trust House Forte Hotels Ltd (1980) ICR 721 — 134

Bowden and others v Tuffnel Parcels Express Ltd (2001) IRLR 838 — 67

Bowen v Millbank Estate Management Organisation (2007) All ER D 143 Jul — 136

Bracebridge Engineering Ltd v Darby (1990) IRLR 3 — 97

Bradford Hospitals NHS Trust v Al-Shabib (2002) EAT 709/01 — 89

Bristow and Roberts v Pinewood Studios Ltd (1982) EAT 600/81–601/81 — 157

British Aerospace v Green and others (1995) IRLR 433 — 158

British Airways v Starmer (2005) IRLR 862 — 90

British Airways Engine Overhaul Ltd v Francis (1981) ICR 278 — 118

British Gas Services Ltd v McCaull (2000) IRLR 60 — 124

British Home Stores v Burchell (1978) IRLR 379 — 131

British Nursing Association v Inland Revenue (2002) IRLR 480 — 76

British Sugar plc v Kirker (1998) IRLR 624 — 158

Brookes and others v Borough Care Services Ltd and others (1998) IRLR 636 — 162

Bullivant Ltd and others v Ellis (1987) IRLR 491 — 196

Bunce v Postworth Ltd t/a Skyblue (2005) IRLR 557, CA — 65

Burton and another v De Vere Hotels (1996) IRLR 596 — 97

Byrne Brothers (Formwork Ltd) v Baird & others (2002) IRLR 96 — 86

Cable and Wireless plc v Muscat (2006) EWCA Civ 220 — 53

Cadman v Health and Safety Executive (2006) IRLR 969 — 104

Cambridge and District Co-operative Society Ltd v Ruse (1993) IRLR 156 — 166

Camellia Tanker Ltd SA v International Transport Workers Federation and another (1976) ICR 274 — 182

Campbell v Union Carbide (2002) EAT 0341/01 — 38

Canniffe v East Riding of Yorkshire Council (2000) IRLR 555 — 106

Capper Pass v Lawton (1977) ICR 83 — 101

Carmichael v National Power (2000) IRLR 43 — 33

Carr v Alexandra Russell Ltd (1976) IRLR 220 — 146

Chessington World of Adventures v Reed (1997) IRLR 556 — 99

Chief Constable of Bedfordshire Constabulary v Graham (2002) IRLR 239 — 108

Chief Constable of Lincolnshire v Stubbs (1999) IRLR 81 — 106

Christie and others v John E Haith Ltd (2003) IRLR 670 — 106

Clark v Nomura plc (2000) IRLR 766 — 149

Clark v Oxfordshire Health Authority (1998) IRLR 125, CA — 65

Collins v Hertfordshire County Council (1947) KB 598 — 52

Commission of the European Communities v United Kingdom (2006) ECJ 7/9/06 (C 484/04) — 32, 72

Commissioners for the Inland Revenue v Ainsworth (2005) IRLR 465 — 70

Commotion Ltd v Rutty (2006) ICR 290 — 19, 60

Connex South Eastern Ltd v National Union of Rail, Maritime and Transport Workers (1998) IRLR 249 — 176

Coote v Granada Hospitality Ltd (1998) IRLR 656 — 96

Copland v United Kingdom (2007) ECHR 62617/00 — 186

Cornwall County Council v Prater (2006) EWCA Civ 102 — 33

Courtaulds Northern Spinning Ltd v Sibson (1988) ICR 451 — 40

Craigie v Haringey Council (2007) EAT 0556/06 — 54

Croft v Consignia plc (2002) EAT 1160/00, IRLR 851 — 114

Cruickshank v VAW Motorcast Ltd (2001) IRLR 24 — 110

Cunningham v BMS Sales Ltd (2007) Equality Tribunal of the Republic of Ireland — 121

Dacas v Brook Street Bureau (UK) Ltd and another (2004) IRLR 190 — 52

Dalgleish v Lothian and Borders Police Board (1991) IRLR 422 — 193

Davey v Daybern Co Ltd (1982) EAT 710/81 — 134

Delaney v Staples (1992) IRLR 191   74
Devonald v Rosser (1906) KB 728   41
Discount Tobacco and Confectionery Ltd v Armitage (1990) IRLR 15   124
Discount Tobacco and Confectionary Ltd v Williamson (1993) IRLR 327   73
Driskel v Peninsula Business Services (2000) IRLR 151   98
Dryden v Greater Glasgow Health Board (1992) IRLR 469   41
Dugdale and others v Kraft Foods Ltd (1977) ICR 48   101
Dunnachie v Kingston upon Hull City Council (2004) EWCA Civ 84   144

Eaton Ltd v King and others (1996) EAT 1353/96   158
Egg Stores v Leibovici (1976) ICR 260   128
Enderby v Frenchay Health Authority (1993) IRLR 591   103
Etam plc v Rowan (1989) IRLR 150   94

Faccenda Chicken Ltd v Fowler (1986) IRLR 69   196
Federatie Nederlandse Vakbeweging v Staat der Nederlanden (2006) IRLR 561   70
Felix Palacios de la Villa v Cortefiel Services SA (2007) C-411/05   122
Fleet v Matheson (2005) ICR 1132   66
Four Seasons Healthcare Ltd v Maughan (2004) EAT 0274/04   128
Fyfe v Scientific Furnishings Ltd (1989) IRLR 331   145

Galaxy Showers Ltd v Wilson (2005) EAT 10/11/05   19
Gascol v Mercer (1974) IRLR 155   48
Gibbs v Harris (2007) EAT 23/07   19
Gough v Country Sport (Wales) Ltd (1989) ET Case No 01075/89   79
Government Communications Staff Federation v Certification Officer and the Council of
    Civil Service Unions (1992) ICR 163   189
Gozdzik & Scopigno v Chlidema Carpet Co Ltd (1979) EAT 598/78   130
Green and Son (Castings) Ltd and others v ASTMS and AUEW (1983) IRLR 135   156
Greer v Sketchley Ltd (1978) IRLR 445   195
Gregory v Tudsbury Ltd (1982) IRLR 267   79
Gunton v London Borough of Richmond-upon-Thames (1980) IRLR 321   149

H J Heinz Co Ltd v Kenrick (2000) ICR 491   114
Halford v United Kingdom (1997) IRLR 471   199
Hare v Murphy Brothers Ltd (1974) ICR 603   146
Harrington v Kent County Council (1980) IRLR 353   128
Harris and another v Courage (Eastern) Ltd (1982) IRLR 509   132
Harrison v Kent County Council (1995) ICR 434   118
Haseltine Lake & Co. v Dowler (1980) IRLR 25   127
Hayward v Cammell Laird (1984) IRLR 463   103
Henry & others v London General Transport Services Ltd (2002) IRLR 472   48
Hepworth Heating Ltd v Akers & others (2003) EAT 846/02   62
High Table Ltd v Horst and others (1998) ICR 409   166
Hindle v Percival Boats (1969) WLR 174   153
Horkulak v Cantor Fitzgerald International (2003) EWHC 1918 (QB)   146
Horsey v Dyfed County Council (1982) IRLR 395   124
Hoyland v Asda Stores Ltd (2006) IRLR 468   86
HSE v Zeneca Ltd (1999)   3
Hudson v Ridge Manufacturing Co. Ltd (1957) QB 348   203

Husain and another v Bank of Credit and Commerce International SA (2002) EWCA Civ 82   45
Hutchison 3G UK Ltd v Mason (2003) EAT 0369/03   124

Igen v Wong (2005) ICR 931   92
Intel v Daw (2007) IRLR 346   208
International Packaging Corporation (UK) Ltd v Balfour and others (2003) IRLR 11   62
Irani v Southampton and SW Hampshire Health Authority (1984) IRLR 203   149
Irving and another v The Post Office (1987) IRLR 289   124
Isle of Wight Tourist Board v Coombes (1976) IRLR 413   45

Jagdeo v Smiths Industries Ltd (1981) ICR 47   203
James v Greenwich Council (2007) CA   53
John Lewis plc v Coyne (2000) IRLR 139   146
Johnson v Unisys Ltd (2001) ICR 480   144
Johnstone v Bloomsbury Health Authority (1992) QB 333   40, 212
Jones v Associated Tunnelling Company (1981) IRLR 477   48
Jones v Tower Boot Company (1996) IRLR 168   99
Jones v University of Manchester (1993) IRLR 218   90
Junk v Kuhnel (2005) IRLR 310   155
Jupiter General Insurance Company Ltd v Shroff (1937) ER 67   152

Kerr v Atkinson Vehicles (Scotland) Ltd (1973) IRLR 36   130
Kettle Produce v Ward (2006) EAT 0016/06   90
King and others v Eaton Ltd (1995) IRLR 199   155
Kuzel v Roche Products Ltd (2007) EAT 0576/06/CEA   198

Landeshauptstadt Kiel v Jaeger (2003) ECR 1-8389/IRLR 804   69
Langston v AUEW (1974) ICR 180   42
Latimer v AEC Ltd (1953) AC 643   203
Law Society v Bahl (2004) IRLR 799   92
Leeds Rhinos Rugby Club and others v Sterling (2002) EAT 267/01   93
Leicestershire County Council v UNISON (2005) IRLR 920   155
Leisure Employment Services v HMRC (2007) EWCA Civ 92   77
Levett v Biotrace International Ltd (1999) IRLR 375   165
Lewis v Motorworld Garages Ltd (1986) ICR 157   141
Lister v Romford Ice and Cold Storage Ltd (1956) AC 555   46
Little v Beare & Son Ltd (1980) EAT 130/80   160
Lock v Cardiff Railway Company Ltd (1998) IRLR 358   146
London Underground v Edwards (1998) IRLR 364   106
London Underground v National Union of Rail, Maritime and Transport Workers
    (1995) IRLR 636   175
Long and others v SP Dataserve Ltd (2005) ET 103200/05   186

Maidment and Hardacre v Cooper and Co (1978) IRLR 462   101
Malik and another v Bank of Credit and Commerce International SA (1997) IRLR 462   45
Mandla v Dowell Lee (1983) IRLR 209, 2 AC 548   109
Mansfield Hosiery Mills Ltd v Bromley (1977) IRLR 301   130
Marshall v Land Nordrhein-Westfalen (1998) IRLR 39   95
Marshall v Harland and Wolff Ltd (1972) WLR 899   128

Martin v SS Photay & Associates (2007) ET 1100242/07   135

Matthews and others v Kent and Medway Towns Fire Authority and others (2006) UKHL 8   56

McCartney v Oversley House Management (2006) IRLR 514   69

McDonagh v Johnson & Nephew (Manchester) Ltd (1978) EAT 140/78   146

McMeechan v Secretary of State for Employment (1997) ICR 549   51

Meadows v Faithful Overalls Ltd (1977) IRLR 330   75

Mears v Safecar Security Ltd (1982) IRLR 183   48

Melhuish v Redbridge Citizen's Advice Bureau (2005) EAT 1030/04   66

Midland Cold Storage v Turner (1972) ICR 230   168

Millar v Inland Revenue Commissioners (2006) IRLR 112   110

Montgomery v Johnson Underwood Ld (2001) IRLR 269   51

Moonsar v Fiveways Express Transport Ltd (2004) IRLR 9   98

Moores v Bude-Stratton Town Council (2000) IRLR 676   48

Morgan v Electrolux Ltd (1990) IRLR 89   146

Morland v London Borough of Tower Hamlets (2003) High Court 1.5.03   212

Morrish v Henley Ltd (1973) ER 137   45

Morton Sundour Fabrics Ltd v Shaw (1966) ITR 84   127

Moyhing v Barts and London NHS Trust (2006) IRLR 860   89

Mugford v Midland Bank plc (1997) IRLR 208   165

Murray and another v Foyle Meats Ltd (1999) IRLR 562   165

Navy, Army and Air Force Institutes v Varley (1976) IRLR 408   105

NCB v Galley (1958) 1 WLR 16   38

Nerva and others v United Kingdom (2002) IRLR 815   77

News Group Newspapers Ltd v SOGAT '82 (1986) IRLR 227   182

Norton Tool Co. Ltd v Tewson (1972) ICR 501   144

O'Hanlon v Commissioners of HM Revenue and Customs (2007) IRLR 404   113

O'Neill v Symm & Co Ltd (1998) ICR 481, IRLR 233   113

Ogilvie v Neyrfor-Weir Ltd (2003) EAT 0054/02   146

Ottoman Bank v Chakarian (1930) AC 277   45

Outlook Supplies v Parry (1978) IRLR 12   104

Palacios de la Villa v Cortefiel Servicios SA (2007) C-411/05   122

Panama v London Borough of Hackney (2003) IRLR 278   146

Parker Foundry Ltd v Slack (1991) IRLR 11   144

Pay v Lancashire Probation Service (2003) ICR 1138   188

Pearce v Governing Body of Mayfield Secondary School (2003) IRLR 512   97

Pepper v Webb (1969) WLR 514   152

Perera v Civil Service Commission (1983) ICR 428   106

Philip Hodges & Co v Kell (1994) IRLR 568   81

Pickford v ICI (1998) WLR 1189   204

Polkey v A E Dayton (1987) AC 344   137, 145

Port of London Authority v Payne and others (1992) IRLR 447   119

Post Office v Union of Communication Workers (1990) IRLR 143   182

Potter v Hunt Contracts (1991) IRLR 108   73

Purdy v Willowbrook International Ltd (1977) IRLR 388   75

Quinlan v B&Q plc (1998) EAT 1386/97   111

Quinn v Calder (1996) IRLR 126 — 48

R v Attorney General for Northern Ireland (1999) IRLR 315 — 71
R v Central Arbitration Committee ex parte BTP Tioxide Ltd (1981) IRLR 60 — 172
R v Secretary of State ex parte Equal Opportunities Commission (1995) 1 AC 1 — 8, 26, 90
R v The Mansfield Justices ex parte Sharkey & others (1984) IRLR 496 — 3
Raspin v United News Shops Ltd (1998) IRLR 9 — 150
Ready-Mixed Concrete v Minister of Pensions (1968) ER 433 — 34
Reaney v Hereford Diocesan Board of Finance (2007) ET 1602844/2006 — 115
Reed and another v Stedman (1999) IRLR 299 — 124
Reiss Engineering v Harris (1985) IRLR 23 — 4, 194
Roberts v Toyota (GB) Ltd (1981) EAT 614/80 — 133
Rolls-Royce Ltd v Walpole (1980) IRLR 343 — 130
Royal Bank of Scotland v McAdie (2007) EAT 0208/06 — 24

Safeway Stores plc v Burrell (1997) IRLR 200 — 154
Sagar v Ridehalgh (1931) Ch 310 — 40
Sahatciu v DPP Restaurants Ltd (2007) EAT 0177/06 — 146
Sanders v Parry (1967) ER 803 — 46
Scally v Southern Health and Social Services Board (1991) IRLR 522 — 44
Scott v London Borough of Hillingdon (2001) EWCA Civ 2005 — 124
Scott & Co v Richardson (2005) EAT 0074/04 — 134
Scott Packing and Warehousing Co Ltd v Paterson (1978) IRLR 166 — 133
Scottbridge Construction Ltd v Wright (2002) IRLR 21 — 76
Secretary of State for Employment v ASLEF (1972) QB 443 — 46
Shergold v Fieldway Medical Centre (2006) EAT 0487/05 — 19
Shirlaw v Southern Foundries (1939) ER 113 — 48
Shultz v Esso Petroleum Ltd (1999) IRLR 488 — 18
Silvey v Pendragon plc (2001) IRLR 685 — 165
Somjee v United Kingdom (2002) IRLR 886 — 185
Spijkers v Gebroeders Benedik Abattoir CV and another (1986) CMLR 296 — 162
Spring v Guardian Assurance plc (1994) IRLR 460 — 42
Springboard Sunderland Trust v Robson (1992) IRLR 261 — 102
St Helens Metropolitan Borough Council v Derbyshire (2007) UKHL 16 — 96
Stanley Cole (Wainfleet) Ltd v Sheridan (2003) IRLR 52 — 140
Stedman v United Kingdom (1977) 23 EHRR CD 168 — 199
Stevenson v MacDonald (1952) 1 TLR 101 — 32
Stewart v Moray Council (2006) IRLR 592 — 181
Strathclyde Regional Council v Porcelli (1986) IRLR 134 — 96
Sutcliffe & Eaton Ltd v Pinney (1977) IRLR 349 — 133
Sutherland (Chairman of the Governors of St Thomas Becket RC High School) v Hatton, and other cases, Court of Appeal (2002) IRLR 263 — 206
Süzen v Zehnacker Gebäudereinigung GMBH Krankenhaus Service and Lefarth GMBH (1997) IRLR 255 — 162
System Floors (UK) Ltd v Daniel (1985) IRLR 475 — 37

Taylor v Connex South Eastern Ltd (2000) EAT 1243/99 — 161
TFS Derivatives Ltd v Morgan (2004) EWHC 3181 — 196
TGWU and Economic Skips Ltd (2002) TUR 1/121 — 182

Thanet District Council v Websper (2002) EAT 1090/01   140, 212
Thomas v Farr plc and Hanover Park Commercial Ltd (2007) EWCA Civ 118   196
Thomas v National Union of Miners (South Wales) (1985) IRLR 136   178
Timeplan Education Group Ltd v National Union of Teachers (1997) IRLR 457   174
Torith Ltd v Flynn (2002) EAT 0017/02   68
TSB Bank plc v Harris (2000) IRLR 157   43

UNIFI and Bank Tejerat (2002) TUR1/144   182
United Bank v Akhtar (1989) IRLR 507   48
Universal Fisher Engineering Ltd v Stratton (1971) ITR 66   160

Vento v Chief Constable of West Yorkshire Police (2003) IRLR 102   93

Walker v Northumberland County Council (1995) IRLR 35   4, 206
Waltons & Morse v Dorrington (1997) IRLR 488   204
Webb v EMO Air Cargo Ltd (1994) IRLR 482   79
Webley v Department for Work and Pensions (2004) EWCA Civ 1745   58
Western Excavating (ECC) Ltd v Sharp (1978) IRLR 27   48, 140
Whitefield v General Medical Council (2003) IRLR 39   185
Whitfield v Cleanaway UK Ltd (2005)   89, 115
Whitehouse v Chas A Blatchford & Sons Ltd (1999) IRLR 492   163
William Ball Ltd v Wood and others (2002) EAT 89/01   103
William Hill Organisation v Tucker (1998) IRLR 313   42
Williams v Compair Maxam (1982) IRLR 83   157
Williams and others v Whitbread Beer Co LN (1996) CA   23
Williams-Drabble v Pathway Care Solutions Ltd (2005) ET 2601718/05   90
Wilson v Racher (1974) ICR 428   152
Wiluszynski v London Borough of Tower Hamlets (1989) IRLR 279   4

Yemens v Noakes (1881)   32
YMCA Training v Stewart (2007) IRLR 185   146
Younis v Transglobal Projects (2005) EAT 0504/05   34

Useful websites

www.acas.org.uk Advisory, Conciliation and Arbitration Service

www.berr.gov.uk Department of Business, Enterprise and Regulatory Reform

www.cac.gov.uk Central Arbitration Committee

www.cbi.org.uk Confederation of British Industry

www.cipd.co.uk Chartered Institute of Personnel and Development

www.curia.eu.int European Court of Justice

www.dfes.gov.uk Department for Education and Skills

www.dwp.gov.uk Department for Work and Pensions

www.echr.coe.int European Court of Human Rights

www.employmentappeals.gov.uk Employment Appeal Tribunal

www.equalityhumanrights.com Equality and Human Rights Commission

www.ets.gov.uk Employment Tribunals Service

www.europea.eu.int European Commission

www.europarl.eu.int European Parliament

www.hse.gov.uk Health and Safety Executive

www.incomesdata.co.uk Incomes Data Services

www.irsonline.co.uk Industrial Relations Service

www.lawreports.co.uk Incorporated Council of Law Reporting

www.scottishlaw.org.uk Scottish Law

www.scottishparliament.co.uk Scottish Parliament

www.tuc.org.uk Trade Union Congress

Preface

It is nearly four years since the first edition of this book, and in that time there have been a significant number of changes in employment law. This book has been thoroughly revised to take account of all those changes.

The book has been written specifically for non-lawyers. It presumes no prior knowledge of the subject, and is particularly suitable, therefore, for those studying employment law as part of a non-law degree such as Human Resource Management or Business Studies. It covers the entire syllabus set by the Chartered Institute of Personnel and Development for its Employment Law elective, and is thus also suitable for students studying towards CIPD membership.

Students who are required to study employment law in more depth but have no prior knowledge of the subject might also find it useful to read as an introductory text. Understanding the basic principles of employment law is a very important grounding for further study.

To make the subject of employment law more accessible for such students, legal cases referenced in the book are explained in some detail, bringing the subject to life and giving a clear illustration of each legal point in question.

In addition to understanding the facts of employment law it is also important that students take time to examine the impact of employment law on organisations. To stimulate such evaluation the book has a number of specific features:

TASK

These are activities that the student can carry out to understand more of how employment law impacts on an organisation. Many of the tasks are specifically focused on an organisation within which the student works, or an organisation with which the student is familiar.

EXPLORE FURTHER

These sections give suggestions for further study and stimulate further thought for students who wish to examine a particular issue in more detail. The sections are supported by ideas of further cases to read which are given at the end of each chapter.

EXAMPLES TO WORK THROUGH

At the end of each chapter are organisational scenarios, giving the students the opportunity to apply the legislation they have learned.

CASE SUMMARIES

At the end of most chapters there are brief summaries of additional cases which might be of interest to the student.

CHAPTER 1

The formation of employment law

CHAPTER OBJECTIVES

The objectives of this chapter are:

- to introduce the workings of employment law
- to highlight the differences between criminal and civil law
- to examine the sources of employment law
- to examine the impact of European institutions on UK employment law
- to determine the role of key institutions
- to define and explain terms commonly used in employment law.

AN INTRODUCTION TO EMPLOYMENT LAW

Employment law is one of the fastest-changing areas of the law in the UK. In the past 20 years there has been a steady increase in the introduction of legislation.

In 1979 the Conservative Government came into power with a reforming agenda. Under Margaret Thatcher's leadership it took the view that the balance of power in the employment relationship had swung too far in favour of the employee. The miners' strike in 1984/5 was a key example of this struggle of power. As a result of this concern over the balance of power a series of new employment legislation was introduced in the 1980s and 1990s. One of the key elements of this was legislation that reduced the power of the trade unions and introduced new individual rights.

In 1997 the Labour Government returned to power. Firstly, it opted into the Social Charter. The Social Charter is a declaration of member states of the European Union that they will bring in a level of basic rights (not just in relation to employment) as laid out in the 1957 Social Chapter (which is in the original Treaty of Rome). The basic rights include such things as a basic wage, the rights to be consulted by employers and the rights to join or not join a trade union. The signing of the Charter has led to the introduction of a series of changes in employment law. One of the first examples of this was the introduction of the National Minimum Wage in 1998.

It was also widely expected that the Labour Government would reverse much of the legislation introduced by the Conservative Government which curbed the powers of the trade unions. In fact, it has done very little reversal, but it has continued with the ongoing introduction of new legislation. There have been specific themes to some of these introductions. For example, the concern over the increasing difficulty for employees in balancing home and work life led to the introduction of a number of pieces of legislation known as 'family-friendly' policies.

In recent years there has been yet more legislation introduced, making some significant changes to employment practices. A good example of this is the Employment Equality (Age) Regulations 2006 that were introduced in October 2006.

This relentless change has serious implications for those involved with employment law. Employers complain that there is a never-ending amount of bureaucracy to face, and HR practitioners struggle to keep up with the changes. In this book we examine current legislation, anticipate some of the planned changes – and try to understand the impact on organisations of the major pieces of legislation.

TASK

Find out how recent changes in employment law have impacted on policies and procedures within your organisation, or an organisation with which you are familiar.

It is clear that employment law is affected by a number of external factors, and one of these is the political party that is in government. In looking at the development of employment law it is important to consider the stance taken on employment issues by the main political parties. The stereotypical view is that the Conservatives are the party of the 'employer' and Labour is the party of the 'employee'.

However, this stereotypical view might have been supported by policies in the past, but is certainly not as clear in today's political climate. Indeed, in the election manifestos during the 2005 General Election there were very few significant differences, relating to employment policies, between the major parties.

It is certainly true, however, that the development of legislation does impact on the way that the employer and employee manage their relationship. Many employers would argue that employees now have too many rights. As we work through the book, think back to this point – and think about whether the balance in the employment relationship brought about by legislation is fair or not.

EXPLORE FURTHER

All the major political parties have their own websites. Browse through the sites of the main parties, paying particular attention to their policies and manifestos. What would be the likely impact on employment law if one of the opposition parties came into power?

CRIMINAL AND CIVIL LAW

Employment law is primarily governed by civil law. However, there is some criminal law that relates to employment matters, and for that reason the issue of criminal law cannot be ignored.

CRIMINAL LAW

Criminal law focuses on the punishment of crimes, usually through proceedings brought by the Crown Prosecution Service. There is also the possibility of proceedings being brought by other bodies, such as the Health and Safety Executive. The punishment brought by criminal proceedings can be imprisonment or fines. In employment law the main cases of criminal law are brought through:

- the **Trade Union and Labour Relations (Consolidation) Act 1992**, some aspects of which relate to illegal activity during industrial action (we examine this in Chapter 10)

- the **Data Protection Act 1998** – for improper use of confidential and personal data (we examine this in Chapter 11)

- the **Health and Safety at Work Act 1974** – for criminal breaches of health and safety legislation (we examine these in Chapter 12)

- the **Racial and Religious Hatred Act 2006**, which makes it unlawful to incite racial hatred. Although the legislation relating to racial and religious discrimination (see Chapter 7) is likely to cover most situations in the workplace, there is the possibility that proceedings could be brought under this legislation as well

- the **Corporate Manslaughter and Corporate Homicide Act 2007**, which allows companies to be prosecuted if a fatality occurs as a result of serious breaches of health and safety responsibilities (see Chapter 12).

Criminal proceedings are usually first brought in the Magistrates Court. Serious offences can be referred directly to the Crown Court. Appeals on issues of fact go to the Crown Court, whereas appeals on issues of law go to the Divisional Court. From here any further appeals go to the Court of Appeal and then on to the House of Lords.

Examples of criminal cases relating to employment law are:

- *HSE v Zeneca Ltd* (1999)

  A breach of the Health and Safety at Work Act (1974) led to the Health and Safety Executive bringing a case against Zeneca Ltd. While preparing to decant a highly flammable liquid an employee suffered facial burns after electrostatic ignition of the liquid. A lack of training in electrostatic awareness was identified. Zeneca was fined a total of £5,000.

- *R v The Mansfield Justices ex parte Sharkey and others* (1984) IRLR 496

  Nine striking miners, who were members of the Yorkshire National Union of Miners, were arrested under the Public Order Act 1936. They were remanded on bail, with the condition that they did not visit any place for the purposes of picketing in relation to the existing employment dispute. They were allowed, however, to picket peacefully at their usual place of work.

TASK

During your studies take note of any employment cases you read of which relate to criminal law. It is unlikely that you will find a great number of such cases, because most employment cases will relate to civil law.

CIVIL LAW

Most employment law will fall under the remit of civil law. Civil law is concerned with resolving a dispute between two parties. Most employment disputes will be resolved in the employment tribunal – which deals only with civil cases. In resolving the dispute a monetary award can be given to the wronged party (referred to as 'compensation' or 'damages'), and in some cases an injunction can be made. Civil law is based on the law of *contract*, of *tort*, and of *property*.

Contract

In employment law a contract is made between the employer and the employees, consisting of a number of obligations on both sides of the agreement. If one of those obligations is breached in some way, there can be a dispute under the law of contract. For example:

- *Wiluszynski v London Borough of Tower Hamlets* (1989) IRLR 279

  Following a dispute between the employer and the recognised trade union, Wiluszynski refused to carry out all his duties as agreed under his contract of employment. Although he carried on performing other duties the employer decided to withhold all his wages. The Court of Appeal ruled that the employer was allowed to take this action because Wiluszynski was not acting in accordance with his contract of employment.

Tort

A tort is a wrong, such as the wrong of negligence. If an employee is injured at work through the negligence of the employer (the employer has provided inadequate equipment, for example), a claim would be made based on the law of tort. For instance:

- *Walker v Northumberland County Council* (1995) IRLR 35

  In this case Walker was employed as a social worker by Northumberland County Council. Because of the stressful nature of his work, and the lack of support he received, he suffered a nervous breakdown. While he was absent from work due to this breakdown he agreed with his employers a series of measures to help him in his work. He returned to work, but the support agreed was withdrawn. Walker suffered a further breakdown. It was found that his employers had been negligent in not giving him the support that he needed to carry out his duties. (We examine this case in more detail in Chapter 12.)

Property

If an employee uses inventions designed at work – under the employer's copyright – for personal gain, there can be a claim under the law of property. For example:

- *Reiss Engineering v Harris* (1985) IRLR 23

  Harris was a sales manager working for a company that sold valves. Reiss Engineering did not have a research and design department, and had never designed a valve or improvements or modifications to a valve. Harris invented a new type of valve. Reiss Engineering claimed that the patent for the new valve should belong to them, because they claimed Harris had invented it during the course of his normal duties. The court held that it had not been part of Harris's normal duties to invent anything, and hence the patent belonged to Harris. (We examine this case in more detail in Chapter 11.)

In employment law most cases are first heard in an employment tribunal. If there is an appeal, which must be based on a point of law, it is referred to the Employment Appeals Tribunal. Any further appeal is directed to the Court of Appeal and then to the House of Lords.

A civil law claim that is not related to employment is first brought in the County Court. Any appeal is then directed to the Court of Appeal and finally the House of Lords.

Not all employment-related issues must start in an employment tribunal. For example, certain cases of wrongful dismissal (see Chapter 9) can be brought in the County Court or the High Court, as well as in the employment tribunal.

SOURCES OF LAW

Legislation is created in a number of different ways:

STATUTE

Statutes are Acts of Parliament, and they are the main source of legislation. Recent examples of statute are the **Employment Relations Act 2004** and the **Employment Equality (Age) Regulations 2006.**

An Act of Parliament has to go through a lengthy process before it is finally accepted as statute. Typically, it starts as a Green Paper, which is a consultation document. This Green Paper will pass through a number of parliamentary committees, depending on the range of its content. When all comments have been received and considered, it is issued as a White Paper – which is a statement of the government's policy. This White Paper (known as a bill) is then discussed and reviewed by the House of Commons, and then the House of Lords, before being finalised. It becomes a statute when it receives royal assent.

Some statutes are implemented immediately. However, it is more common for there to be a time-lag between the royal assent and the enforcement of the content. This is usually for the practical reason that employers need time to implement the requirements.

For example, the Employment Act came into existence in October 2002. Within the Act there were new provisions relating to maternity leave that were only enforced for women whose babies were due after 6 April 2003, and new dismissal, disciplinary and grievance rules that did not come into force until October 2004.

Statute is created for a variety of reasons. Some are directly related to the political policies of the party in government – eg the National Minimum Wage Act 1998 was a result of a manifesto promise of the Labour Government to put in place a minimum basic wage (which was also driven by the signing of the Social Charter).

Some statute results from British membership of the European Union – as we discuss later in this chapter.

Some statute results from concern regarding specific aspects of working life in the UK. For example, a significant part of the Employment Act 2002 relates to family-friendly policies (which the Labour Government highlights as a major concern). Prior to introducing this legislation the

Government undertook a survey of working life. It picked up on concerns about the quality of family life, and concerns about the amount of time parents were spending with their children. The content relating to maternity leave, paternity leave, adoption leave and flexible working were all intended to address this issue of the balance between working and family life.

CODES OF PRACTICE

Codes of practice are not law, but if they are broken, the court would expect to see a good reason for such a breach. They are, therefore, important and should be breached only if there is good reason for doing so. The most commonly quoted example of a code of practice, although not relevant to employment law, is the Highway Code.

Employment codes are issued by a number of bodies such as Acas (see below).

TASK

Look at the Acas website and read one of the codes of practice that are there: www.acas.org.uk. Become familiar with the style and content of codes of practice.

COMMON LAW

This is also known as case law. Case law is law based on precedents following from judgments in previous cases. A precedent set by a court can be 'binding' or 'persuasive'.

It is 'binding' if it is set by the Court of Appeal, House of Lords or European Court of Justice. This means that any court hearing a case based on similar principles has to make its judgment in accordance with the principle that has already been set. This only changes if an appeal is made against a decision that results in a change in the decision, or if future statute alters the principle that has been set.

It is 'persuasive' if the judgment comes from the ruling of a lower level of court. In such a situation due respect must be given to a previous judgment but, if there is good reason, the principle of the ruling does not have to be followed.

Most cases give judgments specific to the person before them. For example, I could take a case to the employment tribunal saying that my contract of employment expressly stated that I should be paid my full holiday entitlement on leaving the company. The company did not pay that holiday pay. There is no dispute over the calculation of the holiday pay: the only issue is whether the money should have been paid. The tribunal reads the contract, agrees that the money is owed and orders that it should be paid. That judgment affects me alone.

However, a case could be brought to the Court of Appeal where there is a disagreement over the legal definition of holiday pay (as defined in the Working Time Regulations 1998). In determining what the correct definition of holiday pay is, the Court of Appeal is determining how the law should be interpreted – and is setting a precedent that is then binding on any subsequent cases relating to the definition of holiday pay. This is case law.

Case law is interpreted by the most senior court in the relevant legal system, so if a decision is overturned by an appeal court, that decision forms case law and not the decisions of previous courts. And if one of the parties thinks that the decision made in an employment tribunal is wrong, it can appeal to the Employment Appeals Tribunal (EAT). The EAT reviews the decision made by the employment tribunal and either supports it or changes it. If the EAT changes it, the EAT's interpretation takes precedence over the employment tribunal, and the case law is based on the EAT's decision.

If one party is unhappy with the reversal of the decision made by the EAT, he/she can appeal to the Court of Appeal. Any decision made by the Court of Appeal overrules the EAT. Ultimately, a decision of the House of Lords overrules all previous decisions.

THE ROLE OF EUROPE

The UK has been a member of the European Community since 1973. As already noted, the Labour Government signed the Social Charter on coming into power in 1997. The Social Charter is a declaration that the member state will adhere to a basic level of rights as spelled out in the 1957 Social Chapter. These basic rights include a right to a basic wage, the rights to join or not join a trade union, the right to strike, and the right to be consulted by employers. The Social Chapter is important because it is the basis for many of the Directives that have been introduced by the EC.

European law is given precedence over UK national law. Therefore, if there is any dispute between UK national law and European law, the European law will be enforced. There are four main sources of European law:

- *Treaties* are the primary source of all European law. A treaty is a framework within which a member state can implement legislation. The first treaty was the Treaty of Rome (1957) which created the European Economic Community (as it was then named). Subsequent treaties include the Maastricht Treaty (1992) and the Treaty of Amsterdam (1997).

- *Regulations* automatically become part of the national laws of the member state by virtue of treaties previously entered into. There might be a requirement for the member state to pass legislation to incorporate them. Examples of Regulations are the Working Time Regulations 1998 and the Part-time Workers (Prevention of Less Favourable Treatment) Regulations 2000.

- *Directives* lay down objectives that the member state is 'directed' to implement by making them part of national law. The member state decides exactly how it will achieve this. There is usually a time period given in which to carry out the implementation, and there have been occasions on which an extension to this time period has been negotiated. If the member state does not implement the Directive in the given time period, it can be forced to pay damages to any individual who has suffered loss as a result of the non-implementation. Examples of Directives are the Working Time Directive 1993 and the Information and Consultation Directive 2002.

- *Decisions* relate to specific member states, individuals or organisations. They are binding.

TASK

Find further examples of Treaties, Regulations, Directives and Decisions. Consider the impact that each of your examples had on UK legislation

Within the European Community the European Commission introduces new legislation. The European Parliament has the right to be consulted over any proposals but, unlike the UK Parliament, cannot introduce any proposals.

The European Court of Justice (ECJ) has an important role in defining and interpreting EC law. The final court of appeal in a member state can refer a case to the ECJ for an interpretation of a specific aspect of European law. The ECJ makes the ruling and then returns it to the courts in the member state for that ruling to be acted upon.

A good example of this is *R v Secretary of State ex parte Equal Opportunities Commission* (1994) 1 AC 1.

In this case the Equal Opportunities Commission (EOC) claimed that the differing qualifying periods to bring a claim of unfair dismissal for full-time and part-time employees was discriminatory. At the time full-time workers had to have two years' continuous service to bring a claim for unfair dismissal, whereas part-time workers had to have five years' continuous service.

The EOC showed that significantly more women than men have part-time jobs, and the law therefore discriminated against female employees. The case was referred to the ECJ who judged that the different qualifying periods were discriminatory against women, and so had to be changed. The ruling was referred back to the UK, who subsequently introduced new legislation eliminating the difference in qualifying period for full- and part-time workers.

(Note: the current qualifying period is one year for both full- and part-time workers.)

 EXPLORE FURTHER

What do you think the impact would have been on UK law if the ECJ had not been there to rule in the case of *R v Secretary of State ex parte Equal Opportunities Commission* (1994)? What ongoing repercussions might this have had?

The ECJ carries out a number of additional functions including:

- hearing challenges that a member state has failed to fulfil some aspect of a treaty. An individual or a group of individuals can bring these challenges
- hearing complaints regarding the way in which European law has been interpreted and applied.

The European Court of Human Rights (ECHR) is the court that hears any claims that an individual or groups of individuals has suffered a violation of the European Convention on Human Rights 1950. Much of this Convention has been incorporated into the Human Rights Act 1998. In the same way as with the ECJ, any legislation of a member state that is found to be incompatible with European law is referred back to the government of the member state for amendments to be made to national legislation.

A recent example of a ruling by the ECHR is *ASLEF v UK* (2007) ECHR 110022/05.

In this case the trade union ASLEF had refused membership to members of the British National Party, claiming that their values did not correspond with the values of ASLEF. The BNP members had challenged ASLEF, stating that they had a right to freedom of expression (Article 10 of the Human Rights Act 1998) and freedom of assembly and association (Article 11), and so could not be refused because of their views. The ECHR ruled that ASLEF was allowed to refuse membership to the BNP members – stating that the right of ASLEF to choose its members outweighed the right of the BNP members to freedom of expression.

The Human Rights Act 1998 contains a number of articles that are explored in detail in Chapter 11.

 EXPLORE FURTHER

Look at recent changes in employment legislation in the UK. Distinguish which are the result of European Directives and which are not. Are there underlying differences relating to the two sources of legislation? Now select any other member state of the European Union. Contrast and compare key areas of legislation of this member state and of the UK. Are there any areas of commonality appearing? If there are not, how can that be explained?

KEY INSTITUTIONS

There are a number of institutions within the UK that have a direct impact on the creation and workings of employment law. These include:

Acas

Acas (the Advisory, Conciliation and Arbitration Service: www.acas.org.uk) is a service funded by the government but independent of any government control. Acas is run by a council of 12 members from business, unions and the independent sector. It has about 800 employees working from 11 regional offices, and a head office in London. It has been in existence since 1974.

Acas is a service for both the employer and the employee. Its duty is to remain impartial, and to try to help both sides find solutions to their difficulties. Specifically, the functions include:

- advice – Any person can phone Acas for advice about an employment-related matter. For example, an employer might phone to ask for information about recent developments in employment law, or an employee might phone asking for advice in taking a claim to the employment tribunal. In 2006/7 Acas dealt with 9,839,335 telephone enquiries. According to the Acas annual report, the top three topics that people rang the helpline about were: discipline/dismissals/grievance (24%), redundancy/lay-offs/business transfers (17%) and contracts (12%). Acas can also be asked to carry out employment-related surveys or more lengthy projects.

- conciliation – Conciliation is the process of bringing both sides of a dispute together, and helping them to find a solution to their difficulties. Acas might perform this role before any conflict has actually occurred, or when it has already commenced.

  In particular, Acas tries to help both parties in an employment dispute to resolve the dispute before the case reaches the employment tribunal. All cases lodged with the employment tribunal are copied to Acas, and it will contact both parties and try to help them to reach an agreement. In 2006/7 Acas helped to settle 24% of cases before they reached a tribunal hearing.

- arbitration – Arbitration is the process of bringing in an independent body (eg Acas) and letting it evaluate the situation and determine a solution. Although there is not always a legal requirement to implement the recommended solution, there is a moral obligation. This process can only work if both sides agree to be bound by the process of arbitration.

In addition, Acas publishes codes of practice, runs training sessions, and is involved in consultation with the government about new initiatives relating to employment.

TASK

Look through the Acas website (www.acas.org.uk) and make sure you are familiar with the range of services that it provides. You might find it particularly interesting to read its annual report.

THE CENTRAL ARBITRATION COMMITTEE (CAC)

The CAC (www.cac.gov.uk) is an independent body with statutory powers, whose specific role is to determine the outcome of applications relating to the statutory recognition or derecognition of trade unions for collective bargaining purposes (see Chapter 10). The CAC is also responsible for determining the outcome of disputes between employers and employees over the disclosure of information for collective bargaining purposes, and in dealing with complaints relating to the establishment of works councils in the UK. All these issues are looked at in more detail in Chapter 10.

The Committee consists of a chairman, ten deputy chairmen, 16 members representing workers, and 16 members representing employers. The Secretary of State for Trade and Industry appoints the Committee after consulting with Acas.

THE EQUALITY AND HUMAN RIGHTS COMMISSION

The Equality and Human Rights Commission (www.equalityhumanrights.com) was set up in October 2007 as a result of the Equality Act 2006, and replaced three former organisations:

- the EOC (Equal Opportunities Commission)
- the CRE (Commission for Racial Equality)
- the DRC (Disability Rights Commission).

The three former organisations had all worked to combat discrimination, but with the growing range of discrimination legislation (which is explored in Chapters 6 and 7) it was perceived that there was a need for one organisation that covered all aspects of discrimination. It was also considered that one organisation would be able to have greater impact than three separate organisations.

The benefits of the single organisation are:

- bringing together equality experts and acting as a single source of information and advice

- being a single point of contact for individuals, businesses and the voluntary and public sectors

- helping businesses by promoting awareness of equality issues, which may prevent costly court and tribunal cases

- tackling discrimination on multiple levels – some people may face more than one type of discrimination

- giving older people a powerful national body to tackle age discrimination.

The role of the key institutions relating to health and safety (the Health and Safety Executive and the Health and Safety Commission) is detailed in Chapter 12.

TASK

It is important that throughout your studies you keep abreast of the changes and developments in employment law. This can be achieved by reading such publications as the CIPD periodical *People Management*, reading quality newspapers, and browsing websites such as www.berr.gov.uk and the websites already listed for specific employment institutions. Decide now what will be your main sources of reference and be sure to make regular referrals to them.

It is important to note that both the employer and the employee can seek advice and support from all the bodies outlined above. They operate without bias, and are not permitted to promote the interests of one side of the employment relationship.

EXPLANATION OF COMMON TERMS

There are some standard terms that are used in employment law which it is important to understand:

An Act is always cited in a standard way – that is, the name of the Act followed by the date the Act was passed. For example: the **Employment Act 2002.**

The person who brings a case to a tribunal is called the **claimant.**

The employer who defends a case in the tribunal is called the **respondent.**

The person who brings a case to the appeal court is called the **appellant.**

The person who brings a case in the civil court is called the **claimant** (until 2000 the person was known as a *plaintiff*).

A case is always described as one party 'versus' the other party, and the date it was heard in the court follows in parentheses (round brackets). For example: *Delaney v Staples* (1992).

If a case is brought by the state, it is listed as *R v A N Other* (2003), where *R* stands for 'Regina' (the queen, as head of state).

Ex parte literally means 'from a party' – meaning that only one party is making the initial application. So in the case *R v Secretary of State ex parte Equal Opportunities Commission* (1994) the challenge was coming from a party called the Equal Opportunities Commission.

When cases are cited in literature, only a brief description of the facts is usually given. To read the full report you must refer to the given source. For example, *Delaney v Staples* (1992) IRLR 191 means that the full script can be found in the Industrial Relations Law Reports (www.irsonline.co.uk). A case followed by 'ICR' is reported in the Industrial Case Reports (www.lawreports.co.uk). (The printed versions of these reports can be found in many university libraries.)

KEY LEARNING POINTS

- Employment law is a rapidly changing area of law.
- Employment law is primarily governed by civil law, although there are situations in which criminal law might be applied. Civil law is based on the law of contract, tort and property.
- Legislation is created by statute, common (case) law and the influence of codes of practice.
- European law has precedence over UK law.

FURTHER READING

USEFUL WEBSITES

www.acas.org.uk	Advisory, Conciliation and Arbitration Service
www.cac.gov.uk	Central Arbitration Committee
www.equalityhumanrights.com	Equality and Human Rights Commission
www.berr.gov.uk	Department of Business, Enterprise and Regulatory Reform
www.cbi.co.uk	Confederation of British Industry
www.cipd.co.uk	Chartered Institute of Personnel and Development
www.dfes.gov.uk	Department for Education and Skills
www.echr.coe.int	European Court of Human Rights
www.curia.eu.int	European Court of Justice
www.tuc.org.uk	Trades Union Congress

It is important to note that some legislation and legal terms are different in Scotland from those in England and Wales. A number of the websites direct Scottish students to particularly relevant information. In addition, it might be helpful to access the following specific websites:

www.scottishparliament.co.uk

www.scottishlaw.org.uk

EXAMPLES TO WORK THROUGH

1 Is it true that employment law in the UK is primarily driven by initiatives from the European Union? Justify your answer.

2 Explain the disadvantages and advantages of replacing the Commission for Racial Equality, the Disability Rights Commisson and the Equal Opportunities Commission with the Equality and Human Rights Commission.

3 Explain how Acas can support both the employer and the employee.

CHAPTER 2

The Employment Tribunals and the Employment Appeals Tribunal

CHAPTER OBJECTIVES

The objectives of this chapter are:

- to analyse the history of the employment tribunals
- to explain the operation of the employment tribunals
- to outline the impact of the Employment Appeals Tribunal
- to examine the Acas Arbitration Scheme
- to consider the future of the employment tribunals.

THE HISTORY OF THE EMPLOYMENT TRIBUNALS

The employment tribunals were created by the Industrial Training Act 1964 (and at this stage were named 'industrial tribunals'). They were initially created to hear appeals relating to the assessment of training levies under this 1964 Act. Over the next three years their brief was extended to include such things as the determination of the right to a redundancy payment and issues surrounding the lack of, or inaccuracy of, a written statement of terms and conditions of employment.

In the mid-1960s the government became concerned about the number of unofficial strikes, wage inflation and the general existence of restrictive practices in industry. It commissioned Lord Donovan to lead an investigation into these issues. As a result of the investigation the Donovan Report was published in 1968 and gave a comprehensive overview of industrial relations at the time. In particular, the Report observed two systems of industrial relations that had developed. There was the formal system of negotiation at industry level and the informal level happening more locally within the organisation. Donovan suggested that many of the problems identified by the government were due to the conflict between these two systems. His main recommendation was the formalisation of industrial relations systems at organisational and industry level.

As part of those recommendations Donovan saw the need for an industrial tribunal system to which employees could bring their grievances. He described this system as needing to be easily accessible, informal, speedy and inexpensive.

At first the industrial tribunal system was just this. However, over the years the workload of the tribunals has increased significantly, and many believe the system has moved far from the ideal that Donovan initially described.

It is easy to see some of the key reasons that the workload increased so dramatically. When the Donovan report was published, there was no legislation relating to unfair dismissal (introduced in 1971), sex discrimination (1975), or race discrimination (1976). Today, more than half of the claims to the employment tribunals relate to these areas of legislation.

Despite this increasing workload it was still hoped that the employment tribunals system could meet Donovan's ideal. The idea was that an employee who felt he/she had been badly treated by an employer should have the means to get an independent judgment on the issue, quickly and without cost. How are those criteria met today?

EASILY ACCESSIBLE

The Donovan Report suggested that there should be employment tribunals operating in all major industrial centres, making them easily accessible. In 1971 employment tribunals were heard in 84 locations. Today there are 31 permanent centres at which employment tribunals are heard. In addition to this there are a number of hearings that take place at non-permanent centres. There is also the ability to hear cases almost anywhere if people have particular needs (eg disability) that make it difficult to attend a permanent centre. It is difficult, therefore, to give a specific number of centres, but the system is certainly still very accessible to those who want to use it.

Accessibility can also refer to the ease of registering a claim with the employment tribunal. The system is open to everyone, and the actual process of registering a claim is relatively straightforward (as we see later in this chapter). Forms to apply to the employment tribunals (ET1) are readily available at places such as the Citizens' Advice Bureau. It is also possible to complete the ET1 on line through the employment tribunals' website (www.ets.gov.uk).

INFORMAL

This is maybe the area which now least meets the original Donovan ideal. There are definitely ways in which the employment tribunals system is much less formal than other court systems. There are no wigs and gowns, and the hearing-rooms are less imposing than many courtrooms. In higher courts the parties are expected to present their case, and challenge the case of the opposite side. An unrepresented applicant who is struggling to explain his/her case in the employment tribunal is usually given some assistance by the Employment Judge to make sure that all facts are communicated.

However, it is widely accepted that the employment tribunals have moved away from the picture of the potentially wronged employee presenting his/her grievance in a simple manner, with the employer responding to the accusations. It is now very common for one or both parties to be represented by solicitors or barristers, and the simple arguments are often weighed down by substantial legal arguments. This has impacted on the aspect of informality – but is probably inevitable, given the growing amount of legislation relating to employment issues.

SPEEDY

The original Donovan ideal was of a very quick resolution to the grievance. This allowed the employee and employer to put the issue behind them and continue with a good working relationship or, if the employee had left the employer, allowed the employee to leave the issue and move on to find new employment.

All the employment tribunals have targets to hear claims speedily. However, typically, many months elapse between the application to the employment tribunals and the hearing. The actual time-lapse will depend on the area of the country where the application is lodged and the expected length of the hearing. There are simply too many applications for the process to work any quicker. In the late 1960s there were around 9,500 applications registered at the employment tribunals each year. In the year 2006/7 176,434 applications were received.

INEXPENSIVE

There is currently no charge for bringing an application to the employment tribunals – although we will see when we review the future of the employment tribunals that this might change in the future.

If an employee chooses to represent himself/herself, and many do, there are obviously no legal costs. If the employee chooses to seek legal representation, then legal aid is not available, and so the employee must meet those costs. If the employee is a member of a trade union, that union will typically represent the employee, presuming that they do not feel the case is totally unfounded. In some cases the employee might get representation or support from one of the bodies described in the last chapter – such as the Equality and Human Rights Commission.

In many courts the unsuccessful party has to meet all or part of the costs of the opposing side. In the employment tribunals this is unusual, although the practice is increasing. In 2006/7 costs were awarded in just 509 cases (166 times to claimants and 343 times to respondents). The average amount of costs awarded was £2,079.

We can see, therefore, that there are ways in which the 'Donovan ideal' is far away from the reality of today. However, the employment tribunals are still a court at the lowest rung of the court hierarchy, and there is still a desire to ensure that the employee is able to bring his/her case and present it in a simple format.

 EXPLORE FURTHER

How relevant do you think the 'Donovan ideal' is for today's world of employment? Are the issues of accessibility, informality, speed and expense of primary importance? Any students particularly interested in this should read the original Donovan Report. Compare and contrast that Report with the report of the Employment Tribunal System Taskforce, which is referenced at the end of this chapter.

An application to the employment tribunals is usually brought by an individual (although there are cases when a group of employees with the same grievance bring a joint claim). This focus on the individual reflects the increasingly individualised nature of employment rights. As we work through the various areas of employment law in this book you will notice that the majority of the legislation gives right to the individual, rather than rights to a group of individuals (eg a trade union). We note later in this chapter that the increase in legislation is regarded as one of the reasons that applications to the employment tribunals have grown so rapidly.

THE PROCESS OF THE EMPLOYMENT TRIBUNALS

The employment tribunal consists of an Employment Judge (formerly known as a Chairperson) and two lay members. The Employment Judge is a fully qualified lawyer who either works full-time as a Employment Judge or practises law part-time. The lay members are appointed by the Secretary of State for Trade and Industry. They have extensive experience and knowledge of employment issues. In each employment tribunal one lay member will come from an 'employee' background (eg a trade union official) and one from an 'employer' background (eg an HR manager). The three members of the employment tribunal have an equal vote in deciding the outcome of each case.

In certain cases the Employment Judge can sit alone to hear a case. These are specific claims under legislation such as the Pension Schemes Act 1993 and the National Minimum Wage Act 1998.

The employment tribunals have jurisdiction to hear cases relating to over 80 different pieces of legislation. In 2006/7 the most common types of claims were reported as:

	Number of claims (total 176,434)
Unfair dismissal	38,376
Working Time Directive	33,607
Wages Act	23,624
Breach of contract	23,504
Equal pay	7,854
Sex discrimination	18,909
Redundancy pay	6,643
Disability discrimination	4,345
Race discrimination	3,117

Source: the Employment Tribunals Annual Statistics 2006/07

BRINGING A CLAIM TO THE EMPLOYMENT TRIBUNALS

An employee makes a claim to the employment tribunals by completing the claim form known as an ET1. This form must be lodged at the employment tribunals within three months of the alleged incident occurring.

For example, if the employee has been dismissed, the claim form must reach the employment tribunals within three months of *the date of dismissal*. If the employee is alleging that an act of sex discrimination has occurred, the claim form must reach the employment tribunals within three months of the last date of the alleged act of discrimination.

There are certain claims where the three-month rule is extended. These include:

- unfair dismissal for unofficial industrial action (six months from date of dismissal)
- redundancy payment (six months from relevant date)
- equal pay (six months from termination of employment).

If the claim form is presented after this date, and the claimant can show a justifiable reason for the delay, the claim can be referred to a preliminary hearing of the employment tribunals to consider whether the reason is indeed justifiable and whether the case should go forward to a full hearing.

The possible reasons for a late claim include (although these will not necessarily be accepted as justifiable reasons – it will depend on the details of each case):

- ignorance of rights
- ignorance of the time-limit
- advisers not being aware of the time-limit, or not giving clear advice regarding it
- the claimant's being ill or too distressed to make a claim
- the claimant's being disabled and needing to seek help, which has taken time to arrange
- waiting for internal procedures within the organisation to be completed
- claim forms being lost or delayed in the post
- waiting for the outcome of other legal proceedings.

It is not possible to have clear rules on when a claim presented out of time could still be accepted, because the details of each claim will vary. The following cases illustrate this issue.

- *Avon County Council v Haywood-Hicks* (1978) ICR 646

  In this case the claimant was a polytechnic manager. He had been dismissed, and he claimed it had been an unfair dismissal. His claim form was received by the employment tribunal six weeks after the three-month period had elapsed. He claimed that he was not aware of the existence of employment tribunals, and the possibility of bringing a claim, until he read an article in a newspaper. The employment tribunal ruled that he ought to have investigated his rights and ought to have claimed in time. They ruled that the idea that a well-educated and intelligent man had no idea of his rights 'offended their notion of common sense'. The time-limit was therefore not extended in this case.

- *Shultz v Esso Petroleum Ltd* (1999) IRLR 488

  The claimant became depressed during the last six weeks of the three-month period for making a claim, and claimed he was too depressed to instruct solicitors. The employment tribunal and the employment appeal tribunal both found in favour of the respondent. However, the Court of Appeal held that it had not been practicable for the claimant to lodge a claim. The Court of Appeal stressed that the issue of practicability was paramount.

The Employment Act 2002 introduced statutory dismissals and statutory disciplinary and grievance procedures (see Chapter 8 for more detail). Part of the requirements of these procedures is that an employee must raise a grievance with the employer and wait at least 28 days before bringing a claim to the employment tribunal. (This does not apply to claims of unfair dismissal where, clearly, the employment has come to an end.)

If the employer responds to the grievance, it is quite possible that the grievance process will take more than three months to complete. If a grievance has been lodged with the employer within three months of the event being complained about, the employment tribunal can extend the claim time by a further three months.

The Employment Appeals Tribunals have taken a relatively relaxed view of what can be counted as a letter expressing a grievance (Step 1 of the procedure). For example:

- *Galaxy Showers Ltd v Wilson* (2005) EAT 10/11/05

  The employee sent the employer a resignation letter, and in this explained the reasons that he was unhappy and therefore resigning. It was held by the EAT that the explanations of his reason for resigning was sufficient for it to be seen as a letter raising a grievance.

- *Shergold v Fieldway Medical Centre* (2006) EAT 0487/05

  The employee resigned and, in the letter of resignation, complained about the treatment she had received from her line manager. The EAT accepted that this letter was sufficient to be treated as Step 1 of the statutory grievance procedure.

- *Aspland v Mark Warner Ltd* (2005) ET 2200483/05

  The employee's solicitor set out her grievances in a letter to the employer. This was subsequently found to comply with Step 1 of the statutory grievance procedure.

- *Commotion Ltd v Rutty* (2006) ICR 290

  The employee successfully argued that her written request for flexible working constituted Step 1 of the statutory grievance procedure, even though she had not formally labelled it as such.

These cases, and other similar ones, suggest that the courts are taking a fairly broad view of what complies with Step 1 of the statutory grievance procedure. However, it is important to note that an ET1 itself cannot be a 'grievance' for the purposes of the statutory procedure. In *Gibbs v Harris* (2007) EAT 23/07 the EAT held that the ET1 cannot be Step 1 one of the statutory grievance procedure because grievances and litigation are two different things.

RESPONDING TO A CLAIM IN THE EMPLOYMENT TRIBUNAL

The relevant regional office of the employment tribunal receives the claim to the tribunal and a copy is sent to the respondent. The respondent is also sent a form known as an ET3 to complete and return to the employment tribunal within 28 days. As well as confirming details of the claimant and the respondent, the ET3 requires the respondent to outline its defence of the claim. In accordance with the Employment Tribunal (Constitution and Rules of Procedure) Regulations 2004, if the respondent wants to request an extension to the time-limit to make a response, it must do so within 28 days of receiving the claim form.

When the 28-day period has elapsed, the case will be listed for a hearing in the employment tribunal. If the respondent does not respond within the 28-day period, the case will still be listed, and the respondent has lost its right to take any further part in the proceedings. A copy of the completed ET3 is sent to the claimant by the employment tribunal.

The Employment Tribunal (Constitution and Rules of Procedure) Regulations 2004 prescribe that all claims and responses must be made on the ET1 and ET3 forms. The employment tribunals will reject any submissions that are not on these forms.

TASK

Find out what preparations each party needs to make before a hearing. Looking at the employment tribunals website (www.ets.gov.uk) will help in doing this.

HEARINGS PRIOR TO A FULL HEARING

There are circumstances in which an application can be listed for some form of review prior to a full hearing. These are a *pre-hearing review* or a *case management discussion*.

Pre-hearing review

The purpose of the pre-hearing review is to act as a deterrent to a party to pursue a claim that has little or no chance of success or to consider a point that determines whether a claim can proceed – such as whether the claimant is actually an employee, or whether the claim was brought within the prescribed time.

If the conclusion of the review is that either the claim or the response has no realistic chance of success, the employment tribunal (or the Employment Judge sitting alone) has to decide whether to order one party to pay a deposit before proceeding. If that party goes on to lose the case and is ordered to pay costs, the money will be deducted from the deposit. The maximum deposit that can be ordered is £500.

Case management discussion (CMD)

This discussion is held by a Employment Judge sitting alone, and is held in private. The purpose of the discussion is to prepare the case so that it runs smoothly on the day – so it is more likely that a CMD is held before a complex case. Issues such as the numbers of witnesses, the issues that need to be addressed and documents that need to be available could all be discussed. It is not unusual for the CMD to be held as a telephone conference call.

SETTLEMENT PRIOR TO THE HEARING

In most employment law cases Acas has a statutory duty to contact both parties and try to reach a conciliated settlement. According to the Employment Tribunals Services Annual Report 2006/7, settlements of claims through Acas in that year were:

Unfair dismissal	35%
Disability discrimination	46%
Breach of contract	28%
Race discrimination	38%
Wages Act	28%
Working Time	11%
National Minimum Wage	32%
Sex discrimination	12%
Redundancy pay	17%
Religious belief discrimination	35%
Sexual orientation discrimination	41%
Equal pay	6%

In total, Acas reached a conciliated settlement in 24% of all cases.

It is important to note that a further 31% of all claims were withdrawn before reaching a hearing, and an additional 23% were disposed of otherwise. Only 21% of claims actually went to a hearing. Just 12% of all claims made were successful in an employment tribunal hearing.

It is usual for the conciliation to involve a payment of some financial sum, although reinstatement or re-engagement can occur in some cases. When both sides have agreed a settlement, it is confirmed on a form COT3 and the case is then withdrawn from the employment tribunal. The signing of the COT3 prohibits either side from pursuing any issue relating to the case.

Outside of the Acas process a compromise agreement can be reached. These agreements have the same status as a COT3 (ie the parties cannot take the claim any further) but are not negotiated through Acas. A compromise agreement must be in writing and can only be reached when the employee has received advice from a relevant, independent adviser. An independent adviser is a qualified lawyer, a certified adviser from an independent trade union or a worker at an advice centre who has been certified as an adviser for this purpose.

In addition, the applicant can withdraw his/her application at any stage.

The number of cases withdrawn before a full hearing is very significant. There are likely to be a wide range of reasons that claimants withdraw their claims. These could include the claimant's worrying that he/she has no real prospect of success, or being very nervous of appearing in the tribunal.

THE OPERATION OF THE EMPLOYMENT TRIBUNALS

Before the case is listed an Employment Judge will have reviewed the file and estimated how long the case will take to hear. The majority of cases are listed for one day (or part day), but it is quite possible for a hearing to go beyond this time, especially if there are a group of claimants bringing a case against a respondent. Unless there are good reasons, all hearings are open to the public. Exceptions to this include situations where national security might be at risk, or where a juvenile is involved in some way.

After all the evidence has been presented, and all witnesses have been heard, the employment tribunal retires to reach a verdict. The verdict has to be a majority view, not necessarily a unanimous view. The employment tribunal can give its judgment in summary form (ie identifying just the key facts and concluding with the judgment) or give extended reasons. Extended reasons give a thorough summary of the facts of the case, an explanation of the reasons behind the decision of the employment tribunal and a summary of the merits of the case. A party requiring extended reasons must request them within 21 days of the summary reasons being given. It is not unusual for summary reasons to be given before the parties leave the tribunal building. This will depend on the time available and the complexity of the case.

TASK

Find out more about the procedure that is followed during an employment tribunal hearing. You will find useful information on the tribunal website (www.ets.gov.uk).

The decision of the employment tribunal is not only who has 'won' the case, but also what remedies are to be made. The remedies will vary according to the type of claim brought. For example, if the claim brought is for an unlawful deduction of wages, and the employment tribunal finds that there has been an unlawful deduction, the remedy will be to pay the money that has been unlawfully deducted.

In cases such as unfair dismissal (when employment has ended) there are three options available to the employment tribunal:

- reinstatement – The employee returns to the job he/she had. This is a rare remedy because the relationship between the employee and the previous management is usually too badly damaged for a working relationship to be resumed. In addition, it is quite possible that the employee has gone on to find new employment while waiting for the hearing.

- re-engagement – The employee returns to the company, but in a different role. Again, this is rare because of the damage that has been done to the employment relationship.

In 2006/7 reinstatement or re-engagement was the remedy in just 0.3% of unfair dismissal cases that proceeded to a hearing.

- compensation – The company is ordered to pay an amount of money to the employee: this was awarded in 39.3% of unfair dismissal cases in 2006/7. (The remaining cases were settled before coming to the employment tribunal.)

Compensation awards for unfair dismissal are currently (2008) capped at £63,000. This figure is reviewed in February each year. There is no maximum compensation for a successful discrimination claim. However, large awards are still relatively rare. In 2006/7 average awards of compensation were:

	£
Unfair dismissal	£7,974
Sex discrimination	£10,052
Race discrimination	£14,049
Disability discrimination	£15,059

TASK

Attend the local employment tribunal. Hearings typically start at 10am, so arrive at least 15 minutes before. Explain to the Clerk the purpose of your visit, and ask advice for a suitable hearing to watch. Try to attend the full hearing, and (if the decision is given that day) stay to hear the decision.

THE ROLE OF THE EMPLOYMENT APPEALS TRIBUNAL

Both the claimant and the respondent have the right to appeal against the decision of the employment tribunal. An appeal is referred to the Employment Appeals Tribunal (EAT). It is usual for the composition of the EAT to be one legally qualified Employment Judge and two lay members. In this case, however, the Chairperson is a judge from the High Court or the Court of Appeal nominated by the Lord Chancellor. As with the employment tribunal, one lay member comes from an 'employer' background and one from an 'employee' background. On rare occasions (usually when a matter of great importance is being heard) a Chairperson might sit with four lay members, two from each side.

An appeal can only be made on a point of law or on a claim that the finding of the employment tribunal is 'perverse'. In addition, there can be an appeal if the decision has been subject to some fundamental flaw, as when one member of the employment tribunal has been found to be known to one of the parties, or a member of the employment tribunal behaved in a way that clearly demonstrated bias, or if the employment tribunal refused to hear a witness, to allow cross-examination or to take note of a piece of relevant evidence. An appeal is also allowed if a member of the employment tribunal falls asleep during the hearing!

An appeal must be lodged within 42 days of the date that the extended reasons were sent to the appellant. The appeal is lodged by serving a notice of appeal along with a copy of the tribunal's decision and a copy of the extended reasons.

All appeals are listed for a preliminary hearing/directions (PHD). The main purpose of the PHD is to determine whether there are adequate grounds for appeal and, if there are, to give directions to both parties on preparation for the full appeal hearing.

In claiming that a finding was perverse, the appellant must show that the conclusion reached by the employment tribunal was one that no reasonable tribunal could have reached. This is very difficult to present successfully. For example:

● *Williams and others v Whitbread Beer Co Ltd* (1996) CA [IDS Brief 572]

Williams was attending a works-related course and after a course session went to the hotel bar. He had a number of drinks and became loud and abusive to a fellow employee. When his manager told him to 'tone it down' he became loud and abusive towards his manager. Whitbread held a disciplinary hearing and Williams was summarily dismissed for gross misconduct.

The employment tribunal found that the dismissal was not within the band of reasonable responses of a reasonable company, and hence concluded that the dismissal was unfair.

Whitbread appealed and the appeal was upheld because the EAT concluded that a reasonable employment tribunal could have concluded that dismissal was a fair response.

The Court of Appeal overturned the EAT's decision, stating that the role of the EAT was to determine whether the tribunal had reached a conclusion that no reasonable tribunal could have reached. They ruled that the tribunal's conclusion was reasonable, and even if it was not the conclusion the EAT would have reached there was no evidence of 'perversity' and hence the decision of the employment tribunal had to stand.

An example of an appeal on a point of law can be found in:

- *Royal Bank of Scotland v McAdie* (2007) EAT 0208/06

  McAdie was dismissed on the grounds of ill-health. However, she claimed that her dismissal was unfair because much of her illness had been caused by the poor way that her employer had dealt with grievances that she had raised. The employment tribunal agreed that her dismissal was unfair, because they concluded that no reasonable employer would have addressed the grievances in the way that they had been addressed, and the situation should therefore never have arisen.

  However, the EAT ruled that the ET had focused on the wrong point. Although it was certainly the case that there was a link between the grievance and the ill-health, it did not mean that a dismissal could not be fair. The question was not whether the illness had been caused by the grievance, rather whether the dismissal could be fair. Given the situation of the long-term illness, it found that the dismissal was fair.

In 2007 Acas extended its conciliation services to cover certain categories of EAT cases, at the EAT's invitiation. The type of cases where conciliation may be appropriate includes cases where:

- the employment relationship is ongoing
- a case might be referred back to the employment tribunal
- an appeal relates to monetary awards.

 EXPLORE FURTHER

Many of the cases we will study in this book have been referred to appeal – some to a higher level of appeal than the Employment Appeals Tribunal. Look at a number of these cases and note the reasons that the appeals were made. What are the most common reasons that you encounter? Do you think there is any way in which the procedure of the employment tribunals ought to be changed in order to reduce the number of cases that go to appeal?

INCREASING CLAIMS TO THE EMPLOYMENT TRIBUNALS

As we noted earlier in the chapter, claims to the employment tribunals have grown overall across the years. Figure 1 shows how the level of claims varies from year to year.

Although there has at times been a slight drop in applications, the current employment tribunals system is one that was originally designed to cope with a very limited range of legislation, and a few thousand claims each year. It is now coping with an increasingly wide range of legislation and well over 100,000 claims each year.

WHY HAVE THE CLAIMS INCREASED?

- Every time new legislation is introduced, there are new claims that can be brought to the employment tribunal.

  For example, in October 2006 legislation making discrimination on the grounds of age illegal was introduced. In the six months of 2006/7 that this legislation was in place, there were 972 claims relating to age discrimination. That implies the potential for a huge number of additional claims that the employment tribunal would be required to hear.

Figure 1 Claims to the employment tribunal

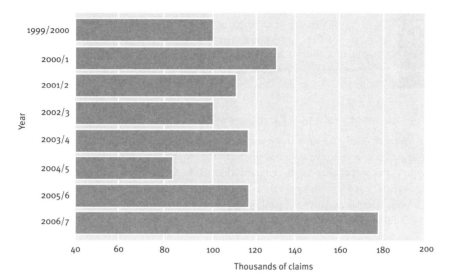

- Initiatives to reduce claims do not work, or actually result in more claims.

  As mentioned earlier, the Employment Act 2002 introduced statutory procedures to be followed when handling disciplinary or grievance situations in the workplace – these were introduced in 2004. One of the primary purposes of these two procedures was to push the resolution of differences in employment back into the workplace. The idea was that this would then reduce the number of claims to the employment tribunal because issues would be resolved without being escalated to this level.

  In February 2007 the Gibbons Report was published on research into the efficiency of the statutory procedures. The report concluded that the procedures have resulted in increased claims and any advantages that they might have brought have been outweighed by the problems.

  Part of the reason for the increased claims was the need for the courts to develop case law to clarify aspects of the legislation – for example, determining what constitutes raising a grievance (as explained earlier). Another reason is that any failure to follow the dismissals and disciplinary procedure results in automatically unfair dismissal – and employees have brought claims on this basis that they could not have brought previously.

  The conclusions of the Gibbons Report were that the statutory procedures as they currently exist should be abolished. In response to this the Department of Business, Enterprise and Regulatory Reform launched a consultation process about the future of the statutory procedures. At the time of writing this consultation is still taking place.

TASK

Read the Gibbons Report (available on the Department of Business, Enterprise and Regulatory Reform website) to understand the key concerns that were expressed. Keep up to date with the progress of the consultations and the outcomes by looking at the website (www.berr.gov.uk).

- More people can bring claims to the employment tribunals.

  Until February 1995 part-time employees had to have five years' continuous service before they could bring a claim for unfair dismissal to the employment tribunals. As we see in Chapter 6, this was challenged as being discriminatory against women – because significantly more women than men work part-time. Thus, under the Employment Protection (Part-time Employees) Regulations 1995 the qualifying period for part-time employees was brought into line with full-time employees.

  Up until 1999 full-time employees were required to have two years' continuous service before they brought a claim to the employment tribunals. In a similar way to the part-time case explained above, the two-year rule was challenged on the grounds of indirect discrimination. In *R v Secretary of State for Employment ex parte EOC* (1995) it was shown that, on average, women have significantly shorter periods of continuous service than men, and therefore the two-year rule discriminated against women. On this basis the qualifying period was reduced to one year in 1999 (Unfair Dismissal and Statement of Reasons for Dismissal (Variation of Qualifying Period) Regulations 1999). Again, we look at this case in more detail in Chapter 6.

- Employees are more aware of their rights.

  It is certainly true that employees are more aware of their rights. They might not be certain exactly what those rights are, but they know enough to be prompted to go and find out more. It is more likely, therefore, that employees will think about the possibility of bringing a claim.

 EXPLORE FURTHER

Can you think of any reasons that the claims to the employment tribunals might have fallen previously? Would you predict that the number of claims will fall again in the next few years, or do you think that there will be a continued increase? What are the reasons for your predictions? Make sure you read the next annual report of the Employment Tribunals Service to see if you are right.

THE ACAS ARBITRATION SCHEME

The Employment Rights (Dispute Resolution) Act 1998 introduced a new scheme to try to reduce the pressure on the employment tribunals system. It is known as the Acas Arbitration Scheme. The scheme was launched in May 2001 and it was hoped that it would take the strain off the employment tribunals system. In reality it has had little impact – indeed, it only handled three cases in 2006/7, six in 2005/6, five in 2004/5 and eight in 2003/4. However, it is an important step and requires examination.

The Acas Arbitration Scheme only addresses unfair dismissal cases and claims made in relation to requests for flexible working. Although that limits its jurisdiction, we must remember that nearly half of all claims to the employment tribunals do relate to unfair dismissal.

The main advantage of the scheme is that it will hear claims quickly, it will be informal and it will be speedy – maybe going back to the Donovan ideal we examined at the start of this chapter.

The initial lodging of the claim is still to the employment tribunals through submitting an ET1. If both parties agree, the claim may then be taken out of the employment tribunals process and directed to the Acas arbitration process. At that stage an Acas Arbitrator (not an Acas member of staff but an independent person appointed by Acas who is deemed to have specialist relevant knowledge) is appointed to the case. The Acas Arbitrator then arranges a time for the hearing as quickly as possible, with a target of being heard within a period of two months.

The hearings are conducted informally and as locally as possible to the parties. There is no cross-examination of witnesses (witness statements may be presented, but the witnesses are not questioned), no formal pleadings and the proceedings are confidential. The two parties simply explain their side of the case to the Acas Arbitrator, bringing his/her attention to any relevant documents. Each party is also allowed the opportunity to comment on the other party's written submission. The Acas Arbitrator then questions both parties and also seeks views on any remedy that might be awarded. Both parties are then invited to make closing statements. The Acas Arbitrator determines the outcome. The decision is not given at the hearing, but is communicated to both parties in writing after the hearing.

The decision of the Arbitrator is final – there is no route of appeal unless there is a challenge on the grounds of substantive jurisdiction or on grounds of serious irregularity.

Why has the system been so little used?

The limited focus of jurisdiction can be a problem. It is not unusual for a claim to relate to more than one area of legislation. For example, there could be a claim for unfair dismissal and unlawful deduction of wages. If such a claim went through the Acas arbitration route, only the part relating to unfair dismissal could be heard. The matter relating to unlawful deduction of wages would have to be referred to the employment tribunal, meaning that the parties would have to attend two hearings. This is unlikely to be popular with claimants or respondents.

In addition, if there are any disputes relating to the claim – eg was the applicant actually dismissed, was the application to the employment tribunal made in time? etc – the Acas Arbitrator cannot hear the claim. Again, it is not unusual for these types of issues to accompany a claim for unfair dismissal.

The potential to appeal is very limited. Although this means the claim is finalised more quickly, people might be apprehensive about committing themselves to a scheme in which there is no appeal – especially as there is an alternative (ie the employment tribunal) where there is the right of appeal.

The hearings are in private and hence representatives are not able to assess how effective the process is and decide if they want to use this route. In reality, this is a small issue because there have been so few hearings. However, a representative has a responsibility to give the best advice possible to his/her client. So he/she might find it difficult to recommend a process he/she has never seen in operation and knows relatively little about.

The Acas Arbitrator is not required to be legally qualified. Although the Acas Arbitrator will be thoroughly trained, and will have been selected for his/her depth of knowledge and experience, some claimants or respondents might feel uncomfortable that no formal legal qualification is required.

Whatever the reasons for the poor uptake, the scheme is currently under review. There could be alterations made to it, or it could simply be relaunched with more publicity and more explanation.

TASK

Relate the Acas Arbitration Scheme back to the 'Donovan ideal'. On the basis of that analysis, do you think the scheme is well designed? What would you alter to make the scheme more attractive?

THE EMPLOYMENT TRIBUNALS (CONSTITUTION AND RULES OF PROCEDURE) REGULATIONS 2001 AND 2004

The Acas Arbitration Scheme only addresses unfair dismissal claims and claims relating to requests for flexible working. In addition, it only provides an alternative route to the employment tribunals. It does not help to resolve some of the difficulties with the tribunal system itself.

In the light of the increased cost and workload of the employment tribunals system there have been a number of measures taken to try to make the system more manageable.

The Employment Tribunals (Constitution and Rules of Procedure) Regulations 2001 introduced the possibility of awarding costs – which is rarely used, as we have already seen.

The Regulations broadened the range of situations in which costs can be awarded. This included giving the opportunity to award costs when the application or the conduct of the proceedings has been 'misconceived'. 'Misconceived' means that the case has no reasonable prospect of success. The maximum level of costs that can be awarded is £10,000.

Those who bring misconceived cases are mostly employees who are not represented who have a real (but misplaced) belief that the employer has acted in some illegal manner. The potential for costs to be awarded should encourage employees to seek more advice before pursuing a claim. However, this does presume that employees realise they might have a weak case, and that they need that advice. It could be argued that if they realised they had such a weak case, they might never have considered a claim in the first place!

The 2004 Regulations further addressed this point – and allow for the ability of the parties to be able to pay any costs awarded to be considered when making a costs award. In addition, costs awards can be made specifically against representatives who are deemed to have acted vexatiously, abusively or otherwise unreasonably.

The awarding of costs against the unrepresented employee does require a change of attitude of the employment tribunals. Although the 'Donovan ideal' might be very distant from today's reality, there is still the underlying idea that tribunals are there for the employee to bring a case against the employer in a simple way, looking for an independent judgment on the issue. Awarding costs might deter the employee who has genuinely been treated badly, going against the whole philosophy of the employment tribunals.

As we have already noted, the employment tribunals can require an applicant to pay a deposit, following a review of the case at a pre-hearing review. The regulations increased this deposit from £150 to £500 – again trying to reduce the number of weak claims to the employment tribunals. However, deposits are rarely awarded and this increase will be of no relevance unless deposits become more widely used.

Prior to the Regulations an employment tribunal could 'strike out' a claim on the basis that it was 'scandalous, frivolous or vexatious'. As with the definitions relating to costs, the term 'frivolous' was replaced with the term 'misconceived' in these Regulations. As before, this covers cases that the employment tribunal judges deem to have no reasonable chance of success. This aspect of the Regulations does give more powers to the employment tribunal but is largely thought to be unlikely to have much effect. Not only are employment tribunals reluctant to judge a case before all the facts have been presented, but the strike-out could be challenged under the Human Right Acts 1998 – specifically the right to a fair trial.

In reality, the 2001 Regulations did not result in a significant reduction in the number of claims. The 2004 Regulations were then introduced which aimed to simplify the process. The main changes in those Regulations were:

- New ET1 and ET3 forms were introduced. As already noted, these have to be used for all claims and responses. However, they have been greatly criticised for being too complicated, and one of the recommendations of the Gibbons Report is that they are simplified.

- Acas's duty to conciliate became limited to a fixed period. The purpose of this was to encourage parties to settle at an earlier stage, rather than just before a hearing takes place – which wastes valuable employment tribunal resources.

  If the claim relates to unauthorised deductions of wages, wrongful dismissal, statutory redundancy pay, guarantee payments or unpaid medical suspension pay, the conciliation period is limited to seven weeks. In all other cases it is 13 weeks (unless it relates to whistleblowing, equal pay and discrimination cases, for which there is no limit).

  However, the employment tribunal Employment Judge can extend the seven-week limit to 13 weeks, and the Acas Conciliation Officer can extend the 13 weeks to 15 weeks, if it is deemed to be appropriate.

  The Gibbons Report concludes that the fixed conciliation periods have not brought the perceived benefits and should be abolished.

- The rules on costs were further extended. When making a costs award the employment tribunal now has a duty to consider the ability of the parties to pay. Costs have also been extended so that an award can be made against a representative who has caused a case to take longer than necessary, or who has persisted in defending the indefensible.

KEY LEARNING POINTS

- The employment tribunals system was originally intended to be easily accessible, informal, speedy and inexpensive.

- The employment tribunals have jurisdiction to hear cases relating to over 80 pieces of legislation, the most common being unfair dismissal.

- A claimant lodging an ET1 at the tribunals within three months of an alleged incident occurring starts the process of a claim to a tribunal. The respondent must reply to this claim within 28 days, using an ET3.

- The Employment Appeals Tribunal reviews cases when there is dispute over a point of law, or the judgment of the employment tribunals is viewed as 'perverse'.

- There has been a significant increase in the numbers of cases coming to the employment tribunals. This is because of increased legislation, more people being eligible to bring claims, and an increased awareness of employee rights.

- The Acas Arbitration Scheme was introduced to reduce the number of claims being heard by the employment tribunals, focusing only on unfair dismissal claims and claims relating to the right to request flexible working. To date, it has not been widely used.

- The Employment Tribunals (Constitution and Rules of Procedure) Regulations 2001 and 2004 were brought into effect to try to address specific problems within the tribunal system.

- The Gibbons Report has made a number of suggestions about the future of the Employment Tribunals Service, and these are currently being reviewed.

EXAMPLES TO WORK THROUGH

1 In this chapter you have read about a number of initiatives that have been taken to reduce the number of claims to the employment tribunals. Which do you think have most likelihood of success? Justify your answer.

2 Do you think that the 'Donovan ideal' is relevant for organisations today? Justify your answer.

3 You have received an application by an ex-employee to the employment tribunals which was received by them four months after he was dismissed. Explain how you should proceed.

CHAPTER 3

Contract of employment

CHAPTER OBJECTIVES

The objectives of this chapter are:

- to describe and explain the tests used in law to determine whether a person is an employee
- to examine the component parts of the contract of employment
- to outline the detail to be contained in the statement of initial employment particulars
- to define and list the duties of the employee and the employer
- to outline the concept of continuity of employment.

WHO IS AN EMPLOYEE?

This is an important question, because much of the legal protection we look at in this book relates only to employees. For example, an employee can make a claim for unfair dismissal but someone else who is working in an organisation and who is not an employee cannot make a claim, even if they are dismissed in exactly the same way. Some legislation extends to both employees and those working within an organisation without employment status – discrimination legislation is an example.

There are two alternatives for those that work in an organisation. They can be hired to work under a contract *of* service (an employee) or under a contract *for* services (an independent contractor).

Section 230 (1) of the Employment Rights Act 1996 defines an *employee* as 'an individual who has entered into or works under a contract of employment'.

Section 230 (3) of the same Act states that a *worker* is 'an individual who either works under a contract of employment or works under any other contract where that individual agrees to personally perform work or services for another party'.

Although these definitions are of some use, they do not tell us exactly who should be given a contract of employment. This is primarily because situations of employment are very varied so that there can be no one clear rule.

Where there is any doubt over employee status, it is the responsibility of the courts (usually the employment tribunals) to take each individual case and to apply its judgment. They do this through a mix of using case law and applying a number of tests that have been developed over the years. This task is often carried out in a pre-hearing review – to determine, for example, whether a claim for unfair dismissal can be heard because the respondent is claiming that the claimant was never an employee.

Tests used by the courts to determine an employment relationship have been control tests, organisation tests, 'ordinary person' tests, mutual obligations tests, and a combination of tests known accordingly as multiple tests.

Control test

This test originates from a judgment in 1881 in the case of *Yemens v Noakes*. The judge stated that 'An employee is subject to the command of his master as to the *manner* in which he shall do his work.'

The idea was that if a person was being told how to do his work, he was an employee. This is an outdated test for two main reasons. Firstly, we have a much more skilled workforce than nearly 130 years ago, and many employees are expected to work without specific instructions, using their skill and expertise. Secondly, an independent contractor could be told specifically what to do if hired for a specific project (eg a company could hire an electrician to help with a rewiring project, and give very specific tasks).

Organisation test

In *Stevenson v MacDonald* (1952) 1 TLR 101 the judge, Lord Denning, stated that 'A person is an employee if that person is an integral part of the business.'

This is of more use than the control test because it overcomes the problem of skilled people having control over their own work. However, it does not help us in the example of the electrician – if the company is carrying out a refurbishment project, completing the rewiring is an important part of the overall process. If there is no other electrician, the person who has been hired could be seen to be an 'integral part of the business' (under Lord Denning's ruling). This does not necessarily mean that he has become an employee.

Ordinary person test

In *Collins v Hertfordshire County Council* (1947) KB 598 the judge posed the question, 'Was a contract a contract of employment within the meaning which an ordinary person would give to those words?'

This is also known as the 'man in the street' test – in other words, what would ordinary common sense conclude? However, such a simple test does not give us any guidelines over what should be used to determine an employment relationship and what should not. On that basis, the test is of little help.

Mutual obligations test

This test looks at the nature of the relationship between the employer and the person in question, and considers whether there is sufficient mutuality for an employment relationship to exist. There are two levels of mutuality to consider. Firstly, is there an obligation to provide work (and an obligation to carry out that work)? Secondly, is there a promise of future work (both a promise to provide it [employer] and a promise to carry it out [employee])?

This test definitely helps us to understand the definition of an employee more clearly, but there are still some difficulties. If we go back to our electrician example, he could go on to be hired for a series of future refurbishment projects. Although he has no written contract of employment he starts to assume that he is an employee because there is always work for him, and he always carries it out. The employer then runs out of work for him and simply states he is no longer required. The electrician protests that he is an employee, and hence must be made redundant (see Chapter 9). The employer replies that he has always been an independent contractor, and there has never been an obligation on the employer to provide work for the electrician. It has simply been coincidence that a series of projects followed one after the other. So is the electrician an employee?

The following case helps us to examine this further:

- *Carmichael v National Power* (2000) IRLR 43

    In this case Mrs Carmichael and her colleague worked at a power station as visitor guides. The work was part-time. There was some correspondence between the ladies and National Power that the ladies relied on as a contract of employment. The relationship between the ladies and National Power was described as that of a 'station guide on a casual as-required basis'. National Power argued, therefore, that the work was on a casual basis and that there was no obligation to provide work. On that basis the relationship was not one of employer and employee. It was also noted that on 17 occasions Mrs Carmichael had been unable to work, and her colleague had been unable to work on eight occasions. On none of these occasions had National Power taken any disciplinary action.

    The employment tribunal agreed that there was no employment relationship. Eventually, the Court of Appeal overturned this decision. National Power appealed against this decision and the House of Lords found in favour of the employer – so the relationship in this case was not one of employer and employee.

    The basis for the decision was that the relationship, as described, failed the first stage of the test of mutuality. National Power had no obligation to provide work, and Mrs Carmichael and her colleague had no obligation to work even if there was work available.

A decision that seems to contrast with this is that of:

- *Cornwall County Council v Prater* (2006) EWCA Civ 102

    Prater was a teacher working with children who were unable to attend school. She worked under a series of contracts, with no obligation to take a further contract once one had been completed – and the Council were under no obligation to offer her any future contracts. There were some breaks between contracts, but both parties accepted that they would not be seen to break her continuity of employment if she were found to be an employee.

    The Court of Appeal held that Prater was working under a series of contracts of employment and that they added together to give her sufficient service to accrue employment rights.

They distinguished this case from Carmichael by stating that the Carmichael case was determining whether there was an 'umbrella' contract that amounted to employment – rather than focusing on the actual status of Carmichael when she was working. In the case of Prater the focus was on her status when she was actually working, and it was found that this status amounted to employment.

The length that the relationship has been in place might also be relevant:

* *Younis v Transglobal Projects* (2005) EAT 0504/05

  Younis was engaged to generate sales over a three-year period. His engagement was subject to a 60-day notice period. He was paid a small retainer plus commission. He worked for other organisations and there was no contractual obligation on him actually to do any work for Transglobal Projects during his three years.

  Despite this, the EAT concluded that there was mutuality of obligation – and hence an employment relationship – because the contract had been operating for three years' duration.

  These cases further underline that each case is decided by the courts on its individual facts, and that there is a limit to general principles that can be applied.

Multiple test

The experience of using the tests we have examined has shown the courts that it is not possible to focus on one particular aspect of the working relationship and to use that to determine whether or not there is an employment relationship. On that basis, the most commonly used test in the courts today is the multiple test.

In using the multiple test the courts look at every aspect of the relationship as described, and use them to determine the nature of that relationship. This is best illustrated in the following case:

* *Ready-Mixed Concrete v Minister of Pensions* (1968) ER 433

  Ready-Mixed Concrete decided to separate the making of concrete from the delivery of the concrete. It put in place a system of 'owner-drivers' – in other words, the delivery men would own their own vehicles and would be self-employed.

  In determining whether or not the drivers were self-employed the courts looked at a number of aspects of their employment. In favour of the drivers' being employees was:

  – they had to wear company uniforms (suggesting a level of control from the employer)

  – their lorries had to be available for company work at certain hours (an obligation to work)

  – they could only use the lorries for company business (again, suggesting a level of control)

  – they had to obey the foreman's orders (definitely an issue of control)

  – they could sell the lorries back to the company at an agreed valuation (not typical of an independent relationship).

  In favour of the drivers' being self-employed was:

  – the drivers were responsible for the maintenance and running costs of the lorries (suggesting that the expenses of employment were their own)

  – the drivers could employ a substitute driver (there was no obligation on the driver to be personally available for work)

- the drivers could own more than one lorry (suggesting that they could work for more than one employer)

- the drivers paid their own tax and NI contributions (an employer typically deducts tax and NI from the employee's pay).

Although there were factors suggesting both types of relationship, the court decided that there were three crucial conditions to meet for a contract of employment to exist:

- Did the employee agree to provide his own work and skill?

- Had the employer got some element of control?

- There must not be any term inconsistent with a contract of employment. (Inconsistency with a contract of employment could be such things as the employee's being responsible for payment of his own tax and NI contributions – typically the employer deducts these from the employee's pay. However, that one point alone would not necessarily be enough to determine employment status.)

The court found that the first two conditions were met. However, the third condition was not met because there were factors inconsistent with a contract of employment, and on that basis the drivers were to be classed as self-employed. The relevant factors are those listed above as being in favour of the drivers' being self-employed.

In determining the nature of a working relationship in the courts today those three crucial conditions are usually addressed, and the decision is made based on the answer to them.

 EXPLORE FURTHER

Do you think that the courts have arrived at a satisfactory solution to the issue of deciding who is an employee? If not, what potential problems do you see with the current situation? What type of test might improve the current situation?

Even if you think that the courts have not arrived at a satisfactory solution to determining who is an employee, it is important to consider whether the solution that is in place is fair to both the employer and the employee.

It is unlikely that there can ever be a clear-cut test that gives an objective formula to determine employment status. This is because all employment relationships differ in some way. This becomes increasingly true as we see a wider use of atypical contracts – which we look at in the next chapter. Because we have an increasingly flexible workforce, we have increasing variations on employment relationships.

Although, therefore, we might conclude that there never will be a perfect solution to this dilemma, we must not underestimate the importance of the decisions made. An employee has a wide range of rights, which a non-employee simply does not have. It is often advantageous to be classified as an employee. However, we must remember that an employee also has a wide list of duties to the employer, and not everyone might want to be bound by these duties.

THE CONTRACT OF EMPLOYMENT

The contract of employment describes the basis of the employment relationship. It can be in writing or it can be agreed orally. It is of great importance in the event of any dispute, because the contract of employment explains the way in which the employer and employee have agreed to work together. The contract of employment is a legal document, and employers should therefore take care in determining the content.

The terms of the contract of employment can be classified as:

● express terms

● implied terms.

Express terms are terms that have been discussed and agreed between the employer and employee. They might not be in writing. It must be emphasised that express terms cannot diminish statutory rights. We examine statutory rights in more detail later in this chapter, but in essence they are rights expressed in law (in statute). So, for example, the National Minimum Wage (NMW) is determined by statute. Potentially, the employer can offer a wage of a lower level than the NMW and the employee can accept this. However, if the employee then challenges this wage in the court, the employer cannot argue that it is fair because it was agreed between the two parties – because it has diminished the employee's statutory rights.

Implied terms are those that have not been specifically agreed between the employer and employee but are derived from the following sources:

● collective agreements

● statute

● custom

● the courts

● work rules.

WRITTEN STATEMENT OF INITIAL EMPLOYMENT PARTICULARS

Sections 1 to 7 of the Employment Rights Act 1996 set out the right of all employees to receive a written statement of initial employment particulars not later than two months after the beginning of employment. The statement must include:

● the names of the employer and the employee

● the date when employment began

● the date when continuous service with the employer began (ie taking into account any previous service with the employer prior to this appointment)

● the job title, or a brief description of the job duties

● the rate of remuneration, the way in which it is to be calculated (eg the terms of a bonus scheme) and the periods at which the employee will be paid – this includes all financial benefits as well as basic pay

● terms and conditions relating to hours of work (eg this should include basic hours, shift patterns and rules regarding overtime)

- terms and conditions relating to holiday pay (eg this must specify the numbers of days' holiday to which the employee is entitled each year, and the period in which it is to be taken)

- the place of work, or the employer's address if the employee will be moving between a number of places of work

- terms and conditions relating to payments given if incapacitated due to sickness or injury

- details of pension schemes

- the length of notice the employee is required to give, and the employer is entitled to receive, to terminate the contract of employment

- where the employment is not intended to be permanent, the period for which it is expected to continue, or if it is a fixed-term contract the date it is to end

- any collective agreements that will directly affect the employee including, where the employer is not a party, the persons by whom they were made

- if the employee is required to work outside the UK for more than one month, the duration of the period of work outside the UK, the currency of the remuneration while abroad and any additional remuneration or benefits applicable to the work; in addition, any terms and conditions relating to the eventual return to the UK

- details of disciplinary rules that apply to the employee

- details of grievance procedures, and the name of the person the employee should apply to if he/she is dissatisfied with any disciplinary decision or to air a grievance.

TASK

Look at the statement of initial particulars issued by your organisation, or one with which you are familiar. Does it meet all of the above criteria?

Despite this lengthy list of contents, the statement is not the full contract of employment, it is simply a statement of the main terms and conditions of employment. Indeed, it should be noted that the law does not actually require employees to sign the statement or to give any indication that they have received the statement. The statement is the employer's version of the terms and conditions, and is not an indication of any agreement being reached between the employer and the employee. If the employee works in accordance with the terms and conditions, it could be argued that the employer's version has contractual effect because of the lack of any challenge. In practice, a court will usually accept that the statement is strong evidence of the terms agreed by the employer and employee. However, because the statement is not a contract either party can challenge the accuracy of the statement – as happened in the following case.

- *System Floors (UK) Ltd v Daniel* (1985) IRLR 475

  Daniel brought a claim of unfair dismissal against System Floors. System Floors challenged his right to bring the claim, stating that he had insufficient continuity of service. They challenged the date when employment commenced, declaring that it was actually one week later than cited in the written statement of initial employment particulars. The EAT allowed the employer to show that the actual starting date was different from the one stated, although it did emphasise that it is a 'heavy burden' to show that actual terms differ from the statement.

IMPLIED TERMS

COLLECTIVE AGREEMENTS

A collective agreement is an agreement made between the employer and the employee's trade union or association. As the term suggests, the agreement applies 'collectively' to all employees covered by the negotiating group. Typical topics for collective agreements are pay, bonus schemes, shift patterns, redundancy agreements, and disciplinary and grievance procedures.

A collective agreement can be incorporated (become part of) a contract of employment by *express incorporation* or *implied incorporation*.

Express incorporation

Here there is a clear statement that the employer and employee agree to be bound by a collective agreement. This is typically a statement within the collective agreement that expressly incorporates the collective agreement into the contract of employment. An example of express incorporation is found in the following case.

- *National Coal Board v Galley* (1958) 1 WLR 16

  The pit deputies working for the National Coal Board (NCB) had contracts of employment that stated that they were regulated by any national agreements. After negotiation with the trade unions a national agreement was revised, and a clause requiring pit deputies to work on such days as reasonably practicable was inserted. This could potentially involve working on Saturdays. Galley refused to work on Saturdays and was held to be in breach of his contract. This was because his contract of employment stated that his employment was governed by national agreements, and the revised collective agreement had been expressly incorporated into his contract.

Implied corporation

If there is no express term, an alternative is to claim that the collective agreement has been incorporated into a contract of employment by 'implication'. If the employer and employee have always conducted the employment relationship in accordance with the collective agreement, then it can be implied that they agreed to be bound by that agreement. However, this is less certain than a term that has been expressly incorporated, because the intention to be bound by an agreement can always be challenged. For example:

- *Campbell v Union Carbide Ltd* (2002) EAT 0341/01

  Campbell was employed as a chemical plant operator, initially with ICI. ICI entered into a collective agreement with the recognised trade union that included a clause covering redundancy payments that was stated to be legally binding, and another clause headed 'discretionary severance in non-redundancy cases'. The part of ICI in which Campbell worked was transferred to Union Carbide Ltd, along with all terms and conditions of employment. After a period of time Campbell was given notice of termination on the grounds of ill-health. He claimed that he was entitled to payments under the 'discretionary severance in non-redundancy cases' clause because these payments had been made by the organisation in all previous cases when an employee had been terminated following a lengthy period of sickness absence. Union Carbide refused to make the payment, stressing that the payments were classed as 'discretionary'.

The EAT ruled that although the payments had always been made, this did not give rise to incorporation by implication or evidence of a contractual term. The important question was whether there was evidence that both parties intended the payments to form a term of the contract. Because the payments had specifically been called 'discretionary' payments, it ruled that the employer had indicated that there was no intention for the payments to be contractual – and so there was no requirement to make the payments.

TASK

What collective agreements exist in your organisation (or an organisation with which you are familiar)? Are they expressly incorporated into the contract of employment? If they are not, is there evidence that they have been incorporated by implication?

STATUTE

As already noted, a contract of employment cannot diminish any rights of the employee determined by statute. Any relevant statute automatically forms a part of the contract of employment. Two examples are:

- the **National Minimum Wage Act 1998** (see Chapter 5): the employer must pay at least the minimum wage as determined by the Secretary of State.

- the **Working Time Regulations 1998** (see Chapter 5): the employer must allow all employees covered by this legislation the breaks, holidays, rest periods and maximum weekly hours as laid out in the Regulations.

CUSTOM AND PRACTICE

Before written particulars and written contracts of employment were widely used, custom and practice was of importance because looking at the 'way it has always been done' gave a good indication of the terms by which the employer and employee intended to be bound. Since the introduction of written documents, custom and practice has become less important.

However, it can still be argued that if there is a definite practice that is reasonable and is generally applied, it could form part of the contract of employment. In determining whether the practice has become part of the contract a full range of issues must be considered, including such issues as how long the custom has been in place, whether the policy regarding the custom has been brought to the attention of employees by management, and whether there is evidence that both parties intended the custom to be part of the contract of employment.

Custom and practice can be useful in helping the courts to interpret a contractual term that is not clear.

If we look back at the case of *Campbell v Union Carbide Ltd* we see the issue of custom and practice highlighted. Although Union Carbide had always paid the ill-health severance payment (evidence of custom and practice), it was judged not to have formed part of the contract because it was clearly highlighted as discretionary.

- *Sagar v Ridehalgh* (1931) Ch310

In this case a weaver working in the mills in Lancashire challenged the company for reducing wages for faulty work. Although this practice had never been brought to the attention of the employee there was a clear custom of trade showing that reductions were always made for faulty work. In this case, custom and practice was judged to form part of the contract of employment.

Although this is an old case, it is a useful illustration of a factor that could be considered to form part of the contract of employment through custom and practice.

TASK

Are there any practices that could be incorporated by custom and practice into the contracts of employment in your organisation (or one with which you are familiar)? What are they? Are they important to the organisation? Should they be expressly agreed between the employer and employee?

THE COURTS

The role of the courts in determining implied terms has developed through a series of cases. The initial view was based on the 'officious bystander test' (derived from *Shirlaw v Southern Foundries* (1939) ER 113 – see Case summaries at the end of this chapter). This test questioned whether a term would be implied if an officious bystander asked two parties who had a contract if a term that they had not specifically mentioned was part of the contract. If they replied 'of course', then the term was implied.

This is a very limited way of looking at implied terms, and the courts now take a much wider view. One issue to be considered is 'reasonableness':

- *Courtaulds Northern Spinning Ltd v Sibson* (1988) ICR 451

Sibson resigned from the trade union, and because the trade union operated a closed shop (all employees had to join the trade union – a practice no longer allowed in law) the trade union insisted he be moved to another site. Sibson was offered employment one mile from his current place of work, but he refused to go and resigned claiming unfair and constructive dismissal (see Chapter 8). The Court of Appeal ruled that the agreement to move sites should be implied if it was satisfied that both parties would have agreed to it if they were being reasonable. It was judged that a move of one mile was reasonable, and so there was no dismissal.

A more recent decision is

- *Johnstone v Bloomsbury Health Authority* (1991) QB 333

Johnstone was a Senior House Officer in a hospital. His contract gave a standard working week of 40 hours, and he had to be available on call for an average of 48 hours each week. As we will see when we examine the duties of the employer, there is an implied term that the employer will take reasonable care of the employee's health and safety. In stating an average of 48 hours per week, it was actually possible for Johnstone to work over 100 hours in a week, which breached that implied term. The Court of Appeal ruled that the right for the employer to request overtime work had to be limited by the implied term of care for the employee's health and safety. However, one judge dissented, declaring that however burdensome the requirements might be, they were express terms of the contract of employment.

In summary, the courts will look at all factors regarding the employment relationship, and determine whether there is an implication that both parties would agree to be bound by the term under question. They will then look wider than this, and consider whether the implied term is reasonable. They will also consider a wider approach, and determine whether the implication of the term is necessary, or of benefit to, the contract of employment.

WORK RULES

Many organisations have a set of rules governing the way in which they require employees to act. These might cover such things as not smoking, not bringing alcohol or drugs onto the site, the correct way to wear uniforms, etc. Such rules are clearly devised by management and, unlike collective agreements, do not require any prior negotiation.

If a rule has been expressly incorporated into a contract of employment, it will be contractual. For example, if the rule of not smoking on company premises is expressly written into a contract of employment, that requirement is contractual. However, if something is simply contained in the set of rules and is not referred to in any contractual documents, it is not part of that contract.

- *Dryden v Greater Glasgow Health Board* (1992) IRLR 469

  Greater Glasgow Health Board introduced a smoking ban in the workplace (a new work rule) and Dryden resigned and claimed constructive dismissal. It was held that the introduction by the employer of a smoking ban did not constitute a breach of contract. It was also held that there was no implied right to smoke (despite the employee's trying to argue custom and practice). In addition, it was held that the employer did have the right to make rules for the conduct of employees, even changes such as a smoking ban.

IMPLIED TERMS OF LAW

As well as terms that can be implied into the contract of employment, there are also obligations placed on both the employer and the employee by law. These obligations are implied into the contract of employment.

DUTIES ON THE EMPLOYER

To pay wages

There is a duty of the employer to pay the employee during the period of employment.

- *Devonald v Rosser* (1906) KB 728

  The employer closed the works (tinplate) through lack of business. Two weeks later the employer gave all employees one month's notice of the termination of this contract. Devonald claimed pay for the two weeks before the notice was given. This was granted because there was an implied duty that the employer would pay the employee.

To provide work

This duty is unclear. It is possible that the failure to provide work might be a breach of contract if :

- earnings depend on work being provided (eg a sales person remunerated by commission)
- the employee needs the opportunity to practise skills (eg a trainee).

- *William Hill Organisation Ltd v Tucker* (1998) IRLR 313

  Tucker had been involved in developing a new approach to betting. When he gave notice of his intention to resign, William Hill tried to put him on 'garden leave' (to stay away from work while on full pay) for six months. During that period he would not be allowed to work. Tucker challenged this on the basis that he needed to keep practising his skills, and six months was too long a period to be away from work. He was successful in his claim.

However, provided that the employee is paid, it *can* be concluded that there is no duty to provide work:

- *Langston v AUEW* (1974) ICR 180

  When the employee worked on night shifts or worked overtime he was paid his basic wage plus premium payments. His employers suspended him without pay, and thus took away his opportunity to earn the premium payments. It was judged that although they had no obligation to provide work, they did have an obligation to make the payments.

To provide references

An employer has a duty to take care when writing references, and the following case highlights the difficulties that can arise in this area:

- *Spring v Guardian Assurance plc* (1994) IRLR 460

  Spring was a sales representative for an insurance company, which was sold to Guardian Assurance. Upon the sale Spring and the new management felt unable to work together and he was subsequently dismissed. At this time Spring decided to set up in business selling insurance for another organisation. Under the rules of the insurance business, Guardian Assurance was required to give a reference about Spring to the new organisation. The reference was written on the basis of information from Spring's previous superiors and included references to a serious case of mis-selling, and suggested that Spring was not honest and was a man of little or no integrity. On this basis the new insurance company refused to accept Spring as selling for them, and other insurance companies also rejected him. Spring brought an action in the High Court claiming damages for loss of earnings based on malicious falsehood, breach of an implied term of contract, and negligence arising from the preparation of the reference.

  The High Court judge described the reference as a 'kiss of death' to Spring's career in insurance because it was so bad. It was found that the allegations of dishonesty were untrue – Spring had acted incompetently but not dishonestly. The judge found that there was no malicious action, because the reference writers genuinely believed Spring was a 'rogue'. However, it was accepted that Guardian Assurance had a duty to take due care over writing the reference, and had been negligent because they had not checked that the allegations of dishonesty were true. They had thereby breached the duty of due care. This case worked through appeals at the Court of Appeal and then the House of Lords – who upheld the original verdict.

This case confirms the duty of an employer in giving a reference. The employer must take every care to ensure that every detail written in a reference is correct. This must include checking the details before writing the reference. It is also the responsibility of the employer to ensure that the overall impression given by the reference is fair. It is therefore important to consider what is not included as well as what is.

The contractual right to receive a reference was also challenged in *Spring v Guardian Assurance*. In the House of Lords judgment the judges concluded that there was a duty when the kind of employment is such that a reference is normally required. In this instance, the insurance business requires that organisations seek a reference from previous employers, and so it would seem that a contractual right for a reference could exist. However, the law on other jobs where the same rigour of reference-taking does not exist is still unclear.

Although there is a clear requirement to state the truth in giving references, the truth must be related to matters that have been thoroughly investigated and are therefore believed to be true.

- *TSB Bank plc v Harris* (2000) IRLR 157

  Harris worked for the TSB. During her employment, there had been 17 complaints about her by customers. Surprisingly, Harris was unaware of these complaints. Harris applied for a job with the Prudential, and they sought a reference from the TSB. In the reference the TSB stated that there had been 17 complaints against Harris: four had been upheld and eight were still under investigation. The Prudential declined to employ Harris.

  On hearing of the reference Harris resigned from the TSB and claimed unfair constructive dismissal (see Chapter 8). The EAT upheld Harris's claim, stating that the TSB had breached the implied term of trust and confidence by not ensuring that the complaints cited in the reference were fair and reasonable.

  In this case the TSB had reported the facts relating to Harris as they understood them. However, by not bringing the complaints to her attention they had not investigated them thoroughly, and so they could not be certain they were true.

Although the obligation to give a reference might not be clear, there is a clear requirement to ensure that the content is correct. It is also important to note that under the Data Protection Act 1998, the employee does have a right to see anything written about him/her. However, in bringing a claim that a reference has damaged an employee's ability to seek alternative employment, the employee must be able to show that it was the reference that harmed his/her prospects and not any other factors.

 EXPLORE FURTHER

As we have seen in this section, the giving of references is fraught with potential difficulties. Look in the HR and business press for any recent cases that have occurred relating to the giving of references. Are you able to draw up any guidelines on giving references that might be of use to your employer?

To take reasonable care for the health and safety of employees

We study this requirement in Chapter 12.

To indemnify the employee against all liabilities and losses incurred in the course of employment

A good example of this is expenses incurred when travelling on company business. Any legitimate business expense should be reimbursed by the employer.

To take reasonable steps to bring to the attention of employees rights of which they would not ordinarily be aware

There are instances where an employee could not be expected to be aware of a particular right. For example, this could be because it has been negotiated with a representative body and the employee was unaware of the negotiations.

- *Scally v Southern Health and Social Services Board* (1991) IRLR 522

   In this case a group of doctors working for the Health Service in Northern Ireland claimed they had not been advised of the ability to purchase extra years that would enhance their pension contributions. When the doctors did find out about the scheme they applied to join, but their application was rejected as being out of time. The House of Lords went on to rule that an employer has an obligation to make employees aware of their rights.

The employer is required to take reasonable steps. It might be deemed reasonable to put notices on a noticeboard. However, if there are employees who are rarely in the building (eg sales representatives who spend most of their time travelling to see customers), it could be argued that it is not a reasonable way of informing that group of employees. In the same way, it would not be sufficient to email information to all employees if some did not have access to a computer.

To give effective support against bullying at work

This can also be linked to the duty to take reasonable care of the safety (and health) of employees. We examine the issues associated with bullying, and the employer's duties, in Chapter 7.

To respect the privacy of the employee

This is explored in Chapter 11.

To deal effectively with grievances

This is explored in Chapter 8.

To take care not to damage the relationship of trust and confidence that should exist between an employer and an employee

This requirement is one that falls on both the employer and the employee. The issue of trust and confidence is seen to be right at the heart of the contract of employment. If there is no trust and confidence, there can be no successful relationship.

One of the first cases outlining this was

- *Isle of Wight Tourist Board v Coombes* (1976) IRLR 413

    Mrs Coombes was the personal secretary to the director of the board. One day they had an argument and in the presence of another employee the director stated, 'She is an intolerable bitch on a Monday morning.' Mrs Coombes resigned and claimed constructive dismissal (see Chapter 8). She was successful in her claim because it was judged that the words of the director had shattered any trust and confidence in the relationship.

The breach of trust and confidence can also be between a group of employees and the employer.

- *Malik and another v Bank of Credit and Commerce International SA* (1997) IRLR 462

    The BCCI collapsed in 1991 after widespread allegations of fraudulent actions. Malik worked for BCCI and alleged that the employer conducting the business in a corrupt and dishonest manner amounted to a breach of the implied term of trust and confidence. The House of Lords held that Malik could bring a claim for damages relating to the stigma of working for BCCI, relating to any damage to future employment prospects.

However, in *Husain and another v Bank of Credit and Commerce International SA* (2002) EWCA Civ 82 another two former employees of BCCI were unsuccessful in their claim for damages related to the stigma. In this situation the Court of Appeal ruled that although the actions of BCCI might well be a breach of trust and confidence, the inability of the individuals to find alternative work related more to personal factors such as inflating their experience and knowledge on job applications.

 EXPLORE FURTHER

The duty of trust and confidence is at the heart of any contract of employment. As we work through this book we will see other situations when this duty is breached. Read these cases carefully. Is there ever a case when the employment relationship has survived such a breach?

DUTIES ON THE EMPLOYEE

To obey all instructions of the employer

It should be noted that the instructions should be reasonable and they should be legal.

- *Ottoman Bank v Chakarian* (1930) AC 277

    The employer instructed Chakarian to remain in Constantinople, although he had previously been sentenced to death there. He disobeyed, and this was found to be justified because the instruction had been unreasonable.

- *Morrish v Henley Ltd* (1973) ER 137

    The employee was instructed to falsify the accounts at the garage where he was employed. He refused and was dismissed. This was an unfair dismissal because the instruction was to carry out an illegal act.

To co-operate with the employer

A clear example of lack of co-operation is the taking of industrial action.

- *Secretary of State for Employment v ASLEF* (1972) QB 443

  ASLEF instructed its members to carry out a work-to-rule. The employees worked strictly according to the company's rules, and caused considerable disruption. The Court of Appeal held that by carrying out the work-to-rule the employees were in breach of the implied term of co-operating with the employer. Lord Denning commented: 'Now I quite agree that a man is not bound positively to do more for his employer than his contract requires. He can withdraw his goodwill if he pleases. But what he must not do is wilfully to obstruct the employer as he goes about his business.'

As we see in Chapter 10, employees do have the right to take industrial action if this action is taken in accordance with relevant legislation.

Fidelity

Employees must not carry out activities that clearly conflict with the duty that they owe to their employer. They must therefore not compete with the employer:

- *Sanders v Parry* (1967) ER 803

  Sanders worked for Parry as an assistant solicitor. He had a major client, and was responsible for all his legal work. Sanders entered into an agreement with the client that he would leave Parry and would set up in practice on his own. The client would then transfer all his business away from Parry to Sanders's new practice. Parry sued Sanders for a breach of the implied term of fidelity. This was successful.

To take reasonable care in carrying out the duties of their contract

If an employee injures another person or property in the course of his/her duties, the employee can be liable to indemnify the employer against any damages. In reality, the issue is typically dealt with through the employer's insurance.

- *Lister v Romford Ice and Cold Storage Ltd* (1956) AC 555

  Lister was a lorry driver who negligently injured a fellow employee (his father) when packing his lorry. The injured employee sought damages from Romford Ice and Cold Storage and was successful (the employer was responsible due to vicarious liability – see Chapter 7). The employer's insurers then brought an action against Lister, in the employer's name, claiming damages for the breach of the implied term that he would exercise reasonable care in carrying out his duties. This claim was allowed.

CONTINUITY OF EMPLOYMENT

The qualification for certain employment rights are dependent on the employee's having had a specific period of continuous employment. An example of this is the requirement to have one year's continuous service before being able to make a claim of unfair dismissal (see Chapter 8).

Section 212 of the Employment Rights Act 1996 defines continuous service as including any week during which all or part of the employee's relationship with the employer is governed by a contract of employment. This section also allows for continuity of employment to continue although the contract is not in existence. These exceptional situations are:

- any week in which the employee is incapable of work through sickness or injury up to a maximum of 26 weeks

- a period of absence due to a temporary cessation of work

- any period during which employment is regarded as continuing due to custom. For example, it could be the custom of the employer to allow compassionate leave in certain situations that is unpaid.

It should be noted that maternity legislation (see Chapter 5) allows for the continuity of employment during the period of maternity leave. It should also be noted that an employee's continuity of employment is preserved when that employment is subject to a transfer of undertaking (see Chapter 9).

In all these cases continuity of employment is preserved, and the weeks during which work does not take place actually count towards the calculation of the period of continuous employment. There are also situations when continuity of employment is preserved, but the weeks when work does not take place do not count towards continuous employment. They are:

- a period of time when an employee is taking part in a strike

- a period of time when an employee is locked out by the employer (this is when an employer refuses to provide work for the employees, with the aim of forcing them to accept certain terms and conditions of employment).

KEY LEARNING POINTS

- There are a number of tests used by the courts to determine who is an employee. The most commonly used test is the multiple test.

- The contract of employment consists of express and implied terms.

- Express terms are those that have been discussed and agreed between the employer and employee.

- The sources of implied terms are collective agreements, statute, custom, the courts, work rules.

- A written statement of initial employment particulars must be given to all employees within two months of commencing employment.

- A collective agreement can be part of a contract of employment through express or implied incorporation.

- A contract of employment cannot diminish any rights of the employee determined by statute.

- The courts can determine whether a term is implied within a contract of employment, through looking at a wide range of factors within the way the relationship between employer and employee is conducted.

- Work rules are only incorporated into a contract of employment if they are specifically mentioned in that contract.

- There are a series of duties on both the employer and the employee that have been imposed by law.

- Continuity of employment includes any week when the relationship between the employee and the employer is governed by the contract of employment, although certain exceptions to this do apply.

CASE SUMMARIES

Shirlaw v Southern Foundries (1939) ER 113 – A term is implied into a contract of employment when if an officious bystander were to make a suggestion to the parties they would reply, 'Oh, of course!'

Mears v Safecar Security Ltd (1982) IRLR 183 – There was a dispute over whether the employee was entitled to sick pay. The employer had never paid sick pay and the employee had never asked for it when he had previously been sick. The Court of Appeal ruled that the only implied term was that there was no sick pay entitlement.

Jones v Associated Tunnelling Company (1981) IRLR 477 – The EAT accepted that there was an implied term that, for reasons of business efficiency, the employer could ask the employee to work at any place within reasonable travelling distance of his home.

Moores v Bude-Stratton Town Council (2000) IRLR 676 – The employer has the implied duty to take reasonable steps to protect employees from bullying or undue interference in their work. In this the employee had suffered verbal abuse and accusations of dishonesty, which had breached the duty of mutual trust and confidence.

Quinn v Calder (1996) IRLR 126 – The employer had paid enhanced redundancy terms to employees for a number of years. However, the enhanced payments had never been incorporated into any policy or communicated formally to employees, so the payments remained discretionary.

United Bank v Akhtar (1989) IRLR 507 – There was a mobility clause within the contract of employment allowing for relocation of the employee anywhere in the UK. The employer gave six days' notice that the employee was to move to Birmingham.

He was unable to comply, resigned, and claimed constructive dismissal. The employee won the case because it was ruled that there was an overriding duty on the employer not to act in such a way as to breach the mutual trust and confidence in the employment relationship, and giving such short notice had breached that trust and confidence.

Gascol v Mercer (1974) IRLR 155 – There was dispute over the hours worked by the employee in relation to the calculation of redundancy pay. The employee claimed that the hours should be determined by his original agreement – but the employer claimed they should be determined by a later written agreement which the employee had signed to indicate his agreement, and had returned a signed copy to the employer. The Court of Appeal held that the later written agreement was relevant because it had been signed to acknowledge acceptance.

Henry and others v London General Transport Services Ltd (2002) IRLR 472 – The employer introduced new working conditions affecting such things as rotas, payment and holidays. The employees signed a petition but continued to work in accordance with the new arrangements 'under protest'. They submitted claims for unlawful deductions from wages two years later. Their claim failed because they had made little protest and had taken so long to register their objections.

Western Excavating (ECC) v Sharp (1978) IRLR 27 – This is the classic ruling defining constructive dismissal (see Chapter 8). For constructive dismissal to take place there must have been a breach of the contract which goes to the very heart of the contract, the employee must resign in response to the breach, and the resignation must be in a timely manner.

EXAMPLES TO WORK THROUGH

1 Joan works as a keep-fit instructor. She teaches at a number of Adult Education classes. Each term she is asked which classes she wants to teach at, and they are advertised in the college literature. If there are enough enrolments, the classes go ahead. If there are insufficient enrolments, the class is cancelled. If she is unable to teach one week, she tells the college that she is not available and they arrange for someone else to take the class. Apply a relevant employment test and determine whether she is an employee.

2 You work in a retail store and the general manager has recently dismissed an employee who worked in your department for gross misconduct – stealing from the shop where you work. However, there was some doubt about his guilt, and you are not comfortable with the final decision that was taken. Today you have received a request for a reference from another shop where the employee has applied to work. How should you proceed?

3 For the past three years your organisation has experienced really good trading results, and the managing director has given the employees a Christmas bonus as a 'thank you'. This year's trading has been poor and the managing director has indicated that he will not be paying a Christmas bonus. The employees are arguing that the bonus is contractual because it has been regularly paid over the past three years. Advise the managing director on how to proceed.

CHAPTER 4

Atypical contracts and the variation of contracts

SPECIFIC CATEGORIES OF EMPLOYEES

The traditional employment contract of 9-to-5, Monday-to-Friday is still common, but it does not have the dominance that it once had. Customers demand certain services 24 hours a day every day of the week, more mothers are returning to work and wanting hours to fit around childcare, and more employees are looking to fit working hours around their other interests to try to achieve some sort of work–life balance. This change in working patterns has also led to an increase in the use of atypical workers. In this chapter we examine some of the issues associated with these contracts.

TASK

Is there a need for a wide variety of types of workers (temporary, part-time, casual, agency, etc, in your organisation (or one with which you are familiar)? Find out how the organisation manages this variety.

EXPLORE FURTHER

In this section we address the legal issues relating to a certain number of atypical contracts. However, there are many more types of contracts being used by organisations (eg annual hours contracts, zero hours contracts). Compile a list of as many of these atypical contracts as you can. Then consider what legislation is relevant to both the employees and employers in specific relation to these contracts. Do you think there is a need for further legislation in some areas? Useful sources of information about changing contracts include the *Labour Force Survey* and *Labour Market Trends*.

AGENCY WORKERS

The employment status of agency workers has been the subject of a number of cases in recent years – and although there have been some consistencies in recent rulings, the guidance on this issue is not clear. Indeed, judges have commented that there will be no clarity without statute addressing this issue – and there are no signs of any statute at present. In this section we explore recent case law and how the current guidance has developed.

Workers provided for an organisation by an employment agency can potentially claim an employer–employee relationship with the employment agency or with the employer they actually work for. To determine if such employment relationships exist, the tests we examined in the last chapter are used.

One of the earlier cases addressing this issue was:

● *McMeechan v Secretary of State for Employment* (1997) ICR 549

In this case McMeechan was a catering assistant who undertook a number of assignments from an employment agency. When the agency entered insolvency, McMeechan claimed entitlement to unpaid wages and redundancy payments from the National Insurance Fund (state funds for employees made redundant – see Chapter 9 – when the employer cannot meet the statutory payments). In favour of his being an employee was that the agency had control over him, because they could terminate his contract and could discipline him. There were also factors consistent with an employment relationship – for example, the agency deducted tax and NI contributions from McMeechan's pay. However, there was a document stating that McMeechan would work as a 'self-employed worker and not under a contract of service'.

This case finally went to the Court of Appeal which found, on the basis of the evidence outlined above, that there was an employment relationship, because there was evidence of control, there was evidence of mutuality, and there was nothing inconsistent with a contract of employment.

It is important to note that the test of mutuality was key to determining the relationship in this case. A case where the multiple test was more evident is:

● *Montgomery v Johnson Underwood Ltd* (2001) IRLR 269

Montgomery was placed in an organisation as a receptionist/telephonist by Johnson Underwood (an employment agency). She worked there for two years and then the organisation asked the agency to terminate the contract. She took a claim for unfair dismissal against both the organisation where she worked and the employment agency. This case went through two stages of appeal and it was eventually concluded by the Court of Appeal that Montgomery was not an employee of either organisation. Crucially, they found that Johnson Underwood exercised 'little or no control, direction or supervision' over Montgomery. On the basis of that conclusion one of the three conditions of an employment relationship was not met, so Montgomery could not be an employee. Although they did exercise control over her work, there were no mutual obligations between her and the organisation, as the contract was between the agency and the organisation. In addition, there were factors inconsistent with an employment relationship – primarily that Montgomery was paid by Johnson Underwood.

Although these two cases give examples of how tests that are widely used to determine employment relationships can be applied, they are not robust in helping to determine whether an employment relationship has developed with the agency itself or with the 'end user' (the organisation in which the employee was placed).

An important ruling came in the following case:

● *Dacas v Brook Street Bureau (UK) Ltd and another* (2004) IRLR 190

Dacas was placed by Brook Street Bureau as a cleaner for a local authority hostel. This was the only work she was assigned to by the Bureau. She worked in this role for six years when she was dismissed following an incident in which she swore at a visitor to the hostel. Dacas claimed unfair dismissal, and took the approach that she had either been an employee of the hostel or of Brook Street Bureau. The employment tribunal had to decide whether she was an employee, and if she was, who was the employer.

The employment tribunal firstly considered whether she was an employee of Wandsworth Council (who ran the hostel). They concluded there was not an employment relationship here because there was no direct contract between Dacas and the Council.

They then considered whether she was employed by Brook Street Bureau. They concluded that although a contract existed between Dacas and the Bureau, they could not be her employers because they had no direct control over her daily work. They concluded therefore that she could not bring a claim of unfair dismissal because she had no employer–employee relationship.

The applicant appealed to the Employment Appeals Tribunal (only against the decision that she was not an employee of Brook Street Bureau), which overturned the decision of the employment tribunal. They determined that Brook Street Bureau exercised control over Dacas because they paid her wages, had the right to exercise disciplinary action and had the right to terminate her contract. They also agreed that mutuality of obligations had been shown. In this case all the other evidence pointed to an employment relationship, and therefore that was what existed. So Dacas was an employee of Brook Street Bureau.

Brook Street Bureau then appealed to the Court of Appeal, which overturned the EAT's finding and ruled that Dacas was not an employee of the Bureau.

In making the judgment the Court of Appeal made it clear that the employment tribunals should always investigate whether an *implied* contract of employment has arisen between the employee and the *end user* (in this case, Wandsworth Council). Importantly, the Court of Appeal stated that in such agency situations the employment tribunals must find that someone is the employer, and it will usually be the end user. It was also noted that one year's employment (which is sufficient to accrue unfair dismissal rights) was sufficient to mean that an implied contract of employment had arisen.

(In this case it was not possible to make a finding that Wandsworth Council was the employer because Dacas had not appealed against the earlier decision regarding this employment relationship.)

This ruling took on considerable importance because of the suggestion that it is not acceptable to conclude that there was an employment relationship but that it was not with any one party. Here the Court of Appeal was clearly saying that there must be an employer – and suggesting that the most likely conclusion was that the employer was the end user.

In 2006 a further – somewhat complex – case went to the Court of Appeal, where the *Dacas* principle (that the end user is likely to be the employer) was applied:

- *Cable and Wireless plc v Muscat* (2006) EWCA Civ 220

  Muscat's original employers (EI) asked him to change from an employee to a contractor. To achieve this EI made him redundant and he set up his own company to provide EI with services. Then EI were taken over by Cable and Wireless. They insisted that Muscat supply his services through an agency which they already used – and would not do business directly with Muscat's company.

  Muscat continued to work through his company, through the agency, for a further eight months until Cable and Wireless decided they no longer required his services. Applying the Dacas principle, the Court of Appeal determined that Muscat was an employee of the end user – in this case Cable and Wireless.

However, soon after the ruling in this case came an EAT ruling which set out some very useful principles about the employment status of agency workers:

- *James v Greenwich Council* (2007) CA

  James was an agency worker who worked for the Council for five years. Her argument was that an implied contract with the Council had arisen. However, the EAT concluded that there was no implied contract because there was no mutuality of obligation in the employment relationship. The EAT went on to give guidelines on when it is appropriate to apply a contract between a worker and end user:

  - If the end user cannot insist on an agency supplying a particular worker, it is not appropriate to imply a contract of employment.

  - It is likely to be a rare situation where there is a contract between the end user and the worker if the arrangements with the agency are genuine and accurately represent the relationship between the parties. If an employment relationship is to be inferred, then there must have been some words or conduct before the relationship started that suggest that the worker is working because of mutual obligations between the worker and the end user, and not because of arrangements with the agency.

  - The length of time that the relationship has been in place does not justify the implication of a contract of employment.

This case was referred to the Court of Appeal, who ruled that it is the role of the employment tribunal to decide – as a question of fact – whether it is necessary to imply a contractual relationship between the end user and the agency worker. This should not be reviewed by a higher court unless there is a clear error of law.

Another decision, soon after this case, also went against the *Dacas* principle – but for different reasons:

- *Craigie v Haringey Council* (2007) EAT 0556/06

  In this case Craigie had been placed to work at Haringey Council by an agency (Aptus). His agreement with Aptus clearly stated that he was not their employee. Craigie admitted that there was no mutuality of obligation with the Council – he did not have to do the work that they were offering.

  He applied for a full-time job with the Council and was offered it, but the offer was later withdrawn due to unsatisfactory references (which were later found to be untrue). Haringey then decided they no longer wanted his services, and he took a claim of unfair dismissal against them.

  In determining whether Craigie was an employee of Haringey, the EAT noted that there was no mutuality of obligation in the relationship. Although Craigie had been working for the Council for two years, the EAT applied the ruling of *James* (the case above) and concluded that time did not determine an employment relationship.

  They then concluded that there was no 'necessity' to imply a contract of employment – that the conduct of the relationship had been consistent with services being supplied to an end user by an agency. Thus, on the basis of 'necessity' no employment relationship was evident.

In conclusion, it appears that the rather mechanical approach that the end user must be the employer is no longer to be followed. It does seem that the employment status tests that we explored in the last chapter are to be our main guide. However, it is likely that we will see more rulings on this topic in the future.

In the *Craigie* case the EAT echoed the comments of previous courts and stated that the law on agency workers is currently unsatisfactory. This is indeed true. However, in early 2007 a Private Member's Bill – the Temporary and Agency Workers (Prevention of Less Favourable Treatment) Bill – was brought before Parliament, but it did not proceed beyond the early debate stages. It is due to return to the House of Commons again . . . but there is no indication that the Government is supporting it, and so it is reasonably unlikely that it will progress at this time.

 EXPLORE FURTHER

Clarification of the status of agency workers has partly been driven by European legislation. Find out how other member states treat agency workers in relation to their agency status. A good starting point is the websites of the European Commission (www.europea.eu.int/comm) or the European Parliament (www.europarl.en.int).

PART-TIME WORKERS

In Chapter 1 we referred to the case of *R v Secretary of State ex parte Equal Opportunities Commission* (1995) 1 AC 1. In this case the ruling that part-time workers needed five years' continuous service to take a claim of unfair dismissal, compared with two years' service for full-time employees, was of indirect discrimination against women. This was because significantly more women than men tend to work part-time. On the basis of this challenge, the qualification period for part-time workers was brought into line with that for full-time workers.

In 1997 the European Union put in place a Directive dealing with the issue of all employment rights for part-time employees. This Directive covered a wide range of contractual issues. Most of the Directive was brought into place as UK law in the Part-time Workers (Less Favourable Treatment) Regulations 2000 (amended in 2002) – which we will refer to as PTW Regulations.

The first stage in considering part-time workers is to determine who they are. Firstly, we have the definition of 'worker' which is the same as that already above from Section 230 (3) of the ERA 1996 – namely, that 'A worker is an individual who either works under a contract of employment or works under any other contract where that individual agrees to personally perform work or services for another party.'

Having determined that the definition of a worker is the same whether they may be part-time or full-time, the next step is to determine what 'part-time' means. The legislation simply states that a part-time worker is one whose normal hours of work, averaged over a period of up to a year, are less than the normal hours of comparable full-time workers.

The comparator is key to these Regulations because they give the right to make a claim of less favourable treatment on the grounds of working part-time. To show that a part-time worker has been treated less favourably, he/she must be able to point to a full-time worker and show that his/her treatment has been different, and that it has been less preferable. For example, the worker might state that he/she does not think the rules regarding access to a pension scheme are fair. If the rules are also applied to full-time workers, then the issue is not the part-time employment. However, if the full-time workers had different pension rules that were seen as preferential, and he/she was able to identify a comparator who was full-time, then the worker could take a claim of less favourable treatment under the PTW Regulations.

The comparator should be someone who is employed at the same time, by the same employer, at the same establishment (or if there are no comparators at that establishment at another establishment of the employer), under the same type of contract and doing the same or broadly similar work (given reference to levels of qualification, skill and experience).

There are straightforward examples. In a call centre there might be a core of staff answering calls who all work a basic week of 35 hours. In addition, there are staff that take the same calls at the same call centre who only work for 15 hours each week – they are clearly classified as part-time.

The more difficult examples are when there is not a clear comparator. For example, the person claiming to be part-time is a cleaner working in a factory where there are no other cleaners, and no other people doing similar work. In this situation the strict definitions do not allow the cleaner to take any claim under the PTW Regulations. This might seem unfair, but the Regulations are focused on different treatment for full-time and part-time working, and any difference that is identified must be clearly attributable to the part-time status. If that clear distinction cannot be shown, then there can be no claim.

There are exceptions to the rules on comparators:

- If a full-time worker reduces his/her hours and becomes part-time, he/she can use the previous terms and conditions of employment as a full-time worker as the comparator.

- In the same way, a worker returning to work after an absence of less than 12 months, who returns to reduced hours, can use his/her previous full-time employment as the comparator.

The regulations give the part-time worker the right not to be treated by the employer less favourably because of the part-time status. This covers contractual issues (eg rate of pay, overtime payments, sickness and maternity pay arrangements, and any other benefits). It also gives the right for the part-time worker not to be subjected to any detriment because of the part-time status. This covers issues such as the possibility of promotion and the access to training. In addition, there must be equal rights to have access to schemes such as pensions and share options and access to statutory leave rights (eg maternity, paternity and parental leave). A worker cannot be selected for redundancy only because of part-time status.

If a worker considers that he/she is being treated less favourably because of part-time status, he/she may ask his employer for a written statement explaining the reasons for the treatment. This written statement can be produced as evidence at any subsequent employment tribunal hearing.

If the worker is not satisfied with the response from the employer, he/she can take a claim to the employment tribunal on the grounds of less favourable treatment or of victimisation. If the worker does take such a claim, the employer has to identify the ground for the less favourable treatment or detriment. The employer is 'vicariously liable' for the actions of its managers, supervisors and other employees. In other words, the employer is responsible for any actions that have been taken by its employees, even if those actions contravene company policy, unless the employer can clearly show that it has taken steps to stop such a situation occurring. (We examine vicarious liability in more detail in Chapter 7.)

If the worker wins the case at the employment tribunal, the possible remedies are that the employment tribunal can order all or one of the following:

- a declaration of the rights of the worker in respect of the complaint

- payment of compensation by the employer to the applicant

- recommended action to be taken by the employer to deal with the issue that has been brought to the tribunal – failure to comply may result in increased compensation being ordered.

TASK

Does your organisation (or one with which you are familiar) employ part-time staff? If so, find out if changes were made to their terms and conditions when the Part-time Workers Regulations were introduced. Do you think any changes have been positive for both the employer and the employee?

- *Matthews and others v Kent and Medway Towns Fire Authority and others* (2006) UKHL 8

The issue of similarity of work was addressed in this case. The fire service operates with full-time fire officers and part-time (retained) officers. The part-time officers usually have other jobs, but are on call for a set number of hours to respond to peaks in demand.

The claimants brought a case arguing that the retained firefighters were unfairly being denied pension, sick pay and additional payment rights that full-time firefighters enjoyed.

Initially, their claim was rejected by the employment tribunal on the basis that the work that they did was sufficiently different from the full-time firefighters for the Part-time Workers Regulations not to apply.

The case eventually went on to the House of Lords where the claim from the retained firefighters was allowed. It concluded that the tribunal had focused too much on the differences. However, when deciding claims under the Part-Time Workers Regulations it is most important to focus on the similarities in the core duties. Because these were broadly the same between the full-time and retained firefighters, the claim was upheld.

CASUAL WORKERS

We have already examined the status of casual workers in looking at the case of *Carmichael v National Power* (2000) IRLR 43 (see the previous chapter).

If a worker is 'casual' in the sense that there is no obligation on the employer to provide work, and no obligation on the employee to carry out any work, it is unlikely that an employer–employee relationship exists. In this situation the casual worker is not entitled to the same benefits as an employee.

TEMPORARY WORKERS

Temporary workers have exactly the same rights as other workers, presuming that they have acquired the relevant statutory period of employment (eg one year's service to take a claim of unfair dismissal). The exceptions are specific temporary contracts to cover maternity leave or to cover an employee suspended on medical grounds.

A temporary worker is usually on a fixed-term contract (see next section) or is an agency worker (which we have already examined) or is a casual worker (which we have also examined).

FIXED-TERM CONTRACTS

There are situations when an employer wants to employ someone, but for a fixed period of time only. For example, there might be a special project to complete, but once that project is completed it is anticipated that there will be no further work for the employees involved. In this situation an employer can issue a fixed-term contract – which clearly states when the employment will end. The following case shows how this can also be abused:

- *Booth v United States of America* (1999) IRLR 16

  This case centred on three employees who worked at a USAF airbase. They were employed on a series of fixed-term contracts. At the end of each contract there was a short break in service after which a new contract of employment was issued. Upon the issuing of each contract they returned to the same job with the same tools and equipment. However, the breaks in employment meant they never amassed sufficient continuity of service to claim statutory rights (such as the right to take a claim of unfair dismissal). The EAT ruled that they had been unable to show evidence of continuity of service. The employer's actions were lawful, if undesirable, and if this loophole was to be addressed it needed to be done through legislation.

The Fixed-Term Employees (Prevention of Less Favourable Treatment) Regulations 2002 introduced new legislation relating to fixed-term contracts. The employee on a fixed-term contract should not receive less favourable treatment when compared to a permanent employee who is employed by the same employer, is engaged in the same or broadly similar work, and is based at the same establishment. If there is no such employee at the same establishment, a comparison may be made by an employee of the employer working at a different establishment. A comparator must be an actual employee, not a hypothetical employee.

Less favourable treatment includes contractual terms (including pay and benefits), opportunities to receive training and secure permanent employment and qualifying periods for benefits.

In addition, the legislation limited the issuing of fixed-term contracts to a maximum of four years. If fixed-term contracts are issued beyond that period of time, the contract will automatically become permanent. Only contracts issued from, or running from, 10 July 2002 are covered by the legislation.

It is also important to note that the termination of a fixed-term contract is a dismissal, and thus should be managed using the statutory dismissals and disciplinary procedure (see Chapter 8). If a contract has a specified end date and the employer wants to terminate the contract prior to that date, there must be some potentially fair reason (eg redundancy or poor conduct of the employee) unless there is a clause in the contract allowing for it to be terminated early.

However, non-renewal of the fixed-term contract does not constitute less favourable treatment, as shown in the following case:

● *Webley v Department for Work and Pensions* (2004) EWCA Civ 1745

Webley was employed on a number of short fixed-term contracts. Her last contract was not renewed, and this resulted in her having an employment length of just less than one year – meaning she could not bring a claim of unfair dismissal.

She claimed that the non-renewal of the contract was less favourable treatment, in comparison to a full-time employee.

The Court of Appeal rejected her claim, stating that if she was right, there could be no fixed-term contracts – because any non-renewal would result in discrimination on the grounds of fixed-term contracts. The law clearly allows for fixed-term contracts, and so the law clearly allows that they can be terminated at the end of the contract.

FLEXIBLE WORKING

The demographics of the workplace have changed greatly over recent years. In particular, there are more women working, and more mothers returning to work after childbirth. In addition, there are more parents raising children alone, and needing to work because they are the only source of income in the family. On average, people are living longer, and this also means that there are more people who have caring responsibilities towards elderly relatives.

It is these changing demographics of the workplace that have prompted the government to consider a number of aspects of legislation to address the needs of family life. As well as the changing statistics there is also the issue of work–life balance and the amount of time that families have to spend together. The government wants to encourage people to work – and wants to encourage women to return to the workplace to use their skills. However, family life is important, and an appropriate balance must be struck between work and outside commitments.

In response to these needs, the government introduced legislation giving a statutory right to request flexible working. The statutory rights are set out in Section 47 of the Employment Act 2002, and the main substance of the rights are found in the Flexible Working (Eligibility, Complaints and Remedies) Regulations 2001 and the Flexible Working (Procedural Requirements) Regulations 2002. The rights came into force on 6 April 2003.

In April 2007 the government extended the legislation to cover carers of adults. The definition of 'carer' is: an employee who is, or who expects to be, caring for an adult who:

- is married to/the partner of/the civil partner of the employee *or*
- is a 'near relative' (parent, parent-in-law, adult child, adopted adult child, sibling [including in-laws], uncle, aunt, grandparent, step-relative) of the employee
- is neither of the above, but lives at the same address as the employee.

The rights of such carers are the same as those that already existed for parents of young children.

It is important to note that the legislation gives a statutory right to *request* flexible working. It does not give a right to be *granted* flexible working hours.

It is also important to note that the rights are only available to those who have a child aged under six years, or a disabled child aged under 18 years, or who meet the definition of an adult carer. This aspect of the Regulations has given employers some concern. With the addition of the adult carers, a potentially large percentage of employees could make a request.

To qualify for the right to make a request for flexible working the employee must have had at least 26 weeks' continuous service on the date of making the request, must be the mother, father, adopter, guardian or foster parent of the child or be married to the child's mother, father, adopted, guardian or foster parent, and must expect to have responsibility for the child's upbringing, or must be an adult carer.

In considering these qualification criteria it is important to note that:

- the legislation is not restricted to women
- the request does not have to be made at the end of maternity leave, it can be made any time that the child is aged under six years (18 for a disabled child)
- the purpose of the request must be to care for the child/adult – it cannot just be because the parent would like to work different hours for their own benefit.

In requesting flexible working employees can request changes to :

- the hours they work
- the times they work
- the place they are required to work.

An employee must write to his/her employer requesting a change to flexible working. There is no prescribed format for this, although the DTI has published some standard forms on its website (www.dti.gov.uk) to suggest the type of information that should be included in the request. For parents, the application must be made at least 14 days before the child's sixth birthday.

Once the employer has received the request, it must arrange a meeting with the employee within 28 days to discuss the request. The employee has the right to be accompanied to this meeting by a fellow worker or a trade union representative. Within 14 days of the meeting the employer must give a written response to the request.

If the request is granted, the changes that have been agreed must be specified in writing, and a date for the start of the changes must be confirmed. This will be a change of contract (see later in this chapter) and will be considered a permanent change. In other words, the employee has no right to expect a change back to the foregoing terms and conditions of employment at some future date.

The legislation sets out a number of grounds on which the employer can turn down the request. They are:

- the burden of additional costs
- a detrimental effect on the ability to meet customer demand
- an inability to reorganise work among existing staff
- an inability to recruit additional staff
- a detrimental impact on quality
- a detrimental impact on performance
- insufficiency of work during the periods the employee proposes to work
- planned structural changes
- any other ground the Secretary of State may specify by regulations.

- *Commotion Ltd v Rutty* (2006) ICR 290

    In this case Rutty was granted a residence order to care for her two-year-old granddaughter and made an informal request to work a three-day week. This was refused, and so she went ahead and made a formal request in line with the Flexible Working Regulations.

    Her request (and her appeal) were turned down because the employer wanted all employees working uniform hours, and it believed that the change would result in a detrimental impact on teamworking. Rutty resigned.

    The employment tribunal, upheld by the EAT, found that the employer had not given a reasonable grounds for the refusal – as set out above. The concerns that they had expressed had not been substantiated.

If the employee is refused his/her request, he/she may appeal against the decision. This must be done in writing within 14 days of the decision being received. The legislation suggests that the appeal should be on the grounds that the procedure was not followed correctly, or that the business reasons are incorrect or that they have not been explained sufficiently. Within 14 days of the request for an appeal there must be a meeting convened, preferably with a more senior manager. Again, the employee has the right to be accompanied. The decision of the appeal should be communicated in writing within 14 days of the appeal meeting.

If the employee's request is still turned down, he/she can refer the issue to an employment tribunal. The employment tribunal has a limited role to play. It cannot challenge the validity of the employer's decision, and it cannot make its own judgment on whether the request should have been granted. Its role is simply to consider whether the employer has given the request serious consideration, whether the reason for refusal was one permitted by the legislation, whether the facts used to assess the request were correct, and whether the employer has acted in accordance with the statutory procedure.

If the employment tribunal finds that the employer has erred in the way it has handled the request, it can either award compensation to the employee (at a maximum of eight weeks' pay –

the statutory definition of a maximum week's pay, currently [as of February 2007] £310, applies) or it can make an order that the request is reconsidered.

It is possible for employees to bring other claims associated with the way they consider the application has been handled. These might include sex discrimination, race discrimination and disability discrimination (we look at all these claims later). It is important, therefore, that the employer is careful to ensure a consistent approach to all requests.

TASK

How has your organisation – or an organisation with which you are familiar – dealt with requests following the legislation relating to flexible working? Do you think the organisation has followed a correct procedure?

An employer has a number of issues to consider when addressing flexible working requests:

- setting precedents – An employer might receive a request from an employee for flexible working, and decide to grant the request. If another employee in the same department then makes the same request, can the employer refuse that employee? Each request is handled separately, so it might be possible to refuse a further request because, for example, the employer was able to reorganise work among existing staff when only one employee was working different hours, but cannot achieve this when two employees are working in this way.

- interpretation of the business grounds – How much inconvenience is the employer expected to accept? It might be possible, for example, still to meet customer demands – although the flexible working of a member of staff makes this more difficult. To what extent must the employer accept a certain level of difficulty before it becomes classed as a 'detrimental effect'?

- expectations of employees – It is true that the legislation was heralded in the popular press as the opportunity for carers and parents of young children to work the hours they requested. Although the legislation does not state that, there is definitely an increased expectation of some level of flexibility. How does the employer address this and maintain good employee relations?

Many employers have addressed these types of issues by formulating a clear policy on dealing with employee requests. Obviously, the policies must incorporate the statutory procedure, but writing a company policy gives time for employer and employees to consider the issues before any conflict occurs.

Concern has been expressed about the strength of the legislation. At the CIPD's annual employment law conference (2003) there was debate over the likelihood of the legislation being flouted. The concern is that employers only have to give a 'business reason' for refusing the request, and that employment tribunals cannot investigate those reasons, they can only instruct firms to 'go back and think again'. It was confirmed by the head of the DTI's employment relations directorate that the government was committed to reviewing the new rights in April 2005, and would consider bringing in some test of objective justification, or possibly a right to flexible working, if there was widespread evidence that the rules were being ignored. To date, no action has been taken on this point.

VARYING A CONTRACT OF EMPLOYMENT

A contract of employment is an agreement between two parties, and for that reason an employer cannot unilaterally vary that contract. If the employer, unilaterally, does make a change to the contract, the employee has two options:

● to resign and seek damages for wrongful dismissal (see Chapter 9)

● to continue working, but try to seek damages for any loss that has been suffered.

If the employee does continue working, without making protest, and continues to work in accordance with the new terms for a significant period of time, it can be interpreted that the employee has accepted the changes to the contract by his/her actions.

If the employee does not agree to the proposed changes, it can be very difficult for the employer to proceed. The options open to the employer are:

● to terminate the contract of employment, and offer new contracts under the new terms. This option runs a strong risk of claims for unfair dismissal from the employee (see Chapter 8)

● to negotiate the proposed new terms with the employee representative body, and to try to seek agreement. If there is a reasonable period ('reasonable' will be the time required for all the issues raised by the employee representatives to be seriously considered and addressed) of negotiation and no agreement can be reached, the employer can give notice that the variation will go ahead, if it can be justified for business reasons. This option will be particularly strong if the majority of employees affected have already agreed to the change.

● *Hepworth Heating Ltd v Akers and others* (2003) EAT 846/02

  280 of the employees at Hepworth Heating were entitled to be paid in cash. Hepworth Heating proposed moving all the employees to pay by direct transfer to a bank account. This had security and cost benefits for the employer. Some of the employees objected on the grounds of inconvenience and security issues surrounding the use of cashpoints. Negotiation took place and was unsuccessful. The employer then wrote to the employees telling them that the change would go ahead, and giving notice of dismissal if the employees refused to accept the change. A number of employees returned the required forms but wrote 'under duress' against their signatures. They carried on working after the cashless pay was introduced.

  The EAT ruled that there had been no 'duress' and so by continuing to work the employees had agreed to the variation in the terms and conditions of their employment.

● *International Packaging Corporation (UK) Ltd v Balfour and others* (2003) IRLR 11

  IPC was experiencing problems with falling orders and reduced its employees' working hours (and hence their wages) without their consent. A number of employees brought claims that this was an unfair variation of contract, leading to an unlawful deduction of wages (see next chapter). The EAT ruled that no implied term existed that allowed the company to unilaterally reduce employees' hours of work (although short-time working had been introduced on two previous occasions with no objections). On that basis, the employees' claim was upheld.

A change should always be preceded by a period of negotiation, when it is hoped that the employer and employee will be able to explore the issues regarding the change. However, the employer does have the right to impose the change. If the employee wants the right to impose his/her opposition, the most effective way is to actually leave employment and claim constructive dismissal. Even if that claim is successful, the employee no longer has a job.

EMPLOYING ASYLUM-SEEKERS, EX-OFFENDERS AND THOSE REQUIRING WORK PERMITS

ASYLUM-SEEKERS

Under the Asylum and Immigration Act 1996 it is an offence for an employer to employ a person aged 16 years or more who has not been given permission to enter or remain in the United Kingdom, or whose permission to stay in the United Kingdom is subject to not taking up any employment.

The employer must check that a prospective employee does have the right to be employed by seeking documentation from that person. Suitable documentation includes papers issued by a previous employer (eg a P45) or a government department (eg the Benefits Agency) which shows a National Insurance number, a passport which shows the right of abode in the UK, a birth certificate issued in the UK or a passport/identity card from a member state of the European Economic Area (EEA). (To clarify the differences between the European Union and the EEA, which are changing, see www.europea.eu.int.)

If an employer is found to have employed someone who is not eligible for work, it can be a defence to show a copy of these documents (so a photocopy should be taken at the time of recruitment).

These requirements have given rise to some concern over possible race discrimination. Employers keen to avoid employing illegal workers might inadvertently treat eligible workers unfairly by rejecting an application out of concern that the workers might be illegally seeking work when they actually had full rights to be employed. As a result of the Immigration and Asylum Act 1999 the Secretary of State issued a code of practice entitled 'Code of Practice for all employers on the avoidance of race discrimination in recruitment practice while seeking to prevent illegal working'. Like all codes of practice, failure to abide by it is not illegal, but not abiding by it would be taken into account should any race discrimination claim be taken. In essence, the code of practice states that all potential employees should be treated the same at each stage of the recruitment procedure. The checks made to ensure that the person is eligible to work should therefore be made of *all* potential employees.

EX-OFFENDERS

The primary legislation relevant here is the Rehabilitation of Offenders Act 1974. The Act focuses on the issue of 'spent' convictions. An ex-offender does not have to disclose any information relating to a spent conviction when seeking employment, unless they are working in occupations such as doctors, nurses, social workers, teachers, becoming registered day-care providers or carrying out any other work with children.

When a conviction is 'spent' it means that the record has been made clean. The timing of the conviction becoming 'spent' is as follows:

	Period of time before spent
Absolute discharges (when an individual is found guilty/admits guilt but is not punished further)	6 months after the sentencing
Probation order, Conditional discharge, Binding over	1 year or until the order expires (whichever is longer)
Fines, Community service orders	5 years
Imprisonment for less than 6 months	7 years
Imprisonment between 6 and 30 months	10 years
Imprisonment longer than 30 months	Never spent

The Act makes it unlawful for an employer to question a prospective employee about a spent conviction, and if such questioning arises, the prospective employee can deny the conviction ever occurred. It is also unlawful to deny employment on the grounds of a spent conviction.

WORK PERMITS

The work permit scheme, along with more than 80 other routes of entry into the UK, was replaced by a new points-based immigration system during 2008. This will not affect nationals of the states of the European Economic Area who have the right to seek work in the UK, and to accept offers of employment. They are also allowed to live in the UK while looking for suitable work.

Citizens of independent Commonwealth countries who have the 'right of abode' in the UK are also allowed to come into the UK and accept offers of employment. These individuals have British Citizenship that may be acquired by birth, adoption, descent, registration or naturalisation.

The new system requires that a worker from overseas must submit a form to the Home Office which will then be scored. Points are awarded for a number of factors, including age, aptitude and experience. There are a minimum number of points required, depending on the category under which entry is being sought. There are five such categories:

Tier 1   Highly skilled
Tier 2   Skilled
Tier 3   Low-skilled
Tier 4   Students
Tier 5   Temporary workers (including working holidaymakers)

Sponsorship by an employer is essential for tiers 2 to 5. Those in tier 1 who meet the points requirement will be allowed to come to the UK to seek work or to pursue self-employment opportunities.

For more details about the system go to www.homeoffice.gov.uk.

TASK

Find out whether your organisation, or one with which you are familiar, has a policy for dealing with asylum-seekers, ex-offenders and those seeking work from overseas. If it does, read it through and see if it meets the requirements outlined in this chapter. If it does not have a policy, make an attempt at writing one!

KEY LEARNING POINTS

- The employment status of agency workers is not clear.

- Part-time workers have the right to be treated the same as full-time workers. To exercise this right they must be able to identify a full-time comparator in the organisation.

- The flexible working regulations give the right to carers of adults, parents of children aged under six years, and disabled children aged under 18 years, to *request* flexible working.

- The employer has a duty to check that all prospective employees have the right to work in the UK.

- Ex-offenders are not required to reveal any details about 'spent' convictions, unless they work in certain professions.

- An employer cannot unilaterally vary a contract of employment. If a change is needed, negotiation must take place. If that negotiation is unsuccessful, the employer can impose the change, but must be able to show it is for sound business reasons.

- If an employee objects to a variation of the contract, he/she can resign and claim constructive dismissal. Alternatively he/she can continue working, and try to seek damages for any losses the change has brought.

FURTHER READING

CASE SUMMARIES

Airlie and others v City of Edinburgh District Council (1996) IRLR 516 – There was a bonus scheme that had been agreed as part of a collective agreement. Within the collective agreement was a provision for the scheme to be reviewed from time to time. The employer negotiated proposed changes with the trade unions, but was unable to reach agreement. It subsequently imposed changes. It was ruled that this was not an unfair variation of contract – because there was provision for the scheme to be reviewed.

Bunce v Postworth Ltd t/a Skyblue (2005) IRLR 557 CA – Bunce worked on a number of short assignments through Skyblue (an agency), most of them jobs for Carillion Rail. He could not expect continuous work and there was no mutuality of obligation. Bunce argued that there was an 'umbrella' contract and that additional contracts were implied each time he took a new assignment. The Court of Appeal dismissed the claim.

Clark v Oxfordshire Health Authority (1998) IRLR 125 CA – Clark, a nurse, worked as part of a 'bank' of temporary workers. She was dismissed and claimed unfair dismissal: the employer argued she was not an employee. It was upheld that she was not an employee because there was no mutuality of obligation and no employment relationship existed in the periods between each period of work.

Fleet v Matheson (2005) ICR 1132 – This case established that an individual working under a 'modern apprenticeship' agreement was not an employee. A traditional apprenticeship was employment, but it had features not part of a modern apprenticeship – a fixed term, and agreement to employ the individual for the entire term and an obligation to educate and train the apprentice to reach the appropriate qualification and then to employ him/her full-time.

Melhuish v Redbridge Citizen's Advice Bureau (2005) EAT 1030/04 – Melhuish worked as a volunteer for the CAB, and wanted to make a claim of unfair dismissal – an option only open to employees. It was ruled that he was not an employee because the very nature of being a volunteer was that he did not have to attend work and was not paid – so there were no obligations on either side of the relationship.

EXAMPLES TO WORK THROUGH

1   Stephen is a graphic designer and he was employed to work with your full-time product development team on a one-year fixed-term contract. The project he was working on has finished after just 10 months, and there is no other work for him to do. Can you terminate his contract early? If you can, how should it be done? If you can't, what other options are available to you?

2   For the past 10 years your organisation has had cleaners supplied by a local employment agency. Most of the cleaners have worked a relatively short period before moving on to other work – and some cleaners have just come for occasional days. However, one cleaner – Daisy – has regularly worked at your organisation for 12 years. You have been made aware that she has had some sort of argument with the agency and is no longer working for them. However, today she has turned up to carry out her cleaning duties, claiming that she really worked for your organisation anyway. What should you do?

3   You have a small shop that has traditionally opened 9am to 5pm Monday to Saturday. However, due to competition from larger stores you have decided that the only way to survive is to extend opening hours to 8am to 7pm. Your existing staff will then be required to work shifts to cover the extra hours, and you will employ one additional person. However, your staff are not happy with the change and are refusing to work the proposed shifts. What should you do?

CHAPTER 5

Individual protection rights

CHAPTER OBJECTIVES

The objectives of this chapter are:

- to examine the provisions of the Working Time Regulations
- to consider various provisions relating to the payment of wages
- to outline the National Minimum Wage Act 1998
- to consider issues relating to payment during sickness
- to explore the impacts of the Work and Families Act 2006
- to examine regulations relating to parental leave
- to outline the legislation relating to adoption leave
- to review situations when the employee is allowed time off work.

THE WORKING TIME REGULATIONS 1998

The Working Time Regulations are the implementation of the Working Time Directive, and of provisions of the Young Workers Directive. Their basis relates to health and safety – that employees are healthier, and less likely to have accidents, if they have at least minimum levels of holidays, rest periods and reasonable working hours.

The original Regulations did not apply to doctors in training, the armed forces and the police. They also did not apply to the activities of air, road, sea, inland waterway and lake transport, sea fishing and other workers at sea. There were also special cases that were excluded – jobs in domestic service, managing executives, family workers and workers officiating at religious services in churches and religious communities.

The transport categories were largely excluded because workers in these sectors are covered by specific regulations relating to their work. However, this did cause some difficulty, because it is largely 'mobile' workers (eg drivers, fishermen, pilots) rather than 'non-mobile' workers (eg clerical/administration) who are covered by the specific legislation. Thus – as shown in the following case – clerical workers can be excluded from the legislation that seems to be most appropriate to their situation.

● *Bowden and others v Tuffnel Parcels Express Ltd* (2001) IRLR 838

Bowden and two colleagues were part-time clerical workers in Tuffnel Parcels Express, which was a business operating in the road transport sector. They were not entitled to paid holidays under their contracts of employment. When the Working Time Regulations 1998 came into force, they asked their employer to give them the minimum holiday entitlement, as defined by those Regulations. They were refused, because the road transport sector was specifically excluded from the regulations. The issue was eventually referred to the European Court of Justice to determine if 'non-mobile' workers within the sector were covered by the regulations. The ECJ ruled that the whole sector had been excluded, and for that reason the clerical staff were also not covered.

However, these exclusions were amended by the Working Time (Amendment) Regulations 2003. In summary, the impact of these amendments is to apply the regulations to non-mobile workers within the transport sector. If mobile workers within the transport sector are not covered by their own specific legislation, these amendments now apply.

Outside the transport sector the amendments also affect doctors in training. The Working Time Regulations apply in full, but the 48-hour week was phased in from 1 August 2004, reaching the 48-hour target on 1 August 2009.

WHO IS A 'WORKER' UNDER THE WORKING TIME REGULATIONS?

The Regulations (Reg 2) state that a worker includes anyone who

has entered into or works under (or where the employment has ceased, worked under) (a) a contract of employment, or (b) any other contract, whether express or implied and (if it is express) whether oral or in writing, whereby the individual undertakes to do or perform personally any work or services for another party to the contract whose status is not by virtue of the contract that of a client or customer of any profession or business undertaking carried on by the individual.

In essence, the definition of a worker therefore covers those employed under a contract of employment and potentially many casual, freelance and self-employed workers. It excludes self-employed people who are genuinely pursuing their own business activity.

This definition is midway between the definition we had in Chapter 2 of a person employed under a contract for services and a contract of service. In *Torith Ltd v Flynn* (2002) EAT 0017/02 the EAT concluded that the regulations have created a 'hybrid' category of a protected worker.

● Flynn worked for Torith as a joiner on one of its building sites. He claimed holiday pay, under the Working Time Regulations. Torith were responsible for deducting tax and National Insurance contributions from his pay, although Flynn was still required to submit an annual tax return as a self-employed person. Flynn received limited supervision in his work. He was supplied with materials and power tools, but supplied his own hand tools. He worked exclusively for Torith, and was expected to work the normal site hours of 39 per week. He was not entitled to holiday or sick pay, and if he did take a holiday, was not guaranteed any work on his return. Subject to Torith's approval, he could provide a substitute to carry out his work.

The EAT ruled that Flynn was covered by the Working Time Regulations. Flynn fell into this category of a 'hybrid' worker because he clearly was not pursuing a business activity on his own account.

WHAT IS WORK?

Work is defined in Regulation 2 as:

- a period when the worker is working, at the employer's disposal and carrying out activities or duties in accordance with usual practice
- a period when the worker is receiving relevant training
- any other period which is to be treated as working time within the Regulations.

Although this might seem straightforward, it has been the subject of considerable debate in case law – mainly relating to time spent on call.

- *Landeshauptstadt Kiel v Jaeger* (2003) ECR 1-8389/IRLR 804

  In this case a doctor claimed that the time he spent on call where he had to remain at the hospital constituted work. It was agreed that although he was allowed to rest during this period if there was no work requiring his attention, it was classed as work because it was time when the employee was 'at the employer's disposal'.

- *McCartney v Oversley House Management* (2006) IRLR 514

  McCartney was a manager of a sheltered housing complex, and was on 24-hour call. She had a house on the premises where she lived. She worked for four days per week and during those days she was required to be on or within three miles of (and in mobile phone contact with) the premises.

  She claimed that the working arrangements meant that she was not receiving the rest periods as set out in the Regulations. The EAT ruled that she was not getting the required rest periods because any time that she was on call counted as work for the purposes of the Regulations.

THE REQUIREMENTS OF THE WORKING TIME REGULATIONS

Annual leave

From 1 October 2007 a worker has been entitled to 4.8 weeks' (24 days') paid leave, which includes four of the public holidays that exist in the UK. From 6 April 2009 this will be extended to 5.2 weeks' (28 days') paid leave – including all eight of the public holidays.

If there is no defined start date for the calculation of holidays (eg many organisations calculate holidays from January to December each year), the leave year runs from the date employment commenced. The entitlement is only to that holiday entitlement which has been accrued – one twelfth of the four weeks being accrued each month.

The workers are entitled to be paid a sum equivalent to a week's pay for each week of leave. This will be the basic week's pay; non-contractual overtime (overtime which is not guaranteed) is not included in calculating the amount.

- *Bamsey and others v Albon Engineering Ltd* (2003) EAT 365/02

  Ten employees brought a claim to the employment tribunal that Albon Engineering had incorrectly calculated their holiday pay. Bamsey worked a basic 39-hour week, but could work up to 9 hours a week in overtime – although that was not guaranteed. His holiday pay had been calculated on just the 39-hour week.

  The EAT ruled that the non-contractual hours could not be included within 'normal working hours', and so the holiday pay had not been calculated incorrectly.

- *Commissioners for the Inland Revenue v Ainsworth* (2005) IRLR 465

  Ainsworth was on long-term sick leave, and was still an employee of the organisation. Because he was still an employee he claimed that he was still entitled to accrue entitlement to holiday pay. The Court of Appeal ruled that holiday entitlement does not continue to accrue while an employee is on long-term sick leave. (This overturned a previous decision in *Kigass Aero Components Ltd v Brown and others* (2002) ICR 697.) The case has now been referred to the ECJ for its ruling on this matter.

Some employers have operated a system called 'rolled up' holiday pay whereby the money that would be paid for holiday pay is 'rolled' into weekly pay and then the employee receives no payment while on holiday leave. There have been a series of rulings on whether this is lawful practice, culminating with a European Court of Justice ruling in April 2006:

- *Federatie Nederlandse Vakbeweging v Staat der Nederlanden* (2006) IRLR 561

  In this case the ECJ ruled that it is unlawful to allow employers to replace the minimum paid holiday entitlement with a pay-in-lieu system. The reasoning was that such a system might encourage employees not to take their full holiday entitlement.

Remember that the Working Time Regulations are based on health and safety – and having adequate rest is a key part of that.

Maximum working week

The number of hours worked, including overtime, must not exceed an average of 48 hours per week over a 17-week reference period. It is therefore not correct to state that a worker cannot work more than 48 hours in any week. He/she can, as long as he/she works less than 48 hours in another week – to give an average of no more than 48 over the 17-week period.

A worker can opt out of this requirement. Any agreement to opt out must be in writing, and either relate to a specific period of time or apply indefinitely. Within the agreement there must be the right for the worker to give seven days' notice (or a greater period of notice, agreed between the two parties – but this must not be more than three months) to terminate the agreement. The employer is also required to keep up-to-date records of all the workers who have signed such an agreement.

However, the opt-out is currently under review, the European Commission challenging the UK over the way it is used. There is the accusation that it has become customary for employees to automatically sign an opt-out, and that the idea of *choosing* to opt out is not what happens in reality.

- *Barber and others v RJB Mining (UK) Ltd* (1999) IRLR 308

Barber and his colleagues were pit deputies working in a coalmine in Yorkshire. They were contracted to work 42 hours per week, but also worked substantial overtime. RJB approached them, asking for them to sign an opt-out agreement from the maximum working week regulations. Due to ongoing pay negotiations, the workers were advised by their union not to sign the proposed agreement.

The pit deputies had already worked more than the 48-hour maximum during the 17-week reference period, and therefore sought a declaration that they did not need to work again until the average fell below the 48-hour maximum. This declaration was granted by the High Court.

Night work

The protection given to night workers is:

- if the work involves any special hazards or physical or mental strain, a maximum eight hours' work in any 24-hour period

- an entitlement to a free health assessment before starting night work, and at regular intervals thereafter

- an entitlement to adequate rest periods if the nature of the work is likely to cause health problems.

If the health assessment shows problems that might be connected with night work, the employer should make every attempt to move the worker to work that is not night work.

In the Regulations 'night work' is defined as a period that is not less than seven hours in length and includes the normal hours of 12 midnight to 5am. A 'night worker' is a worker who normally works at least three hours of working time during this period of 'night work'.

So an employee who normally works a shift from 6pm to 2am is not a 'night worker' because only two hours fall in the period defined as 'night work'. However, an employee who works from 10pm to 6am is a 'night worker' because five hours fall in the period defined as 'night work'.

It is not necessary for the worker to work these night hours each week. It is required that the hours are *a regular feature* of the pattern of work.

- *R v Attorney General for Northern Ireland* (1999) IRLR 315

The employee changed to a shift system that involved working a night shift of 9pm to 7am one week in every three. Clearly, the shift was classified as 'night work' because there were at least three hours worked between 12 midnight and 5am. Although the shift was only worked one week in three, it was judged to be a regular feature of the employee's work, and he was therefore judged to be a 'night worker'.

 EXPLORE FURTHER

Find out how the restrictions imposed on night-time working have affected shifts in various industries. Have a look at the TUC website (www.tuc.org.uk) to see if there is a general policy on how to address negotiations relating to night-time working.

Rest breaks

All adult workers are entitled to at least 11 consecutive hours' rest in every 24-hour period. Young workers (those aged under 18) are entitled to a consecutive rest period of not less than 12 hours in every 24-hour period.

A worker is entitled to at least 24 hours' uninterrupted rest in every seven-day period. The weekly rest period can be averaged over a period of 14 days (eg 12 hours in one seven-day period and 36 hours in the following seven-day period). If a worker's daily work lasts for more than six hours, the worker is entitled to a rest period. The length of time allowed for the break can be agreed in a collective agreement, but it must be for at least 20 minutes, and the worker must be entitled to spend that period of time away from the work station. Young workers are entitled to a break of at least 30 minutes if their working time is for more than four and a half hours.

- *Commission of the European Communities v United Kingdom* (2006) ECJ 7/9/06 (C 484/04)

    In 2006 the trade union Amicus, supported by the European Commission, brought a challenge against the DTI (now the Department of BERR) guidelines on rest breaks issued by the UK Government. The DTI guidelines read that 'Employers must make sure that workers can take their rest, but are not required to make sure they do take their rest.'

    This was challenged on the basis that rests should be obligatory, and that the employer should be responsible for ensuring that they are taken. The challenge was upheld by the ECJ, which agreed that the guidelines did not give the assurance that the minimum requirements of the Regulations would be met. However, in making their judgment the ECJ did comment that there was a limit to the level of 'policing' that the employer was expected to do. As a result of this ruling the guidelines are to be reviewed.

TASK

Find out what alterations your organisation, or an organisation with which you are familiar, had to make in response to the Working Time Regulations. What difficulties did it encounter? Were there any costs involved?

PAYMENT OF WAGES

As we noted in Chapter 3, one of the obligations on the employer is to pay wages. There are also further, more detailed rights of the employee with regard to wages.

THE RIGHT TO AN ITEMISED PAY STATEMENT

In accordance with the Employment Rights Act 1996 (section 8) employees have the right to receive a written pay statement with (or before) each payment of wages or salary. This statement must show the gross and net payments, and the nature of any deductions, and the purpose of those deductions.

If an employee does not receive such a pay statement, he/she can apply to the employment tribunal that can declare the particulars that should have been included. If any unnotified deductions have been made during the 13 weeks prior to the application to the tribunal being made, the tribunal can instruct the employer to refund those deductions.

TASK

Look at your last pay statement. What does it include? Does it show all that is listed above?

AUTHORISED DEDUCTIONS

As we noted in Chapter 2, unlawful deductions from wages is the one of the most common claims brought before an employment tribunal. The only lawful deductions that can be made are:

- those required or authorised by statute (eg PAYE and National Insurance contributions)

- those required or authorised by a provision in the contract of employment, of which the employee has been made aware (eg a payment relating to the use of company tools and equipment)

- those agreed by the employee in writing (eg a contribution to a club or society run by the organisation).

An agreement to a deduction must be made in writing, and it must be made clear that the deduction is to be made from wages – and that the employee agrees to this.

- *Potter v Hunt Contracts* (1991) IRLR 108

  Potter took a HGV driving course that was paid for by the agency he worked for. The agency placed him with Hunt Contracts, who decided to take him on as a permanent employee. As part of the deal with the agency they refunded the cost of the HGV training course. An agreement was drawn up with Potter that he would repay Hunt Contracts for the £545 cost of the course at the amount of £22 per month. One month later his employment was terminated and the outstanding money (£523) was deducted from his outstanding wages. Because this was less than £523 he received nothing in his final pay. The employment tribunal held it was a lawful deduction. However, the EAT overturned the decision of the tribunal because the agreement between Potter and Hunt Contracts did not make it clear that the deduction was to be made from Potter's *wages* – it was therefore an unlawful deduction.

An agreement to a deduction must be made before an event leading to that deduction. (For example, if an employer wants an employee to pay for a training course, this must be agreed between the employee and employer before the employee attends the course.)

- *Discount Tobacco and Confectionery Ltd v Williamson* (1993) IRLR 327

  Williamson was a manager of the respondent's retail outlets. On a number of occasions there had been a shortfall following stocktaking. After a series of shortfalls Williamson signed an agreement that £3,500 would be deducted from his wages at a rate of £20 per week, to compensate for part of the shortfalls. He was then dismissed, due to the shortfalls, and was told his outstanding wages and accrued holiday pay would not be paid to him because they were less than the £3,500 he had agreed to in deductions.

  The EAT supported the tribunal in the finding that the deduction had been agreed to after the event (ie after the shortfalls) and was therefore not a lawful deduction of wages. It was also noted that the respondent had a written procedure for handling shortfalls which had not been followed – and, indeed, Williamson had not been made aware of the procedures.

DEFINITION OF WAGES

Wages are any sum payable to a worker in connection with work done during employment.

- *Delaney v Staples* (1992) IRLR 191

  Delaney was dismissed from employment with Staples, and claimed that she was owed commission, holiday pay and pay in lieu of notice (money relating to the wages she would have earned if she had worked her notice period). It was ruled that the commission and holiday pay had been earned, and so failure to pay them equated to unlawful deductions. However, the pay in lieu of notice was ruled not to be wages because it was not money relating to work done. On this basis it was not possible for the non-payment of pay in lieu of notice to be an unlawful deduction from wages. However, it was ruled that pay in lieu of notice actually equates to damages to compensate the employee for being dismissed without contractual notice (wrongful dismissal – see Chapter 9). Nonetheless, it was noted that if an employee had been given the correct notice but had not been required to attend work (known as 'garden leave'), then that money would constitute 'wages' because a contract of employment still exists.

 EXPLORE FURTHER

As we saw in Chapter 2, unlawful deductions of wages is one of the most common types of claims that come before the employment tribunals. Do you think that the reason for this is a lack of clarity in current legislation? If so, what area of legislation needs clarification? Can you think of any other reasons for this type of claim being relatively common?

GUARANTEE PAYMENTS

Sections 28 to 35 of the Employment Rights Act 1996 state that an employee with one month's continuous service is entitled to a guarantee payment if he/she is not provided with work throughout a day when he/she would normally expect to work, if the reason for the lack of work is:

- a decrease in demand for the employer's business, or for the type of work that the employee carries out

  or

- any other event affecting the employer's normal business (eg a power cut).

The employee loses the right to a guarantee payment if:

- the failure to provide work is related to industrial action
- the employee refuses the offer of suitable alternative work
- the employee does not comply with a reasonable attendance requirement, so that the employer can keep workers together in the event that work can continue (eg vital supplies can be delivered).

- *Purdy v Willowbrook International Ltd* (1977) IRLR 388

  Purdy worked as a trimmer in Willowbrook's coach factory. There was a reduction in trimming work and Purdy was asked to move to the finishing shop – work with which he was familiar. The pay would have been similar to that which he earned as a trimmer, and definitely in excess of any guarantee payment. Purdy refused to move. Subsequently, the trimmers (including Purdy) were moved to a three-day week. Purdy claimed a guarantee payment for the two days of no work, but it was ruled that he was not entitled to the payments because he had refused the opportunity of suitable alternative work.

- *Meadows v Faithful Overalls Ltd* (1977) IRLR 330

  Meadows worked at a clothing factory. On the day in question, when he arrived for work, the heating system was inoperable and the employer was waiting for a delivery of oil to fuel the heating. The employees were asked to wait in the canteen where hot tea was provided. The oil supplier informed the employer there would be a delay in the delivery, and Meadows stated he would only wait until 9.45am. At 9.45am he went home, and the oil delivery arrived just after 10.00am. Meadows claimed a guarantee payment. It was ruled that the request to wait was a reasonable request, and by refusing to do so Meadows had no entitlement to a guarantee payment.

The guarantee payment is for the amount of hours normally worked on the day in question, calculated at the hourly rate. The guarantee payment is paid for a maximum of five days in a three-month period. In 2008 this was subject to a daily maximum of £20.40 (the amount is reviewed in February each year).

THE NATIONAL MINIMUM WAGE ACT 1998

The National Minimum Wage (NMW) Act gives the right for workers to receive a minimum hourly rate of pay. In the Act a worker is described as someone working under a contract of employment or any other contract under which the individual undertakes to perform personally any work or services for another party.

Those who are not covered by the Act include:

- a worker under the age of 26 years who is employed under a contract of apprenticeship and is in the first 12 months of that contract

- a worker who is on a scheme to provide training or temporary work, or a scheme designed to help him/her find work

- a worker who is taking part in work experience as part of a first degree course, or as part of a teacher training course

- a homeless person who is given shelter and other benefits in return for work.

The NMW is paid at two levels. From 1 October 2007 these are:

£5.52 per hour for those aged 22 years and over

£4.60 per hour for those aged 18 to 21 years

£3.40 per hour for those aged 16 to17 years

(These rates are reviewed in October each year. Current rates can be found at www.lowpay.gov.uk.)

Clearly, the rates of pay that are set by the NMW relate to age – and it was therefore expected that the introduction of legislation making age discrimination unlawful from 1 October 2007 might impact on the NMW rates. However, it did not. The government justified this by arguing that removing the three bands of payment might make employers less inclined to employ those in the younger age bracket.

As we will discuss in Chapter 7, a decision to offer rates above the NMW, but using the same age bands, would have to be justified – as would, for example, paying 16-year-olds a different rate from 17-year-olds. If there was no justification, that could potentially be age discrimination.

WHAT COUNTS AS WORK FOR PAYMENT OF THE NMW?

An employee's pay does not always consist solely of a basic rate. There are often bonuses, tips, stand-by payments and other items that make up the total pay. In addition, when calculating an hourly rate a crucial part of the calculation is the number of hours worked. As we saw when looking at the Working Time Regulations, it is not always clear when an employee is actually 'working'. A number of cases have addressed the issue of what should be taken into account when calculating the hourly rate of pay.

- *British Nursing Association v Inland Revenue* (2002) IRLR 480

  The BNA provides a 24-hour service supplying nurses to nursing homes and similar establishments. During the day the bookings are made through the head office. During the night (8pm to 9am) trained nurses work from home, taking calls and placing nurses accordingly. Between calls the nurses can spend their time as they wish. The employment tribunal was asked to determine what hours the nurses were working at night, for the purposes of calculating their wages in accordance with the NMW. The tribunal found (and was supported by the Court of Appeal) that the nurses were working for each hour of their shift. Although they were not taking phone calls all the time, they were required to be available. In addition, they noted that the process during the night was no different from the process carried out during the day. The nurses had therefore to be paid at least the NMW for each hour of their night shift.

- *Scottbridge Construction Ltd v Wright* (2002) IRLR 21

  Wright was a nightwatchman working from 5pm to 7am. He had to respond to telephone calls and the intruder alarm, and was sometimes given some other small tasks. Provided that he carried out these duties he was entitled to spend the rest of the time as he wished, and sleeping facilities were provided. He claimed that he should be paid the NMW for each hour of his shift. The Court of Session supported his claim, ruling that he was required to work at any time during the night should a phone call be made or an alarm be triggered.

In determining whether the worker is working for the purposes of entitlement to the NMW it is important to consider the restrictions placed upon the worker when he/she is not actually carrying out a task determined by the employer (does he/she have to be available?). All aspects of the nature of the work must also be examined to see if it can be properly described as 'work'.

In determining if someone is being paid at least the NMW the current level of gross pay (ie the payment before tax and National Insurance is deducted) must be considered. Added to that can be the cost of accommodation provided to the employee (a formula to account for this is described in the Regulations). Amounts that are not paid through the payroll (eg tips given directly to staff by customers) are not included as part of the definition of pay.

- *Nerva and others v United Kingdom* (2002) IRLR 815

  The applicants were employed as waiters. If customers left cash tips, they were gathered together and shared amongst the waiters. If customers left tips on a cheque or credit card payment, they were also added up and paid through the payroll as 'additional pay'. For the purposes of calculating adherence to the NMW the employer claimed that the tips paid through the payroll counted as wages. The employees brought a claim, which ultimately went to the European Court of Justice. The finding of all the appeal courts was that the employer was entitled to count the tips paid through the payroll as wages. The employer held the legal title to the tips, and they were his money. He was entitled to use them to meet part of the cost of paying the waiters.

- *Aviation and Airport Services v Bellfield and others* (2001) EAT 194/00

  Bellfield worked as a customer care agent. She was entitled to an attendance allowance if strict attendance requirements were met. Due to the introduction of the NMW the employer sought to make alterations to the payment structure. In determining that Bellfield was being paid the NMW the employer relied on the inclusion of the attendance allowance. It was ruled that this could not be included in the calculation because it was not an allowance attributable to the performance (as opposed to being present at work) of the worker in carrying out her work.

- *Leisure Employment Services v HMRC* (2007) EWCA Civ 92

  The employer (which owned the Butlins and Haven camps) supplied employees with accommodation. In addition, it deducted £3 per week from employees for the cost of gas and electricity. The result of this deduction was that the hourly rate paid was below the NMW.

  The employer argued that the weekly £3 actually formed part of the employees' wages, but the Court of Appeal did not allow that argument.

FAILURE TO PAY THE NMW

Employers are required to keep records of payments for a minimum of three years. If a worker believes he/she is not being paid the correct amount under the NMW Regulations, he/she can ask to see these records. If the employer refuses to let the employee see the records, the employee can make a complaint to the employment tribunal. In addition, if the employee believes he/she has not been paid the NMW, he/she can make an application to the employment tribunal for the situation to be assessed.

TASK

List the reasons for and against the introduction of the National Minimum Wage. Do you think that the reasons for and against have been substantiated by evidence gained since the National Minimum Wage was introduced? Has the financial level of the National Minimum Wage been sufficient to have a real impact?

EXPLORE FURTHER

The rate at which the NMW is paid has been raised significantly since it was first introduced. However, many employee groups still believe that it is set too low to be of any real benefit to the employee. Read different opinions on this matter (see www.tuc.org.uk and www.cbi.co.uk as a useful starting point). Having read different opinions, draw your own conclusions on the efficacy of the current rates of the NMW.

PAYMENT AND SICKNESS

STATUTORY SICK PAY

There is no legal requirement on an employer to have a sick pay scheme. However, all employers are required to pay statutory sick pay (SSP) when an employee qualifies for such payments, and cannot contract out of doing so.

Employees who have been continuously sick for four or more calendar days in a row and have average earnings at least equal to the lower earnings limit (the amount at which National Insurance contributions are payable) are entitled to receive statutory sick pay. Any day for which SSP is claimed must be a day on which the employee would ordinarily work. SSP is paid for a maximum of 28 weeks in any 12-month period. If the sickness absence continues once the entitlement to SSP has expired, the employee can then claim incapacity benefit.

SUSPENSION ON MEDICAL GROUNDS

If an employee is suspended from work on medical grounds (eg the employer cannot provide any work for the employee due to health and safety requirements), the employee is entitled to the normal rate of pay for the first 26 weeks of the suspension. Employees who have worked for less than one month, or who have a fixed-term contract of less than three months, are excluded from this entitlement. In addition, an employee is not entitled to the payment if he/she has refused suitable alternative work or has not co-operated with the employer in being available for suitable work. If the employee is incapable of working due to illness, the terms relating to suspension on medical grounds do not apply.

MATERNITY PROTECTION

Maternity protection is an area of employment law that has changed greatly over recent years. The most recent amendment came as part of the Work and Families Act 2006. Maternity protection covers a woman through the periods of ante-natal care, care at work during her pregnancy, and maternity leave.

A pregnant woman is protected against dismissal on the grounds of her pregnancy, discrimination on the grounds of her pregnancy or any other detrimental treatment relating to the pregnancy.

- *Webb v EMO Air Cargo Ltd* (1994) IRLR 482

  Webb was employed to cover another employee who was taking maternity leave. She was taken on six months before the other employee started her leave, so that she could be trained to carry out the duties of the job. Two weeks after her employment started Webb found that she was also pregnant. EMO dismissed Webb because she was not going to be available to them at the crucial time – ie to cover the whole of the period of the other employee's maternity leave. Webb appealed to the employment tribunal, who supported the employer's view. It held that if a man had been recruited to cover, and announced he would be on protracted leave, EMO would also have dismissed the man. The European Court of Justice overruled this finding, ruling that any dismissal relating to pregnancy was sex discrimination, and that it was not right to make comparisons with a 'hypothetical' man.

TASK

Find out if your organisation, or an organisation with which you are familiar, has a maternity policy. Read it and compare it with the statutory requirements covered in this chapter.

ANTE-NATAL CARE

A pregnant woman has the right to take paid time off for ante-natal appointments during working hours. She has the right to be paid for this period of absence. If she is not allowed the time off, she can complain to an employment tribunal that can make a declaration that the refusal was unjustified and order the company to pay the woman an amount equal to that which she would have received for the period of time off requested. If she is allowed the time off but the company refuse to pay her, the employment tribunal can made a declaration to that effect, and order the company to pay her the rightful amount.

The ante-natal treatment must be recommended by a doctor, midwife or health visitor. The woman can be asked to show her employer proof of her appointment (eg an appointment card) for second and subsequent appointments.

A straightforward case showing the right to paid ante-natal appointments is:

- *Gregory v Tudsbury Ltd* (1982) IRLR 267

  Gregory took five consecutive Monday afternoons off to attend ante-natal care and relaxation classes. She produced a medical certificate signed by a doctor and midwife. Her employers allowed her the time off, but refused to pay her for it, although they agreed it was not practical for her to arrange the classes outside working hours. Gregory complained to the employment tribunal and her employer was ordered to pay her for the time spent at the ante-natal classes.

Although there is a clear right to paid time off, this right must not be abused:

- *Gough v Country Sport (Wales) Ltd* (1989) ET Case No. 01075/89

  Country Sport was concerned that Gough was taking off more time than was necessary for ante-natal care. On one occasion Gough had an afternoon appointment, and Country Sport refused to let her also take the morning off to go to the hairdresser. Gough took the whole day off, and was dismissed. The employment tribunal held that it was a fair dismissal, because the reason for the dismissal was Gough's 'flagrant disobedience' and not her pregnancy.

MATERNITY LEAVE

There are three periods of maternity leave:

- *compulsory maternity leave* – No employee may work for her employer for the two weeks (four weeks for factory or workshop workers) immediately following the date of childbirth. This period of two weeks forms part of the period known as ordinary maternity leave.

- *ordinary maternity leave* (OML) – All pregnant women are entitled to take 26 weeks' ordinary maternity leave, regardless of their length of service.

- *additional maternity leave* (AML) – All pregnant women are also entitled to take 26 weeks' additional maternity leave (prior to April 2007 this was only available to women with at least 26 weeks' service). AML starts immediately OML finishes – giving a total leave period of 52 weeks.

Entitlement to maternity leave

Maternity leave (OML and AML) can only be taken by employees (those who have entered into, or work under, a contract of employment that is defined as a contract of service). To qualify for OML the woman must inform her employer no later than the 15th week before the expected week of childbirth (EWC) – in writing if requested – of the following:

- that she is pregnant

- her EWC

- the date on which she wants to start her OML – this cannot be earlier than the beginning of the 11th week before the EWC.

OML is considered to have started on the earliest of:

- the date the employee has notified to her employer as the intended start date of OML

- the day which follows the first day after the beginning of the fourth week before the EWC on which she is absent from work wholly or partly due to pregnancy

- the day that follows the day on which childbirth occurs (OML starts at this point even if the day falls before the beginning of the 11th week before the EWC).

During OML the employee is:

- entitled to the benefits of all the terms and conditions of employment that would have applied if she had not been absent (apart from any terms concerning 'remuneration')

- bound by any obligations arising under those terms and conditions (unless they are inconsistent with the right to take OML – eg the requirement to attend work)

- entitled to return to the job in which she was employed before the OML, with the same seniority and rights as if she had not been absent.

Statutory and contractual holiday will continue to accrue throughout OML, although bank holidays are not included in this. In addition, service for statutory continuity purposes continues to accrue throughout OML.

During AML the employment contract continues, but only certain terms and conditions of employment apply:

- The employer is still bound by the obligation of trust and confidence.
- Any notice provisions still apply.
- Redundancy rights apply.
- Disciplinary and grievance procedures apply.

The Work and Families Act 2006 added in the concept of 'keeping-in-touch days'. During the period of maternity leave the employee is allowed to work for up to 10 'keeping-in-touch' days without losing any entitlement to maternity pay. The employee cannot be forced to work any such days, and must not suffer any detriment for refusing to work any such days. The purpose of the days is to keep some relationship between the employee and the employer going during the period of leave, and to give an opportunity for training or any updating that might occur.

RETURNING TO WORK

When returning from OML an employee is entitled to return to exactly the same job she left and is to be treated as if she had never been absent. She should be paid the amount of pay she would have been paid if she had not been absent (ie inclusive of any pay increases awarded during her absence). If the employer does not allow the woman to return to her old job, this would count as a dismissal, and would be automatically unfair because it would be a dismissal related to pregnancy.

When returning from AML an employee is entitled to return to her old job unless this is not reasonably practicable. In this case an employer must offer a job that is suitable – which will mean the same status and attracting the same terms and conditions of employment.

The exceptions to this are:

- when a woman is returning after two or more consecutive periods of statutory leave, and it is not 'reasonably practicable' for the woman to return to the same job
- where a redundancy situation has arisen during the period of leave. In this situation a woman is entitled to be offered any suitable alternative work.

An example of the issues that can arise relating to redundancy can be found in:

- *Philip Hodges & Co v Kell* (1994) IRLR 568

  Kell worked as a secretary for Philip Hodges & Co. During her maternity leave the firm decided there was no longer a requirement for her role as a personal secretary. They did not give her notice at this time. During her leave they also employed another secretary on an ad hoc basis, but made her permanent and full-time before Kell was due to return to work. The employment tribunal found that Kell worked as a legal secretary, and so was capable of doing the other role that had originally been ad hoc. On that basis, it was unfair to recruit another employee during her maternity leave, and make Kell redundant. They found, therefore, that Kell had been unfairly dismissed.

Notification of returning to work

A woman has the automatic right to return to work following her maternity leave and, unless she says otherwise, it will be assumed that she will return. A woman returning to work after having taken her full maternity leave entitlement is not required to give her employer any notice: she can simply turn up on the day after her period of leave has ended.

If a woman decides not to return to work, she is required to give the notice required in accordance with her contract of employment. This cannot be less than the statutory minimum of one week.

If a woman wants to return to work before the end of her maternity leave (assuming that the period of compulsory leave has passed), she must give her employer at least eight weeks' notice of her intention – specifying the date on which she intends to return.

If a woman wants to return to work, but on reduced hours, she must make her request to her employer in line with the rules regarding flexible working, which we looked at in Chapter 4.

STATUTORY MATERNITY PAY (SMP)

SMP is payable by employers, for a period of 39 weeks, to pregnant employees who have worked for that employer for at least 26 continuous weeks at the 14th week before the EWC (the 'qualifying period'). The payment of SMP cannot start until the employee has ceased working (ie started a period of maternity leave). The employee must earn at least the lower earnings limit for the payment of primary Class 1 NI contributions (£84 for the 2006/7 tax year) as an average payment over the eight weeks up to and including the qualifying period.

SMP is paid at a rate of 90% of average weekly earnings for the first six weeks, and then at £117.18 per week (from February 2008) for the remaining 33 weeks. The employer can choose to pay more than this amount.

The government has announced a commitment to further extend the payment of SMP to 52 weeks. This is likely to be as from 2010, although no definite date has yet been given.

 EXPLORE FURTHER

Maternity legislation has changed greatly over current years. Track the changes that have occurred, and try to determine the reasons for these changes. Do you think that further changes are likely in the future? What changes are most likely to occur?

STATUTORY PATERNITY LEAVE

Statutory paternity leave was introduced by the Employment Act 2002. To qualify for paternity leave the employee must have worked for that employer for at least 26 continuous weeks at the 15th week before the expected week of the birth of the baby. The employee must be the father of the child, or the mother's husband or partner. The employee must expect to have responsibility for the upbringing of the child. (Note: the partner does not have to be male; it can be a female in a same-sex relationship.)

The employee must give 28 days' notice to his employer of the intention to take paternity leave. The period of paternity leave will be of up to two weeks. The paternity leave will be paid at the lower rate of SMP (ie £117.18 per week [as at February 2008]). During the period of paternity leave the contract of employment continues, and the employee has the right to return to his job after the leave ends.

There are currently proposals being considered to introduce further paternity leave – lasting up to 26 weeks. This leave will be known as *additional paternity leave* (APL). The purpose of the leave is to allow flexibility for the mother to return to work early from her maternity leave, and to let the father of the baby take the remainder of the maternity leave period as APL. This would mean that the parents can be the primary carers for the child during its first year of life. APL will not be paid – but if the mother has not used up her full entitlement to SMP, the father can claim the remaining SMP. It is not proposed that the mother and father can take leave together (eg both take 26 weeks' leave at the same time). The purpose of the APL is to extend the time that the child is being cared for by one of its parents.

These are the proposals – there are no specific details at the time of writing. It is unlikely to become part of the legislation before 2010.

ADOPTION LEAVE

The Employment Act 2002 introduced a new statutory right for employees who adopt a child to take time off to build up a relationship with that child. The provisions mirror maternity leave – but either of the parents can take the leave (though not both).

There is therefore a period of *ordinary adoption leave* (OAL), which lasts for 26 weeks, and can be taken by an employee who is the 'adopter' and has been continuously employed for at least 26 weeks ending with the week when he/she was notified of having been matched with the child. The payment during the period of OAL is at the lower rate of SMP.

An employee can choose to commence OAL on the day on which the child is placed with him/her for adoption, or at a predetermined date which is no more than 14 days before the child is expected to be placed, and no later than the day of the placement.

An employee is entitled to *additional adoption leave* (AAL) if the child was placed with the employee for adoption, the employee took OAL in respect of the child and the OAL period did not end prematurely (for example, because of a disruption to the placement of the adopted child). AAL starts the day after OAL ends.

During adoption leave the employee's rights and obligations under the contract of employment continue. The employee is entitled to return to his/her old job with the same seniority and benefits that he/she left.

PARENTAL LEAVE

The Maternity and Parental Leave Regulations 1999 laid down a minimum framework of parental leave rights. Employers and employees have to adhere to the minimum rights, but can work out their own agreement to operate parental leave.

The minimum framework is :

- Employees with at least one year's continuous service with their employer who have responsibility for a child have the right to parental leave.

- Up to 13 weeks' leave may be taken for each child, or 18 weeks if the child is entitled to a disability living allowance.

- The leave has to be for the purpose of caring for the child.

- The right to take leave normally applies during the child's first five years except in relation to parents of adopted children (when the leave can be taken during the first five years of the placement) and disabled children (when the leave can be taken until the child's 18th birthday).

- The employee remains employed while on leave, so the contract of employment continues.

- The employee has the right to return to the same job, or to another suitable job, after the period of leave ends.

The 13 weeks' leave is a total allowance, and under the statutory scheme leave must be taken in blocks of at least one week. An employee cannot take more than four weeks' leave in respect of any individual child during a particular year. Parental leave is unpaid.

If the period of intended leave is two weeks or less, then at least four weeks' notice must be given. For longer periods at least twice the length of leave requested must be given in notice (ie six weeks' notice for three weeks' leave).

TIME OFF FOR DEPENDANTS

The Employment Rights Act 1996 gives a right to enable an employee to take a reasonable amount of time off during working hours to take action which is necessary to:

- provide assistance when a dependant falls ill, gives birth or is injured or assaulted

- make arrangements for the care of a dependant who is ill or injured

- take actions in connection with the death of a dependant

- deal with disruption to or cancellation of arrangements for the care of a dependant

- deal with an incident involving a child at school.

A dependant is the employee's wife, husband, child, parent or someone living in the same house as the employee who is not a lodger, tenant, boarder or employee. The right is not paid, but if the employer has allowed employees paid time off in the past to deal with such issues, it must continue to do so. An employee must make the employer aware of the reason for the absence as soon as is reasonably practical, but there is no requirement to give notice.

TIME OFF FOR PUBLIC DUTIES

Section 50 of the Employment Rights Act 1996 gives employees the right to take time off for certain public duties. They are not entitled to payment from their employer when taking this time off. Duties include meetings of, or work in relation to membership of:

- a local authority

- a statutory tribunal

- a health authority, NHS Trust or health board

- a relevant education body

- a police authority

- the Service Authority of the National Crime Squad or the National Criminal Intelligence Service

- a board of prison visitors or a prison-visiting committee

- the Environment Agency.

In addition, the Right to Time off for Study or Training Regulations 2001 permit employees who are aged 16 or 17 years and are not receiving full-time or further education and have not attained standards of achievement as defined in the Act (eg grades A to C in five subjects at GCSE) a reasonable time off for work for study or training. The same rights are given to employees who are aged 18 years and are undertaking training or study leading to a relevant qualification and who began that study before reaching the age of 18 years.

In Chapter 10 we also note the right to time off for trade union duties, and in Chapter 9 we note the right to time off to seek employment when faced with impending redundancy.

TASK

Find out if there have been any requests for paternity, adoption, parental or dependant leave in your organisation, or an organisation with which you are familiar. How have these requests been addressed? Does the employer feel that the requests have been disruptive to the efficiency of the organisation?

KEY LEARNING POINTS

- The Working Time Regulations were extended in 2003 to cover sectors previously excluded from the Regulations.

- The Working Time Regulations set minimum standards relating to the working week, annual leave, night work and rest periods.

- An employee is entitled to receive an itemised pay statement.

- Deductions from wages are only lawful if they are determined by statute, are agreed within the contract of employment, or if they are agreed between the employer and employee in writing.

- Pay in lieu of notice is not classed as wages.

- Guarantee payments are paid to those who have at least one month's continuous employment, and are not offered work on a day when they would normally be expected to work.

- The National Minimum Wage is paid at three levels, dependent on age.

- The employer has to pay statutory sick pay when the employee qualifies for such payment.

- Maternity leave falls into three categories: compulsory leave, ordinary leave and additional leave.

- A dismissal relating to pregnancy is automatically unfair.
- Paternity leave is allowed up to a period of two weeks.
- Adoption leave mirrors maternity leave, but can only be claimed by one person in relation to each child (known as the 'adopter').
- Parental leave up to a maximum of 13 weeks can be taken in the first five years of the child's life (or in the first five years of an adoption) or a maximum of 18 weeks can be taken in the first 18 years of a disabled child's life.
- Time off to care for dependants can be taken, with as much notice as possible being given.
- Time off is allowed for a range of public duties.

FURTHER READING

CASE SUMMARIES

Hoyland v Asda Stores Ltd (2006) IRLR 468 – This case established that an employee was entitled to a bonus based on sales performance of the whole team, and her own performance. She was absent due to maternity leave and her bonus was reduced pro rata to reflect the days she had worked. She claimed this was unfair. The Court of Session upheld that no reduction should be made for the two weeks of compulsory maternity leave – but she was not entitled to the bonus for the remainder of the maternity leave, because 'remuneration' is not a term and condition of employment that continues during OML and AML.

Anderson v Jarvis Hotels (2006) EAT 0500/05 – The employee worked as a hotel night manager. He was required to sleep on the premises at night and to be on call (and once received a formal warning when he left for 30 minutes during the night). He claimed that he should be paid for the period when he was required to be on the premises. The EAT agreed, claiming that this had to be classed as 'work' because he was at the call of his employers.

Byrne Brothers (Formwork Ltd) v Baird and others (2002) IRLR 96 – This case examined the issue of who is a 'worker' as defined by the Working Time Regulations. The claimants were self-employed builders, but the EAT found that they were workers for the requirements of the Working Time Regulations – if you are researching this, an important judgment to read.

EXAMPLES TO WORK THROUGH

1 You employ a security officer who works at night – from 10pm to 6am. He is required to patrol the site at the beginning and end of his shift, and apart from that his only duties are to answer any emergency calls that are received. He is allowed to sleep on the premises, and a bed is provided. You pay him for the hours that he patrols and for emergency call-outs. However, he is not paid for any time he is resting. He argues that he should be paid for the full shift. Who is correct?

2 One of your male employees received a telephone call at work telling him that his wife had gone into premature labour (five weeks early). He immediately left work and went to the hospital. The baby has been safely delivered and today he has called you and said he wants to take the remainder of the week off as paternity leave. Is he allowed to?

3 You operate a courier business and one of your drivers has had a minor accident in your vehicle – this is his third accident in six months. You have decided to deduct the excess from the insurance claim from his wages, given the number of accidents he has had. Is this allowed? Justify your answer.

CHAPTER 6

Discrimination (1)

CHAPTER OBJECTIVES

The objectives of this chapter are:

- to explore the concept of discrimination
- to analyse the difference between indirect and direct discrimination
- to explore the concept of genuine occupational qualifications (GOQs) and requirements (GORs)
- to outline the concept of 'positive action'
- to consider issues relating to victimisation, harassment and vicarious liability
- to explore the law relating to equal pay.

DISCRIMINATION

Legislation relating to discrimination has developed considerably over recent years. However, the first piece of legislation specifically focusing on issues of discrimination is nearly 40 years old – the Equal Pay Act 1970. That legislation started to address the issue of men and women being paid different rates for the same work – which was not an unusual practice at that time.

This legislation was followed by two major pieces of legislation: the Sex Discrimination Act 1975 and the Race Relations Act 1976. These two Acts made it unlawful to treat employees differently because of their gender or their race. The Acts apply across all areas of employment, from recruitment and promotion to opportunities for training, and dismissal. As we saw in Chapter 2, a significant number of claims brought to the employment tribunal still relate to these two pieces of legislation.

No new areas of discrimination law were introduced until nearly 20 years later, when the Disability Discrimination Act 1995 gave disabled employees the right not to be treated differently in all aspects of employment, in comparison to an able-bodied employee.

In 1999 transsexuals were added to the categories of employees that may not legally be discriminated against, by the Sex Discrimination (Gender Reassignment) Regulations 1999.

In December 2003 two additional pieces of legislation were introduced:

- The Employment Equality (Sexual Orientation) Regulations 2003 made it unlawful to discriminate against employees on the grounds of their sexual orientation.

- The Employment Equality (Religion and Belief) Regulations 2003 made it unlawful to discriminate against employees on the grounds of their religion or belief.

In October 2006 the Employment Equality (Age) Regulations 2006 were introduced making it unlawful to discriminate on the grounds of age.

In addition, there is legislation protecting part-time workers and those working on fixed-term contracts from discriminatory treatment (as we saw in Chapter 4) and protection for trade union members (and non-members) against discriminatory treatment (see Chapter 10).

This brief history of discrimination legislation shows that there has been a move to make it essential to base all decisions relating to employment (from recruitment to dismissal) on the abilities of the employee (or to adapt the requirements of the job so that the employee can perform competently), and not on factors that do not have any bearing on how competently the employee carries out his/her duties.

Indeed, it is important to note that the individuals covered by discrimination legislation is broader than for many other areas of employment law. Not only employees but potential employees, past employees, trainees, the self-employed, the armed forces and the police are covered.

TASK

During your studies ensure that you are aware of any further changes proposed to discrimination legislation, and of new case law as it is reported. Discrimination law is a rapidly moving area of legislation – you must always keep up to date. Useful websites include www.cipd.co.uk (Chartered Institute of Personnel and Development), www.equalityhumanrights.com (Equality and Human Rights Commission) and www.berr.gov.uk (Department of Business, Enterprise and Regulatory Reform).

Discrimination is broadly divided into *direct discrimination* and *indirect discrimination*.

DIRECT DISCRIMINATION

This is where an employee is treated less favourably on the grounds of sex/race, etc, than an employee of the different sex/race, etc. It is important to note that the issue is being treated less *favourably*. Direct discrimination cannot be justified (apart from in certain situations in age discrimination – see next chapter) – and the argument that there was good reason for treating groups differently is not relevant (unless there is a genuine occupational requirement/ qualification – see later). In addition, direct discrimination cannot be justified by the argument that there is no detriment to the employee:

- *Moyhing v Barts and London NHS Trust* (2006) IRLR 860

  Moyhing was a male student nurse who was required to carry out an ECG on a female Asian patient. Because this involved intimate contact he was told that a female chaperone must be present. There was no similar policy for female nurses carrying out an ECG on male patients. He argued therefore that the requirement for a chaperone was direct discrimination on the grounds of his sex. The employment tribunal agreed that there was different treatment, but found that there was no detriment to Moyhing. However, Moyhing successfully appealed to the EAT. The EAT argued that there is no justification to direct discrimination, and assessing there was no detriment did not allow the conclusion that discrimination was justifiable.

If an employee can show that their treatment is unfavourable, then they must be able to point to a comparator of the opposite gender/a different race, etc, and show that this comparator (who is the same as the employee in all other ways) is being treated differently. This comparator can be real or can be hypothetical.

- *Whitfield v Cleanaway UK Ltd* (2005)

  Whitfield was subjected to a series of taunts about his sexuality. He eventually resigned and he was awarded compensation for direct sexual orientation discrimination. In this case the taunting clearly amounted to less favourable treatment.

In some cases it can be difficult to make use of a hypothetical comparator. In the last chapter we looked at the case of *Webb v EMO Air Cargo Ltd* (1994) IRLR 482. In this case Webb was dismissed because she found she was pregnant, and she had only been recruited to cover another employee's maternity leave. The European Court of Justice ruled that any dismissal relating to pregnancy had to be sex discrimination (because only women become pregnant). It ruled that it was not acceptable to make a comparison to a hypothetical man who had announced that he would need to take protracted leave when covering another employee's leave.

- *Balamoody v United Kingdom Central Council for Nursing, Midwifery and Health Visiting* (2002) IRLR 288 CA

  Balamoody was of Mauritian nationality, and was a state registered nurse who owned a nursing home. He was found guilty of mispractice under the Council regulations and his name was removed from the register. However, he claimed that a matron of white ethnic origin was guilty of the offences and therefore applied for his name to be restored to the register. This was refused, and an investigation into the matron found her not guilty of any offences.

  Balamoody then took up a claim of race discrimination. The employment tribunal (supported by the EAT) held that there was no comparator because no one else had been found guilty of any offences. However, the Court of Appeal ruled that a hypothetical comparator should have been used because there was the possibility that the conclusion that the matron was not guilty of any offences was a result of race discrimination.

If an employee can show that there has been less favourable treatment, the next step is to show that the *reason* for the treatment related to the employee's sex/race, etc. This is known as the causation question.

- *Bradford Hospitals NHS Trust v Al-Shabib* (2002) EAT 709/01

  Al-Shabib, a man of Iraqi origin, decided to join the staff gym. After signing an agreement to abide by the rules of the gym, Al-Shabib allowed his wife and child to use the gym, which was in breach of one of the rules. The gym manager reprimanded him. Following an investigation, during which Al-Shabib was not interviewed, it was decided to withdraw his gym membership. Al-Shabib brought a claim to the employment tribunal that he had been subjected to direct race discrimination – believing that the nature of the investigation and the withdrawal of his membership was due to his race. The employment tribunal upheld his claim, stating that his treatment was race discrimination, comparing Al-Shabib's treatment to a hypothetical white employee. However, the EAT overturned this decision, stating that there was no evidence that the treatment of Al-Shabib had been related to his race in any way.

- *Kettle Produce v Ward* (2006) EAT 0016/06

A male manager entered the ladies' toilets and shouted at the female toilet cleaner who was on her break. He accused her of 'skiving'. She brought a claim of sex discrimination. The EAT rejected her claim on the basis that she was not able to demonstrate that the treatment was related to her gender. Indeed, there was no evidence that she would have been treated any other way if the manager had been female.

INDIRECT DISCRIMINATION

This is where (for example, in sex discrimination cases) the employer:

- applies to both sexes a *provision*, *criterion* or *practice*
- which adversely affects a considerably larger proportion of one sex, etc, than another (*adverse impact*)
- and it is to the detriment of the person that he/she cannot comply (*detriment*)
- and it is not a proportionate means of achieving a legitimate end (*justification*).

In summary, this is not deliberate discrimination – but discrimination that has happened indirectly because of a practice imposed by the employer. The intention of the employer is irrelevant, and it is not necessary that the employer realises that the actions are discriminatory.

Provision, criterion or practice

There is no formal definition of 'provision, criterion or practice' – rather the law simply states that it must include a 'requirement or condition'. In reality this is likely to cover most employment practices, including informal arrangements.

An example of a criterion applied to all religions is:

- *Williams-Drabble v Pathway Clear Solutions Ltd* (2005) ET 2601718/05

Williams-Drabble was a practising Christian. The employees were required to work to a new shift pattern that would include Sundays. This would have meant that Williams-Drabble would be unable to attend the church service at her chosen church. She resigned and successfully claimed indirect discrimination on the grounds of her religion, because the new shift patterns would be more difficult for a practising Christian to comply with.

Adverse impact

A case that demonstrates the concept of adverse impact is:

● *Jones v University of Manchester* (1993) IRLR 218

The University advertised for a careers adviser, specifying that the successful applicant would be aged between 27 and 35 years old and a graduate. Jones was aged 46 years, having started her degree as a mature student at the age of 38. In making a claim of indirect sex discrimination she had to specify the pool of people that she was comparing herself against. She sought to claim that the appropriate comparison was between male mature students and female mature students. She showed that female mature students tend to start their degrees at a later age than male mature students, and therefore claimed that the age requirement for the job was indirect sex discrimination. The Court of Appeal held, however, that the correct comparison was between male and female graduates – not mature graduates – and hence there was no indirect sex discrimination, because there was no adverse impact on either men or women.

 EXPLORE FURTHER

This case also illustrates the issue of correctly defining the pool of people against which the comparison is being made. The pool must not be narrowed to a greater degree than the situation has determined. In this case the applicant should have been a graduate. To reduce the pool to mature students creates a different pool from the one specified in the original advertisement. Look at other cases of alleged indirect discrimination to see how the pools have been defined. A useful comparison would be *Price v Civil Service Commission* (1978) ICR 27.

Detriment

The issue of detriment has been the subject of a number of challenges in case law. Some cases have suggested that a 'physical or economic consequence' is required for there to be a detriment. However, recent case law has shown that a disadvantage is sufficient. Also, it has been ruled that a detriment can be emotional or mental. An example of a disadvantage is:

● *R v Secretary of State ex parte Equal Opportunities Commission* (1995) 1 AC 1

In this case the government was challenged by the Equal Opportunities Commission regarding the different qualifying periods (eg to claim for unfair dismissal) for full- and part-time employees. At this time a full-time employee had to complete two years' consecutive employment, and a part-time employee had to complete five years' consecutive employment to qualify for the right. Because a significantly larger proportion of women than men work part-time, this rule was claimed to be indirect sex discrimination. Women suffered the detriment of having to work longer to complete a qualifying period. This claim was upheld and subsequent changes to legislation have introduced identical qualifying periods.

Justification

This case demonstrates that there can be a justification for indirect discrimination:

● *British Airways v Starmer* (2005) IRLR 862

Starmer was a pilot with British Airways, and requested to work part-time (50% of normal hours) following the birth of her child. She was refused on health and safety grounds – British Airways held that pilots who had not flown at least 2,000 hours could not work less than 75% of full time because they did not have sufficient experience.

British Airways argued that there was justification, even if this was indirect discrimination against women. However, the EAT found that it had not sufficiently justified the requirement to work at least 75% of normal hours and hence the discrimination was not justified.

PROOF

If the employee can present facts that suggest that discrimination might have occurred, the respondent has the responsibility to show non-discriminatory reasons for the act that is being complained of.

- *Law Society v Bahl* (2004) IRLR 799

  Bahl was the Vice-President of the Law Society. A complaint was brought against her of bullying and intimidation. An investigation upheld these complaints and she was suspended from the Law Council. She brought claims of race and sex discrimination.

  The Court of Appeal ruled that there had been no discrimination. A useful quote to explain this comes from the judgment:

  All unlawful discriminatory treatment is unreasonable but not all unreasonable treatment is discriminatory, and it is not shown to be merely because the victim is either a woman or of a minority race or colour. Simply to say that the conduct was unreasonable tells nothing about the grounds for acting in that way.

To help with the process of proving discrimination the legislation allows for the use of a questionnaire procedure. The employee can serve a questionnaire on the employer within three months of the alleged act of discrimination (this can be extended by a further three months if the statutory grievance procedure is first used). The employee must explain when he/she thinks the discrimination occured and the reasons he/she thinks the alleged act amounted to discrimination. The employer must then reply to the questionnaire within eight weeks. There is no penalty for not responding, but the tribunal is allowed to draw any inferences from the refusal to comply. In addition, if the employer chooses not to reply to specific questions, inferences can be drawn from the refusal.

- *Barton v Investec Henderson Crosthwaite Securities Ltd* (2003) IRLR 332

  The female employee was concerned that her remuneration package was inferior to a male colleague's. In particular, she was awarded a significantly smaller bonus than her male colleague. The employer held that this was the result of the male colleague in question having been headhunted by a competitor, and the need to improve his remuneration package to keep him. The EAT ruled that once the claimant has shown a potentially discriminatory action, the burden of proof moves to the employer to prove that the acts are not discrimination.

- *Igen v Wong* (2005) ICR 931

  The employee does have to present some level of reasonable suspicion before the burden of proof moves to the employer. Igen was female and recently returned from maternity leave when she was selected for redundancy. This was not enough evidence to suggest that discrimination had occurred.

In giving its judgment on this case the Court of Appeal said that a two-stage process should be followed when the courts consider a discrimination claim:

- The claimant must prove facts from which the tribunal *could* conclude, in the absence of an adequate explanation from the respondent, that the respondent had discriminated against the claimant.

- The burden of proof then moves to the respondent and the respondent must prove that it did not discriminate – that there was some other good reason for the action that is the focus of the complaint.

REMEDIES FOR DISCRIMINATION

If it is found by an employment tribunal that there has been an act of discrimination, the following can be awarded:

- a declaration of the rights of the parties

- an order of compensation that is not subject to a maximum. The compensation should address any loss or damage that has occurred, and can include a sum relating to injured feelings

- a recommendation that the employer should take certain action to ensure that the situation does not recur. If the employer does not take these actions, without reasonable justification, compensation can be increased.

The recommendation must be based on an actual adverse impact suffered by the complainant:

- *Leeds Rhinos Rugby Club and others v Sterling* (2002) EAT 267/01

  Sterling was employed by the Rugby Club on a succession of three contracts. He claimed that the lack of his selection for the first team was on the grounds of his race. The employment tribunal upheld his complaints of race discrimination and victimisation. The tribunal recognised that as a result of the claim, Sterling was less likely to be offered another contract by other clubs because he could be seen as a trouble-maker. To mitigate these consequences the tribunal recommended that the Leeds Rhinos offer the player a new contract. The EAT ruled that this recommendation was not allowed by the Race Relations Act because it was based on a hypothetical outcome and not an actual adverse impact.

As we see here, the purpose of the recommendation is to reduce the adverse effect on the employee.

As noted, the compensation can include an amount for injury to feelings. This is clearly a rather subjective assessment, and guidelines were laid down for the range of compensation that should be offered in the following case:

- *Vento v Chief Constable of West Yorkshire Police* (2003) IRLR 102

  In this case, in which the Court of Appeal was asked to consider whether an award that had been made for sex discrimination was excessive, the following guidelines were set out:

  Top band: between £15,000 and £25,000. Sums in this range may be awarded in the most serious cases, such as where there has been a lengthy campaign of discriminatory harassment on the grounds of sex or race. Only in the most exceptional case should an award of compensation for injury to feelings exceed £25,000.

Middle band: between £5,000 and £15,000. This should be used for serious cases, but which are less serious than those in the top band.

Lowest band: between £500 and £5,000. Awards in this range are appropriate for less serious cases, such as where the act of discrimination is an isolated or one-off occurrence. In general, awards of less than £500 are to be avoided altogether because if there is injury to feelings such a small sum would not be appropriate.

Note that this case was heard in 2003, and it might be regarded as sensible to apply some sort of inflationary increase when applying it in future years.

TASK

Find out if your organisation, or an organisation with which you are familiar, has a policy relating to discrimination in the workplace. Read the policy if it exists, and consider whether it meets the legal requirements. If there is no policy, try drafting one.

GENERAL OCCUPATIONAL QUALIFICATIONS (GOQS) AND REQUIREMENTS (GORS)

As we have seen, there are situations in which indirect discrimination can be justifiable. However, direct discrimination can never be justifiable – unless there is a GOR or GOQ. These are situations in which there is a genuine reason for needing someone of a specific group because of the nature of the role.

Examples of this are:

● The job requires a certain physiology (excluding physical strength) or a certain authenticity in dramatic performances or other entertainment, and a particular gender or race is therefore required.

● The job involves physical contact with people, and it would be inappropriate for this contact to be by a person of the opposite sex.

● *Etam plc v Rowan* (1989) IRLR 150

Rowan, a man, was refused employment at the women's clothes shop Etam because the job would have involved measuring women who were unsure of their size, and this was inappropriate contact. The EAT held that this was a small part of the job, and could have been covered by a female colleague.

● The job-holder has to live on the premises and there are no facilities for providing separate sleeping and other facilities for each sex.

● The job involves a special level of care, and it would be inappropriate for that care to be given by a member of the opposite sex or of a different race/religion.

● The job requires a particular commitment to a religion (eg being a leader in a religious group).

● The job is one of two jobs to be held by a married couple (or those who have a civil partnership).

● The job involves living in a private home and the degree of contact and intimacy involved would be inappropriate with a person of the opposite sex.

- The job involves work outside the UK in countries where laws or customs would mean that the duties cannot be carried out by a woman.

- The job requires authenticity in the provision of food and drink to the public, and for that reason specifying a particular race is allowed

POSITIVE ACTION

In certain situations it might be lawful to positively encourage, for example, members of an under-represented group of employees to apply for a job. Note, however, that there is no such thing as 'positive discrimination'. Action can certainly be taken to encourage under-represented groups to apply for a job, but to then make the recruitment decision on the basis of a factor covered by discrimination legislation would be unlawful.

- *Marschall v Land Nordrhein-Westfalen* (1998) IRLR 39

  This ruling by the European Court of Justice applied to a case in Germany, but the ruling has relevance throughout the EU. Marschall was a teacher in a German school. In the area of Germany where he worked there was a rule that where there are fewer women than men in a particular grade, women are to be given priority for promotion if, on all other factors (eg suitability, performance, etc), the man and woman are equal. Marschall applied for a promotion, and was told that a woman would be getting the job because of this rule. He claimed unfair sex discrimination. The ECJ held that if the rule was working to remove inequalities that affect women's equal opportunities, the rule was lawful. So Marschall's claim failed.

Although this claim was unsuccessful, it must be possible to show that a group of employees is significantly under-represented before making a decision to take positive action to address it.

In addition, public sector employers are subject to the Gender Equality Duty, Race Equality Duty and the Disability Equality Duty. This requires employers to take specific action to remove any existing inequalities and to promote equality.

VICTIMISATION

Victimisation is the term used for the act of penalising employees in some way for exercising their rights under discrimination legislation. Victimisation is unlawful if the employer knows, or suspects that, the person being victimised intends to, or has:

- brought proceedings relating to alleged discrimination

- given evidence or information in relation to a claim of discrimination

- done anything else in reference to discrimination legislation

- alleged that a person has committed an act which would be a contravention of discrimination legislation.

These are all known as 'protected acts'.

In determining whether someone has suffered victimisation their treatment must be compared with the treatment of someone who has not carried out a protected act, and it has to be judged whether that treatment was less favourable. It is also important to consider whether the treatment was that of a 'reasonable and honest' employer.

● *St Helens Metropolitan Borough Council v Derbyshire* (2007) UKHL 16

470 female employees involved in school catering had brought a claim under the equal pay legislation. Around two months before the claims were due to be heard the Council wrote to all the employees telling them that continuing with the claims would have damaging effects on the Council.

The employees brought claims that the letters from the Council amounted to victimisation – that they were a direct result of the employees' taking action under discrimination legislation, and that sending the letters was not the act of an 'honest and reasonable employer'. The House of Lords agreed that the letters were not an act of a reasonable employer, and therefore ruled that victimisation had taken place.

Victimisation can also occur after the employment relationship has ended. This was determined by the following case that was referred to the European Court of Justice for a ruling:

● *Coote v Granada Hospitality Ltd* (1998) IRLR 656

Coote was employed by Granada from December 1992 to September 1993. In 1993 she brought a claim of sex discrimination against the employer that was settled. She left the organisation in September 1993 and was unable to find alternative employment. She believed it was because Granada had refused to supply her with a reference. She challenged this decision in the employment tribunal, which ruled that it could not be classified as victimisation because the employment had ended (although the issue at the centre of the argument was a protected act). The case was eventually referred to the ECJ, which ruled that the employer should be required to give a reference once the relationship had ended, and failure to do so had resulted in victimisation.

TASK

Find out if your organisation, or an organisation with which you are familiar, has a policy relating to victimisation. What training do managers have in this policy?

HARASSMENT

In response to the EC Equal Treatment Directive (amended in 2000) the UK has introduced specific provisions into discrimination legislation protecting workers from harassment across all areas of possible discrimination. Within these provisions a common definition of harassment is given:

Unwanted conduct related to race/sex/disability/etc takes place with the purpose or effect of violating the dignity of a person and of creating an intimidating, hostile, degrading, humiliating or offensive environment.

Harassment can relate to a series of events that add up to an unbearable situation:

● *Strathclyde Regional Council v Porcelli* (1986) IRLR 134

Porcelli was employed as a laboratory technician working in a school. Two male colleagues subjected her to a series of degrading treatment that included making suggestive remarks, deliberately brushing against her, removing her personal belongings, storing equipment where she could not reach it and withholding information from her. They were eventually successful in their aim of forcing her to leave. The tribunal found that this was direct sex discrimination and harassment because the male employees would not have acted in the same way to a fellow male colleague.

And harassment can also relate to one single incident, provided that it is deemed to be sufficiently serious:

● *Bracebridge Engineering Ltd v Darby* (1990) IRLR 3

Darby had been criticised on a number of occasions for leaving work early. On one occasion two male supervisors stopped her as she went to wash her hands, thinking that she was attempting to leave early. She denied this, but they carried her forcefully into a darkened room where they made lewd remarks to her and sexually assaulted her. She immediately complained to a superior, but the general manager decided that no action should be taken against the supervisors. She resigned and claimed sexual discrimination and harassment. The employer argued that harassment had to relate to a series of acts, and not one incident. However, the EAT found that a single incident, if sufficiently serious, can constitute harassment. Because it was judged that the treatment given to Darby would not have been given to a man, it was found that this was an incident of sexual discrimination and harassment.

There has been considerable debate as to whether an employer is liable for harassment which comes from a third party.

● *Burton and another v De Vere Hotels* (1996) IRLR 596

Burton and her colleague were occasional waitresses serving, on this occasion, at a function at one of the hotels. They were of black ethnic origin. The after-dinner speaker was a comedian who was expected to make sexually explicit jokes, but it was known he would also be racially abusive. When the comedian started his act he saw the two waitresses and started to make racially and sexually offensive comments directed specifically at them. This encouraged an atmosphere in which other guests joined in with the abuse. The next day the waitresses complained and their manager apologised to them. However, they also took a claim of race discrimination against the hotel, claiming they had been subjected to racial harassment.

The EAT found that the employer was responsible for racial discrimination because they should have warned the assistant manager who was on duty in the hotel to monitor the act and to withdraw the waitresses if there were any concerns. If the employer had withdrawn the waitresses, the incident would not have occurred and so the employer could have prevented racial discrimination from occurring.

However, the House of Lords ruled that it was not sufficient for the employees to state that the conduct to which they were exposed was racist. They would have to show that they were exposed to it because they were black, and that white waitresses would not have been exposed to something they found objectionable (eg the sexist jokes).

In the case of *Pearce v Governing Body of Mayfield Secondary School* (2003) IRLR 512, the claimant was a teacher who was subjected to taunts from children in the school (a third party) about her sexuality. The House of Lords rejected her claim. It stated that an employer's failure to stop harassment from a third party might be discriminatory behaviour – but only if the employer failed to take action because of the employee's gender.

It is important to note that harassment is a specific form of unlawful discrimination, separate from direct or indirect discrimination. Another important aspect of the definition is the requirement for the conduct claimed of to have the purpose or *effect* of violating the dignity of a person. Existing case law has shown that in determining whether an act violates the dignity of a person it has to be considered from the perception of the complainant. The EC Code of Practice on dignity at work stresses that the individual determines what is, and is not, offensive.

This essential requirement to consider the matter from the view of the claimant is illustrated in the following case:

● *Driskel v Peninsula Business Services* (2000) IRLR 151

Driskel worked as an advice line consultant. In 1995 Huss was appointed the department head, and over a period of time the relationship between Huss and Driskel deteriorated, partly due to the sexual repartee in which Huss indulged. In June 1996 a vacancy for senior advice line consultant arose, and Driskel applied. On the evening before the interview – which Huss was to conduct – he told Driskel to attend the interview in a short skirt and a see-through blouse showing plenty of cleavage to make an attempt to impress him. Driskel did not comment on this at the time, but the next day pointed out that she had ignored his instructions. She subsequently complained of sex discrimination. There was an investigation which the EAT described as involving a good deal of 'to-ing and fro-ing', and eventually Driskel informed the employer that she refused to work unless Huss was moved elsewhere. This was deemed to be impractical and Driskel was told she would be dismissed if she refused to work with her department head. This happened, and Driskel claimed unfair dismissal and sex discrimination.

The employment tribunal rejected her complaints, finding that because she had not complained about the behaviour at the time, and the other various incidents were trivial, the events did not amount to sex discrimination.

The EAT overturned this ruling. It held that the incidents should not have been looked at individually but considered as an overall pattern of treatment. It also held that the tribunal should have considered whether the remarks made undermined Driskel's dignity as a woman. The banter could not be compared to banter between two men, because the perception of the banter by a woman could be totally different.

A further case illustrates the issue of considering the situation from the view of the claimant, and the issue of an 'intimidating, hostile, degrading, humiliating or offensive environment'.

● *Moonsar v Fiveways Express Transport Ltd* (2004) IRLR 9

Moonsar worked in an open-plan office with a group of men. On three occasions she was aware that they were downloading and viewing pornography on a computer in the office. She did not see any of the pornography, and was not asked to become involved in the activity.

After being made redundant she took claims of race and sex discrimination. Her sex discrimination claim related to the instances of the pornography – claiming that the events created an environment that amounted to sexual harassment. The EAT upheld her claim.

It should also be noted that employees who resign from employment as a result of harassment could potentially bring an additional claim of constructive dismissal. We explore this in more detail in the next chapter.

The Protection from Harassment Act 1997 makes harassment, of whatever nature, a criminal offence. In this Act harassment is defined as pursuing a course of conduct that the harasser knows, or ought to know, amounts to harassment or conduct that causes fear of violence in another person. Conduct includes speech. Note also that 'course of conduct' suggests that the conduct has occurred on more than one occasion. Injunctions can be brought, under this Act, against those causing or likely to cause harassment. The Act also allows for the person who has been harassed to seek damages for financial loss and anxiety caused by the harassment.

 EXPLORE FURTHER

Consider the definition of harassment given in the Protection from Harassment Act 1997 and given within discrimination legislation. Does workplace harassment necessarily equate to criminal harassment?

 TASK

Find out what policy your organisation, or an organisation with which you are familiar, has for dealing with alleged incidents of harassment. Do you think the policy addresses all the potential issues sufficiently?

VICARIOUS LIABILITY

'Vicarious liability' means that the employer is held liable for wrongs committed by employees in the course of their employment.

An example to explain this is embodied in the following case:

- *Jones v Tower Boot Company* (1996) IRLR 168

   Jones, a 16-year-old of mixed-race origin, started work at Tower Boot Company. He was immediately subjected to a campaign of physical and verbal assaults from two of his colleagues. This included his being burned with a hot screwdriver and having metal bolts thrown at his head. He resigned after one month and brought a claim of racial discrimination. The employment tribunal found that the employees had been acting within the course of their employment, and so Tower Boot Company was vicariously liable for the actions of the employees. The EAT disagreed that the actions were in the 'course of employment' but the tribunal's findings were supported by the Court of Appeal. It was therefore found that Tower Boot Company were vicariously liable for the claim of race discrimination.

The potential defence of the employer is to show that it had taken every reasonable precaution against the occurrence of the event in question. However, as shown in the following case, if an employer is aware of unpleasant actions being taken by its employees and does nothing to prevent them from continuing, the employer becomes *directly* responsible for the discrimination:

- *Chessington World of Adventures v Reed* (1997) IRLR 556

   Reed, a biological male, announced that she was going to start the process of gender reassignment four years after joining the organisation. Following this announcement a small minority of male colleagues subjected her to a campaign of harassment and ostracism. A series of unpleasant acts took place. Reed attempted suicide and, despite asking for a transfer on her return to work, her employer did nothing to help her. Reed eventually resigned. The EAT found that Chessington World of Adventures was directly liable for the actions of the group of colleagues who had subjected Reed to abuse. The employers argued that they were only vicariously liable for what had occurred, but the EAT found that they were aware of what was happening and had done nothing to stop it. This resulted in direct liability.

THE EQUAL PAY ACT 1970

The Equal Pay Act 1970 (EqPA) legislates against discrimination between men and women in relation to their terms and conditions of employment. Although its name suggests that it focuses only on pay, it does actually legislate across all terms and conditions of the contract of employment. It is important to emphasise that the Act is looking at comparisons between men and women. It is not relevant in addressing grievances of men complaining against their conditions in comparison to other male colleagues, or of women complaining against their conditions in comparison to other female colleagues.

Note that this does not mean that discrimination relating to terms and conditions of employment is allowed on the grounds of race, religion/belief, sexual orientation or age. Such discrimination is specifically cited as unlawful in the relevant pieces of legislation.

Although the EqPA is dated earlier than the Sex Discrimination Act (SDA), the two Acts actually came into force at the same time. They are perceived as complementary pieces of legislation – the SDA dealing with such issues as recruitment, dismissal, promotion and non-contractual benefits, and the EqPA dealing with contractual terms.

The legislation relating to equal pay is greatly influenced by the relevant contents of Article 141 of the Treaty of Rome (1957), and also by the EC Equal Pay Directive (75/117).

The EqPA allows a woman to bring a claim if her terms and conditions of employment are less favourable than a man (and vice versa) if they are employed on:

- like work
- work rated as equivalent
- work of equal value.

LIKE WORK

In the legislation this is defined as 'work of the same or a broadly similar nature'. Generally, the employment tribunals take quite a broad view of this concept. They are not looking for identical work but an overall similarity in the work that is done. It is important that the total work is looked at, and not too much emphasis is placed on small tasks that rarely occur. It is also important that the focus is on what actually happens regularly in the job, rather than a narrow focus on what the contract suggests will happen.

The comparison focuses on the jobs in question, and not on the individuals carrying out the jobs.

The need to take this broad approach is shown in the following case:

- *Capper Pass v Lawton* (1977) ICR 83

  Lawton was employed as a cook working a 40-hour week and being in sole charge of preparing daily lunches for 10 to 20 directors and their guests. She brought an equal pay claim, comparing her jobs with that of two male assistant chefs. They worked a basic 40-hour week with 5½ hours of regular weekly overtime, and they worked one weekend in three. They prepared 350 meals each day in two sittings of breakfast, lunch and tea. The tribunal held that the cook and assistant chefs did 'like work' and thus the equal pay claim was upheld. In supporting this decision the EAT emphasised that a broad consideration of the skill and experiences required to do the job and a general consideration of the type of work required was essential. Although there were clearly differences between the jobs, these were largely trivial.

If there are genuine differences between the jobs, and they are compensated for separately, it does not mean that basic terms and conditions should also vary:

- *Dugdale and others v Kraft Foods Ltd* (1977) ICR 48

  Women quality controllers, working with a food processing company, were paid at a lower rate than the male quality inspectors. The men and women all worked shifts, but only the men were expected to work nights and Sundays. The men were paid an additional shift allowance for Sundays and nights. The employment tribunal found that the differences in shifts were 'differences of practical importance' and so this was not a case of like work. However, the EAT overturned this finding, stating that the work of the men and women was broadly similar. They found that the hours when the work was carried out should be discounted, especially because the men were compensated for the different shift patterns.

However, if there are genuine differences in the work being carried out, the differences cannot be separated from the main duties and ignored in making a claim of like work:

- *Maidment and Hardacre v Cooper and Co* (1978) IRLR 462

  Maidment was a packer who also carried out some clerical duties. She compared her job with that of a male packer who also carried out some storeman duties. The tribunal found that there were significant practical differences in the job, and so there could not be a claim of equal pay.

  Hardacre was a machine operator who compared her job with a male machine operator. They did the same job, apart from the fact that he could set his own machine whereas she could not. Again, the tribunal found that there were significant practical differences that meant there could be no claim for equal pay.

  Both women appealed to the EAT, which supported the tribunal's decision. The women noted that the packer/storeman was paid an additional £2 per week for his store duties, and that the store duties could be seen as a separate activity. They claimed that this activity could be set aside and the remainder of the two jobs could be compared. The EAT did not support this view, and emphasised that the total job must be compared to consider whether like work existed.

WORK RATED AS EQUIVALENT

This can only be used where an analytical, non-discriminatory job evaluation scheme is in place. An analytical scheme is one that breaks jobs down into component parts whereas a non-analytical scheme simply compares whole jobs and does not consider the individual tasks and components that make up the job. There are many ways in which a job evaluation scheme can become discriminatory. Main pitfalls include relying too heavily on subjective judgements rather than objective data, and basing schemes on existing internal benchmark jobs that could perpetuate existing discrimination.

If the points allocated in a job evaluation scheme are directly related to a job grade within the company, the employee should receive the terms and conditions of employment relating to the grade in which he/she is placed:

● *Springboard Sunderland Trust v Robson* (1992) IRLR 261

Mrs R was a team leader, and she compared her terms and conditions to those of Mr R, an induction officer. Following a job evaluation process carried out by the employer, Mrs R's job was evaluated at 410 points, and Mr R's job at 428 points. The company grading scheme stated that jobs with between 360 and 409 points were grade three, and jobs with between 410 and 439 points were grade four. However, the company continued to treat Mrs R as a grade three. The tribunal found – supported by the EAT – that Mrs R had to be treated as a grade four, in accordance with the job evaluation scheme, and that Mrs R and Mr R were therefore carrying out work 'rated as equivalent'.

TASK

Find out if your organisation, or an organisation with which you are familiar, has a job evaluation scheme. Is it analytical and non-discriminatory? Could it be used to defend a claim for equal pay?

WORK OF EQUAL VALUE

The Equal Pay (Amendment) Regulations 1983 added the concept of 'work of equal value'. This amendment was introduced because the existing legislation did not allow for claims of equal value and thus infringed the requirements of the EC Equal Pay Directive.

This category of equal pay claims adds the opportunity to make a claim when there is no like work or work formally rated as equivalent. It is a complicated and lengthy process to prove a case of equal value. An employment tribunal often appoints an independent expert to investigate the claim, and the investigation and writing of the report takes a considerable amount of time.

The Employment Act 2002 has tried to address this issue by reviewing the process of equal pay questionnaires that can be used by the employee to obtain information from the employer. One of the difficulties that many employees face in bringing an equal pay claim is obtaining data about pay within the organisation. Prior to 6 April 2003 employees could only issue a questionnaire seeking relevant information from the employer once a tribunal application had been made. Now a questionnaire can be issued before proceedings are started, and it is hoped that this might reduce the number of equal pay claims that are made. A sample questionnaire has been provided at www.womenandequalityunit.gov.uk which employees may use if they wish. The employer must respond to the questions within eight weeks. The tribunal may draw inferences from a refusal to respond, or from evasive answers.

The employee was successful in showing work of equal value in the following case:

- *Hayward v Cammell Laird* (1984) IRLR 463

  Hayward was a cook employed in the shipyard. She claimed her work was of equal value to that of painters, insulations engineers and joiners working on the same site. The tribunal appointed an independent expert who carried out an investigation into the claim. He supported Hayward, and the claim for equal pay was allowed.

One of the difficulties that the tribunal has in determining whether there is a situation of work of equal value is in deciding how to make this judgment:

- *William Ball Ltd v Wood and others* (2002) EAT 89/01

  Nine female employees (one supervisor and eight cleaner/packers) claimed work of equal value in comparison to work being carried out by picker/packers. The female employees appointed their own expert who carried out a system called 'value check' to determine if the jobs were of equal value. He concluded that they were. This was presented to the tribunal, and the employers brought no alternative evidence. The tribunal worked through the 'value check' system after hearing all the evidence, and altered any scores that they disagreed with, based on what they had heard. They concluded that the jobs were of equal value. The EAT supported their finding, concluding that they had acted fairly on the only constructive approach available to them.

WHAT DEFENCE CAN THE EMPLOYER GIVE?

In some cases it might be possible for the employer to argue that there is a reason for the differences in the terms and conditions of employment. This is known as a 'genuine material difference'. If there is a genuine (significant and relevant) factor, other than sex, which is the reason for the difference, the claim of equal pay will fail. The tribunal must be convinced that the reason given is genuine and not an excuse. There have been a number of cases relating to this point, covering a wide range of different factors.

Different negotiating groups

- *Enderby v Frenchay Health Authority* (1993) IRLR 591

  Enderby, an NHS senior speech therapist, claimed she was employed on work of equal value to that of male principal grade pharmacists and clinical psychologists also employed in the NHS. The NHS claimed that the differences related to the fact that the two groups of employees were represented by different negotiating groups. The case was referred to the ECJ. They ruled that there was a clear difference in pay between the groups, which gave a prima facie case of sex discrimination. They ruled that it was insufficient to rely on the defence that the pay rates were arrived at through separate negotiations. Justification for the actual differences in pay had to be given.

EXPLORE FURTHER

This is an interesting case, and somewhat complicated to follow because of the number of stages of appeal involved. Students wanting to explore this issue further are recommended to read the whole judgment in the case – particularly the ruling of the ECJ. It is particularly interesting to note the reasons that each stage of the court process gives for reaching its conclusions.

COLLECTIVE BARGAINING

Returning to the case of *William Ball Ltd v Wood and others* (2002), part of the defence of the employer was that the rates of pay had been agreed through a process of collective bargaining. The relevant collective agreement categorised workers in the furniture-making industry. It was noted that the agreement pre-dated any equal pay legislation, and the tribunal concluded that it was 'tainted' because for historical reasons it maintained higher pay rates for picker/packers, a job traditionally reserved for men. For this reason, the collective bargaining process (resulting in the collective agreement) was not allowed as a material defence.

Experience

- *Cadman v Health and Safety Executive* (2006) IRLR 969

    Cadman worked as a health and safety inspector. She was paid less than two male colleagues doing the same job. This was justified by the employer because she had less service, and thus less experience, than her male colleagues.

    The case eventually went to the ECJ, where it ruled that an employer does not have to justify differing payments reflecting differing levels of experience, unless there is evidence that suggests that such differences are not being applied fairly. In addition, there is no requirement that the employer demonstrates that the differing levels of service and experience do result in an employee's having different capability in doing a job.

    The case was remitted to an employment tribunal to consider whether there was any evidence that suggested the differences were not being applied fairly.

Red-circling

Red-circling is where one or more employees have their pay protected either for a specific period of time or for the full duration of the remaining period of employment. For example, an employee might need to move to a lighter job for medical reasons, and the employer could decide not to reduce his/her pay accordingly. Alternatively, following a restructuring, there might be a group of employees who are demoted, but again the decision is made not to reduce the pay accordingly. There have been a number of cases examining whether this is a fair defence for a difference in terms and conditions. An interesting ruling is in:

- *Outlook Supplies v Parry* (1978) IRLR 12

    Parry was an accounts supervisor and claimed equal pay with a male colleague who was also an accounts supervisor. The colleague had previously been both a supervisor and an assistant accountant. However, due to ill health he was relieved of some duties and reverted to being an accounts supervisor only. The employer 'red-circled' his pay. This situation had continued for two and a half years. The tribunal concluded it had gone on too long, and allowed the claim. However, the EAT overruled this finding stating that the period of time was actually reasonable. However, it did note that a prolonged period of red-circling could be unreasonable, and it might not be possible to rely on this as a material defence.

Location

- *Navy, Army and Air Force Institutes v Varley* (1976) IRLR 408

Nottingham office staff worked a 37-hour week, whereas London staff worked a 36½-hour week. Varley, a female clerk in Nottingham, claimed that her hours should be brought in line with a male clerk's in London. This claim was not allowed because it was held that the difference was due to location, and not to sex.

TASK

Find out if your organisation, or one with which you are familiar, has significant differences in pay relating to any of the genuine material defences outline above. Do you think they are genuine defences?

ENFORCEMENT OF CLAIMS

A claim can be brought to the tribunal at any time during the period of employment when the comparator is also working, or within six months of leaving employment. The remedy is arrears of pay or damages limited to a maximum of two years before the proceedings were instigated. No payment for injury to feelings is awarded – because this legislation is based on the law of contract (and hence compensates for any contractual payments that have not been paid) and not on the law of tort (as in the case of other discrimination legislation).

 EXPLORE FURTHER

Despite the equal pay legislation there is still clear evidence that the average salary paid to a man is greater than the average paid to a woman. There are factors that influence this (such as women taking career breaks to have children), but overall there still seems to be an underlying difference. Students wishing to explore this issue further would be well advised to read the Kingsmill Report on women's employment and pay (www.kingsmillreview.gov.uk).

KEY LEARNING POINTS

- Discrimination legislation has grown rapidly over the past 30 years.

- Direct discrimination is where an employee is treated less favourably on the grounds of race/sex/etc than employees of a different race/sex.

- Indirect discrimination is where an employer applies a criterion which adversely affects a considerably larger proportion of one group than another and it is to that group's detriment that it cannot apply, and the criterion cannot be justified.

- There are occasions when the employment of someone of a particular race or sex is essential because of the nature of the job – this is known as a genuine occupational qualification or requirement.

- Employees are protected against victimisation for carrying out a 'protected act' as defined under discrimination legislation.

- Harassment is unwanted conduct related to race/sex/disability/ etc that takes place with the purpose or effect of violating the dignity of a person and of creating an intimidating, hostile, degrading, humiliating or offensive environment.

- 'Vicarious liability' means that the employer is held liable for wrongs committed by an employee during the course of his/her employment.

- Equal pay claims focus on a comparator carrying out like work, work rated as equivalent or work of equal value.

- An employer can defend the difference in pay between a man and woman doing equal work if it can prove a genuine material difference other than sex.

FURTHER READING

CASE SUMMARIES

Canniffe v East Riding of Yorkshire Council (2000) IRLR 555 – Canniffe was sexually harassed and assaulted by a work colleague. Before this event it was known that the colleague had carried out inappropriate conduct towards her. The employer argued that it had a discrimination policy that included harassment, and it had brought these to the attention of the employees involved. For that reason, the employer argued, it was not liable for the events. However, the EAT ruled that just having a policy was not enough when there was further action that could have been (and should have been) taken.

Chief Constable of Lincolnshire v Stubbs (1999) IRLR 81 – The claimant was sexually harassed by a colleague who was on secondment to another part of the police force. One incident of harassment occurred at a social function. The EAT ruled that the employer was still liable because seconded officers did remain employees of their home force throughout the secondment. Also, the social function was work-related and so the employer was liable.

Christie and others v John E Haith Ltd (2003) IRLR 670 – The claimants worked packing birdseed. They were ladies and packed bags up to 12kg in weight, for £4.32 per hour. The men packed bags up to 30kg in weight and were paid £4.58 per hour. The men also loaded and unloaded delivery trolleys. The ladies submitted an equal pay claim – but the employer argued that the men's work was more arduous and unpleasant and there was therefore a genuine material defence for the differences. This was upheld.

London Underground v Edwards (1998) IRLR 364 – A new roster of shift patterns was put in place which Edwards was unable to comply with because of her childcare arrangements. Edwards successfully claimed that the criterion was indirect discrimination in that significantly fewer women than men would be able to work the new shifts, because significantly more women than men have childcare responsibilities.

Perera v Civil Service Commission (1983) ICR 428 – Perera, a Sri Lankan, was unsuccessful in obtaining a post as legal assistant. The essential requirement was that he was legally qualified (which he was), and other qualities such as experience of working in the UK and proficiency in written and spoken English were not requirements, rather factors (amongst others) that were judged as 'pluses and minuses' at interview. It was judged that this was not indirect discrimination because these were not essential requirements.

EXAMPLES TO WORK THROUGH

1 Susan is a teacher within a large secondary school. She has always trained the school choir after the school day has finished. She has now been asked to start a further choir for the younger children, again rehearsing after school hours. She has refused to do this because she has her own young children, and staying late on two days causes her childcare difficulties. The head teacher has stated that she is head of the Music Department, and so these duties are part of her job. She is threatening to resign and claim indirect sex discrimination. What is your advice to the head teacher?

2 You are the HR manager and a head of department has informed you that he is concerned about the relationship between one of his senior managers (a man) and a young female employee. He is concerned that some of the behaviour he has witnessed amounts to sexual harassment. He has spoken to the senior manager and explained his concerns – which have been dismissed as 'over-reacting'. What else might you do to ensure that the organisation is not vicariously liable for any harassment that might occur?

3 Your organisation has three different branches – one in London, one in Swindon, and one in Bolton. The wage rates at the London branch are higher than those in Swindon and Bolton. The employees at Swindon are claiming that the 'London allowance' is unfair, because the costs of living in Swindon are similar to those of living in London. They are planning to put in an equal pay claim. What should you do to address this issue?

4 An Indian restaurant has advertised for waiters/waitresses and chefs of Indian origin. Is this allowed?

CHAPTER 7

Discrimination (2)

CHAPTER OBJECTIVES

The objectives of this chapter are:

● to analyse specific issues relating to sex and race discrimination

● to analyse specific issues relating to disability discrimination

● to investigate recent developments since the introduction of legislation relating to discrimination on the grounds of sexual orientation and religion/belief

● to consider the legislation relating to discrimination on the grounds of trade union membership

● to examine the legislation relating to age discrimination.

In the last chapter we looked at a range of issues relating to discrimination legislation. In this chapter we look at each specific area of discrimination legislation in turn.

ISSUES SPECIFIC TO SEX DISCRIMINATION

MARITAL STATUS

Discrimination against employees on the grounds of their married status is prohibited by Section 3 of the Sex Discrimination Act. In law there is no similar protection for people who are living together outside marriage. However, the Civil Partnership Act 2004 does address the issue of those living together of the same sex, as we see later in this section.

● *Chief Constable of Bedfordshire Constabulary v Graham* (2002) IRLR 239

Graham was an Inspector in the Bedfordshire force, and married a Chief Superintendent in the same force. In May 1999 Graham was appointed Area Inspector in the same division that her husband commanded. In June 1999 she was told that her appointment had been rescinded. It was claimed that her appointment was inappropriate in view of the role of her husband in the division. The claims of indirect sex discrimination and direct and indirect discrimination on the grounds of marital status were all upheld. The EAT confirmed that the decision to rescind the job had clearly been on the basis of Graham's marital status.

PREGNANCY

As we discovered in the last chapter, dismissal on the grounds of pregnancy or any matter relating to pregnancy is automatically unfair. We looked at the case of *Webb v EMO Air Cargo Ltd* (1994) IRLR 482. In this case the ECJ ruled that the dismissal was sex discrimination because it was on the grounds of pregnancy – which is gender-related. This does not need to fit with the requirement of the Sex Discrimination Act to have a comparator because any dismissal relating to pregnancy is automatically unfair.

ISSUES SPECIFIC TO RACE DISCRIMINATION

WHAT IS A RACE?

The Race Relations Act 1976 defines 'racial grounds' as being grounds of 'colour, race, nationality or ethnic or national origins'. The Race Relations Act 1976 (Amendment) Regulations 2003 apply to discrimination on the grounds of 'race or ethnic or national origins'. The original definitions of the 1976 Act have, however, not been repealed.

 EXPLORE FURTHER

In reading new cases as they are reported in the personnel and business press, students should note any impact that the revised definition of race brings. It would also be interesting to note any overlap that occurs in bringing claims under the legislation cited above, and the recently introduced legislation against discrimination on the grounds of religion or belief.

A series of cases have helped to define what is and is not a racial group. Sikhs, Jews and Gypsies have all been held to be ethnic groups, but Rastafarians have not. In determining that Sikhs were an ethnic group (*Mandla v Dowell Lee* [1983], IRLR 209, 2 AC 548) it was stated that to be an ethnic group the group must regard itself, and be regarded by others, as a distinct community with long-standing cultural traditions and a shared history. Because Rastafarians have been an identifiable group for only around 60 years, they did not meet this definition. However, Rastafarians would now be covered by the legislation relating to religion or belief.

DISABILITY DISCRIMINATION

The Disability Discrimination Act 1995 (DDA) was the first piece of legislation offering comprehensive protection against discrimination for disabled people. Prior to this there was the Disabled Persons (Employment) Act 1944, which introduced a quota system whereby employers with 20 or more employees had to ensure that at least 3% were registered disabled. However, this Act was rarely enforced, and in reality carried very little benefit for disabled people.

The DDA covers a wide range of protection for the disabled, but here we only concentrate on protection in employment.

DEFINITION OF A DISABLED EMPLOYEE

In the Act a disabled person is defined as having a 'physical or mental impairment that has a substantial and long-term adverse effect on a person's ability to carry out normal day-to-day activities'.

Physical or mental impairment

In the majority of cases this is a relatively straightforward concept. However, there have been cases brought to the employment tribunal for a judgment on less clear illnesses.

- *Millar v Inland Revenue Commissioners* (2006) IRLR 112

  Following a fall at work when Millar hit his head, he developed vision problems primarily including sensitivity to bright lights. This meant that he could not drive at night or on sunny days and could use a VDU only for limited periods of time.

  Despite a number of medical investigations, no cause for his problems could be found, although it was not disputed that the problems existed.

  The Court of Session held that he was disabled in accordance with the definitions of the DDA. He clearly was restricted in relevant day-to-day activities, and reaching the definition of disability does not require reference to cause or to a specific named illness.

The Disability Discrimination Act 2005 further addressed the issue of 'physical or mental impairment' by:

- stating that a mental impairment does not have to be one of a list of clinically recognised illnesses, rather that the impact of the impairment should be considered
- classing all people diagnosed with cancers, HIV or multiple sclerosis disabled from the date of diagnosis.

 EXPLORE FURTHER

Consider what impact this adjustment of the definition of 'physical or mental impairment' has had on disability discrimination claims.

Substantial and long-term adverse effect

An illness is deemed to have had a 'long-term effect' if it has lasted, or is likely to last, at least 12 months or (in the case of a terminal illness) is expected to last for the rest of the employee's life. The definition of a 'substantial and adverse effect' is more difficult. Clearly, it is related to the latter part of the definition – the ability to carry out normal day-to-day activities. However, that amounts to a yardstick, and if the employee is unable to carry out normal duties at work, there is also the possibility that a disability exists.

- *Cruickshank v VAW Motorcast Ltd* (2001) IRLR 24

  Cruickshank developed work-related asthma. He was moved away from his job to working as a fork-lift truck driver, and his symptoms went away. However, a reorganisation resulted in his having to use his fork-lift truck near the area of the fumes that had triggered his asthma, and the symptoms returned. A medical adviser found that the asthma was triggered at work, but not at home. Because there were no other jobs available it was decided to dismiss Cruickshank. The EAT found that although Cruickshank could carry out most normal day-to-day activities, he was unable to carry out normal duties at work. This could not be ignored, and so his illness was to be classified as a disability.

Although an illness might affect some day-to-day activities, and some work activities, it is not typically classified as a disability if the extent of the impact is somewhat limited.

- *Quinlan v B&Q plc* (1998) EAT 1386/97

  Quinlan underwent open heart surgery. As a result of the surgery he was unable to lift the heavy loads that was required of him as a general assistant in the garden centre. He was therefore dismissed. The EAT supported the employment tribunal's view that he was not suffering from a disability because he was still able to carry smaller loads, even though he was not able to carry out the duties required of him at work.

Normal day-to-day activities

These must be normal activities carried out on a regular basis and are listed in the legislation as involving one of the following:

- mobility
- manual dexterity
- physical co-ordination
- continence
- the ability to lift, carry or move everyday objects
- speech, hearing or eyesight
- memory or ability to concentrate, learn or understand
- perception of a risk of physical danger.

As well as relying on any point in this list, it is also required that the activity that is considered is actually part of an employee's normal activities:

- *Abadeh v British Telecommunications plc* (2000) IRLR 23

  Abadeh worked as a telephone operator. One day, while at work, he received a loud screeching noise in one ear, which left him with tinnitus, hearing loss and post-traumatic stress disorder. In deciding whether Abadeh had a disability as defined by the DDA the employment tribunal accepted the evidence that he was unable to travel by underground or on an aeroplane because of his illness. They classified this as a 'normal day-to-day' activity. The EAT found, however, that they had erred in giving any weight to this part of the argument because Abadeh did not live in London and these forms of transport were not part of his normal daily activities.

DISCRIMINATING AGAINST A DISABLED EMPLOYEE

The Disability Discrimination Act 1995 does not include the concept of 'indirect discrimination'. Rather, it has two categories of discrimination: *direct discrimination*, which is treating an individual less favourably because of a disability, and *disability-related discrimination*, which occurs when the employer declines to make reasonable adjustments to accommodate a disabled employee.

An employer is required to make 'reasonable' adjustments to accommodate the needs of a disabled employee. These might include such adjustments as:

- making physical adjustments to the workplace (eg moving a work area to the ground floor of a building)

- allocating some of the duties to another employee (eg in the *Quinlan v B&Q* case the heavy lifting could have been assigned to another employee – if that was operationally possible)

- moving the disabled person to another job (eg VAW Motorcast moving Cruickshank to fork-lift truck driving duties)

- altering the hours of work (eg allowing the employee to start work at a later hour to enable him/her to take advantage of easier travelling arrangements)

- moving the employee to a different place of work (eg moving to a site/office nearer to home, and making travelling easier for the employee)

- allowing time off during working hours for treatment or rehabilitation

- arranging training for the employee (eg to allow him/her to move to a more suitable job)

- acquiring or modifying equipment (eg purchasing a Braille machine to help a partially sighted employee)

- altering instructions or reference materials (eg reprinting them in larger type for a visually impaired employee)

- altering procedures for testing or assessment (eg allowing a longer time to complete the activity)

- providing a reader or a interpreter (eg to help a visually impaired employee)

- providing supervision (eg to help the employee avoid dangerous situations).

TASK

Find out if your organisation, or an organisation with which you are familiar, has made any adjustments as a result of the Disability Discrimination Act. Look at just a few of any such adjustments, and try to understand the reasons that they were necessary.

All these possible modifications have a potential impact on the employer. There is clearly a financial impact in most cases, and some adjustments (although highly preferable) might be impossible for logistical reasons. In determining whether the employer has acted reasonably the employment tribunal will take all these issues into consideration.

- *Beart v HM Prison Service* (2003) EWCA Civ 119

Beart worked as an administrative officer. She had relationship difficulties with her line manager. She discussed the possibility of working part-time, and her line manager took this as meaning she wanted to resign and advertised her job. This left Beart facing demotion and a substantial drop in salary. She went on sick leave suffering from clinical depression. During her sick leave the Prison Service believed she was working in a clothes shop that she owned, and so dismissed her on grounds of gross misconduct. She claimed unfair dismissal and disability discrimination.

In considering her claim for disability discrimination the employment tribunal held that the employer should have considered making the reasonable adjustment of moving her to a different workplace. In not doing so, disability discrimination had occurred. This finding was supported by the Court of Appeal.

- *Archibald v Fife Council* (2004) IRLR 651, HL

Archibald worked as a road sweeper but became unable to walk and therefore unable to do her job. She applied for over 100 administrative jobs with the Council, but was unsuccessful with all the applications. She was eventually dismissed on grounds of capability.

She took a claim for disability discrimination, stating that she should have been offered an administrative post without having to go through the process of competitive interviewing. The House of Lords supported her claim – stating that there is an obligation on employers to make reasonable adjustments for disabled employees, and giving her a job without the process of competitive interviewing was a reasonable adjustment that should have been made.

- *O'Hanlon v Commissioners of HM Revenue and Customs* (2007) IRLR 404

O'Hanlon was absent from work with clinical depression. After a period of time her entitlement to company sick pay ran out, in accordance with the company procedure. She took a claim that failing to pay her full pay during her period of illness was either direct discrimination or disability-related discrimination (not making a reasonable adjustment in light of her disability).

The EAT rejected her claims (this was later upheld by the Court of Appeal). The purpose of a reasonable adjustment is to aid the employee to be part of the workforce. Paying additional monies during a period of sickness absence did not help meet the purpose of reasonable adjustments.

The issue of whether an employer cannot be held responsible for making adjustments has been the subject of case law:

- *O'Neill v Symm & Co Ltd* (1998) ICR 481, IRLR 233

O'Neill worked as an accounts clerk. Three months after starting work with Sym & Co she was dismissed for sickness absence. At her interview she had told them that she had previously suffered from viral pneumonia, but had since recovered. During her period of employment she was diagnosed as suffering from ME – but she did not tell her employers. When she was dismissed she claimed disability-related discrimination, but it was found that the employer could not have discriminated if it did not know that there was a disability.

However, that decision was overturned in the case of:

- *H J Heinz Co Ltd v Kenrick* (2000) ICR 491

  Kenrick had symptoms of chronic fatigue syndrome (CFS), although he was dismissed prior to any firm diagnosis being given. (He was actually dismissed just two weeks before he was due to see a consultant.) The EAT ruled that even though the employer did not know that he was disabled as defined by the DDA, the fact was that he did indeed have a disability. So reasonable adjustments should have been made, and the act of dismissal without making these adjustments was discrimination.

The courts will consider what a reasonable employer ought to have known, or ought to have reasonably investigated.

GENDER REASSIGNMENT

The Sex Discrimination (Gender Reassignment) Regulations 1999 make discrimination against a transsexual for reasons relating to the gender reassignment unlawful. Discrimination is unlawful at any stage of the process of gender reassignment, not just when the process is completed.

Although this legislation has not been reported on in much detail (probably due to the relatively small number of employees who could potentially be affected), there are two interesting cases to consider:

- *A v Chief Constable of West Yorkshire Police* (2002) EWCA Civ 1584

  A was born male, but underwent gender reassignment surgery in May 1996. Since that time she has dressed and presented herself as a woman. In 1997 she applied to join the West Yorkshire Police Force but was told that that the Force had decided not to employ transsexuals because they were unable to perform all the necessary duties. In particular, they would not be able to carry out searches of individuals. A brought a claim of discrimination. The Court of Appeal upheld A's claim, stating that the Force could sensibly have avoided the problem by exempting her from the requirement to carry out searches.

- *Croft v Consignia plc* (2002) EAT 1160/00, IRLR 851

  Croft started work with Consignia in March 1987 as a man. In April 1998 Croft started the process of gender reassignment by taking feminising hormones. At this stage she announced that she would adopt a female role. The way of announcing this to the workforce was discussed, and in particular there was discussion about which toilet Croft should use. It was agreed that she would start by using the gender-neutral disabled toilet, but would eventually move to using the female toilet. Croft was concerned about this, because she wanted to live fully as a female and that included using the relevant toilets. However, the female staff (who had known Croft as a man for many years) were not happy with her using their toilets. Her claim of discrimination was unsuccessful because it was found that Consignia were not refusing to allow her to ever use the toilet, but were trying to deal with a difficult employment relations issue as well as waiting for medical advice.

SEXUAL ORIENTATION

The Employment Equality (Sexual Orientation) Regulations 2003 made it unlawful for employers to discriminate against or harass a person on the grounds of sexual orientation.

The Regulations cover those in employment, those completing vocational training, and job applicants, and also apply to any discrimination or harassment relating to the employment relationship after it has ended. It specifically covers discrimination against people on the basis of their *perceived* sexual orientation as well as their actual orientation.

Sexual orientation is defined as 'a sexual orientation towards persons of the same sex; persons of the opposite sex, or persons of the same sex and the opposite sex'. The Regulations thus cover all aspects of sexual orientation. They do not cover discrimination relating to any particular fetishes (eg sado-masochism) and it cannot be argued that 'orientation' covers orientation towards children (ie paedophilia is not covered by the Act).

To date, the majority of cases that have been heard under this statute have related to harassment on the grounds of sexual orientation:

- *Whitfield v Cleanaway UK Ltd* (2005)

  Whitfield was subjected to a series of taunts about his sexuality, including a manager calling him 'Sebastian' after a homosexual character in the television programme *Little Britain*. Eventually he resigned, and successfully claimed constructive dismissal and sexual orientation discrimination.

The Civil Partnership Act 2004 created a new legal relationship of partnership between two individuals of the same gender. As a result of this Act any benefits that are given to married couples also have to be extended to those in a civil partnership.

In the next section we look at the regulations relating to discrimination on the grounds of religion. There is a specific exemption in Regulation 7.3 of the Act allowing for situation where a particular religious group objects to homosexuality on religious grounds.

- *Reaney v Hereford Diocesan Board of Finance* (2007) ET 1602844/06

  Reaney was a homosexual who applied for a job as youth worker. He was quizzed by the bishop about his sexuality. At the time he was not in a relationship, and he assured the bishop that he would not become involved in any sexual relationship if he was appointed to the job. The bishop's concern was not so much the homosexuality, rather that the teachings of the Church see any sexual relationship outside marriage as wrong. The bishop was concerned that Reaney could not make a commitment that he would be celibate in the future, and he was rejected for the job.

  Reaney successfully won his case of discrimination. This was because the bishop's refusal to accept that the requirements of the job had been met (ie not engaging in sexual relationships outside marriage) was not reasonable.

RELIGION

The Employment Equality (Religion or Belief) Regulations 2003 made it unlawful to discriminate against workers on the grounds of religion or belief.

'Religion or belief' was originally defined as 'any religion, religious belief or similar philosophical belief'. However, in April 2007 the Equality Act 2006 amended the legislation, changing the definition to 'any religion, or religious or philosophical belief' (ie omitting the word 'similar'). Prior to this change political beliefs were excluded from the regulations. In a House of Lords debate on this point it was later suggested that a philosophical belief should cover a 'world view or life stance' – and it is possible that it could be argued that this would encompass political beliefs.

- *Baggs v Fudge* (2005) ET 1400114/05

  Baggs was a member of the British National Party and was not interviewed for a job in a small medical practice because of this. He brought a claim of discrimination on the grounds of religion/belief. The claim was dismissed because the BNP is not a 'religion, religious belief or similar philosophical belief' (ie the beliefs of the BNP are not similar in some way to religious belief).

However, under the new definition it might be arguable that the BNP is a group with a 'philosophical belief' – the removal of the word 'similar' meaning that the comparison to a religious belief is no longer required.

It is clear that people who belong to established religions (eg Christians, Jews, Muslims) are covered. What is unclear is whether those who belong to non-conventional 'religions' such as Druidism or who have 'beliefs' such as animal rights activists are covered. It is also not clear to what extent an employee has to follow a religion in order to be covered by the Act, or the evidence that they need to give to show that they are a member of a religion.

The Regulations state that direct discrimination occurs when an employee is treated less favourably than other employees on the grounds of his/her religion or belief. This covers discrimination on the grounds of:

- the employee's religion or belief
- the discriminator's perception of the employee's religion or belief (even if that perception is wrong)
- the association of the employee with someone of a particular religion or belief
- a refusal by the employee to carry out an act that is discriminatory.

The definition of indirect discrimination is the same as for sex and race discrimination. Although the regulations do not require an employer to provide facilities and time for religious activities, it is possible that requiring employees to work at times or days when the employee's religion require him/her to be at prayer could be indirect discrimination. In the same way, having a certain dress code that clashes with that required by a person's religion could also be seen to be indirect discrimination.

- *Azmi v Kirklees Metropolitan Council* (2007) EAT 0009/07

  A female Muslim teaching assistant was dismissed when she refused to remove her veil when teaching. The Council argued that it inhibited her ability to interact and communicate effectively with the children in her care. Azmi took up a claim of discrimination on the grounds of religion.

The EAT ruled that although the requirement not to wear a veil was a provision, criterion or practice that put her at a disadvantage compared with those who were not of the Muslim religion, it was justified as being a proportionate response to the requirement to give effective education to young children.

TASK

Many organisations do have requirements relating to dress – or to a specific uniform. Find out how these requirements have been adapted to address the needs of different religions.

There are genuine occupational requirements allowed within the legislation. For example, it could be a requirement for a Christian school to employ Christian teachers. However, there must be a genuine need for this requirement. The Acas draft guidance notes suggest that it c ould be a genuine requirement for a teacher to promote a Christian ethos, but questions whether the same requirement could be applied to a maintenance worker employed by the school.

TRADE UNION MEMBERSHIP

REFUSAL OF EMPLOYMENT

It is unlawful (Section 137(1) of the Trade Union and Labour Relations (Consolidation) Act 1992) to refuse employment to people because:

- they are, or are not, members of a trade union

or

- they refuse to accept a requirement that they either become a member of a trade union or that they cease to be a member of a trade union, or they refuse to make payments to the trade union if they fail to join.

It is important to note that this legislation makes the concept of the 'closed shop' illegal. This used to exist in many organisations where, upon starting employment, it was a requirement to join the relevant trade union.

TASK

Try to find someone who was at work in the 1970s who is willing to discuss their experiences with you. Ask them about the 'closed shop'. How did it work? What were the advantages and disadvantages associated with it?

'Refusing employment' covers all of the following:

- refusing to consider a job application or enquiry

- asking the applicant to withdraw an application

- refusing to offer employment

- making an offer of employment which includes terms that no reasonable employee would agree to, thereby making it difficult for the person to accept the offer

- withdrawing an offer of employment after having made it, or causing the applicant to refuse the offer

- including a requirement which goes against that which is listed above (s137 (1)).

An example of 'refusing employment' can be found in the following case:

- *Harrison v Kent County Council* (1995) ICR 434

    Harrison was a social worker working for Kent County Council. He was an active trade union member with a reputation for being a 'strong and forthright' negotiator. He resigned from his job for family reasons, but later re-applied to the Council. He was refused re-employment on the account of his 'confrontational and anti-management approach' in his previous post. The employment tribunal held that this was a fair refusal because it related to previous activities as a trade union member, rather than specifically to trade union membership. The EAT overturned that view, stating that the trade union membership could not be separated from activities carried out because of that membership. The refusal to re-employ Harrison had therefore been unfair.

DETRIMENT

Section 146 (1) of the Trade Union and Labour Relations (Consolidation) Act [TULRCA] 1992 provides for employees not to suffer any detriment by an act (or omission of an act) by the employer if this takes place for the purpose of:

- preventing or deterring him/her from becoming a member of an independent trade union, or penalising him/her for doing so

- preventing or deterring him/her from taking part in the activities of an independent trade union, or penalising him/her for doing so

- compelling him/her to become a member of a trade union.

An example of such a detriment is:

- *British Airways Engine Overhaul Ltd v Francis* (1981) ICR 278

    Francis was a shop steward. She made a statement to the press criticising her trade union for taking so much time to pursue an equal pay complaint by her members. She made this statement during her lunchtime. When the article was published she received a formal warning from British Airways, stating that unauthorised statements to the press were forbidden. Francis challenged the warning in the employment tribunal, stating that it was a detriment based on trade union activities. The employer argued that the statement came about after an informal meeting of union members, and was too remote from Francis's union duties to be classed as trade union activity. The tribunal found, however, that the statement was linked to trade union activity and the warning was therefore unfair because it was a detriment related to such activity.

DISMISSAL

Section 152(1) of TULRCA 1992 defines a dismissal as being unfair if the principal reason was that the employee:

- was, or proposed to become, a member of an independent trade union

- had taken, or proposed to take, part in the activities of an independent trade union

- was not a member of a trade union, and had refused to become a member.

- *Port of London Authority v Payne and others* (1992) IRLR 447

  The Port of London Authority derecognised the TGWU trade union, and also carried out a redundancy process. Employees were selected for redundancy based on a number of criteria, including attitude. Seventeen shop stewards were among those selected for redundancy, and they claimed they had been selected on the grounds of their trade union activities, and that their dismissal was therefore unfair. The tribunal held, and the EAT supported this view, that the shop stewards had been selected by the employer because there was concern that they would become involved in a campaign by the TGWU to restore negotiation rights. Because this campaign was authorised and run by the TGWU, it was held that it must be classified as trade union activity, and the dismissal was therefore unfair.

There is no statutory definition of trade union activity, and therefore in supporting this conclusion the EAT spelled out the process that must be followed to determine if there has been an unfair dismissal relating to trade union activity:

An industrial tribunal must determine the following: the belief held by the employers which formed the basis of the decision to dismiss; whether that belief was genuinely held; and whether the facts upon which that belief was based, judged objectively, fell within the phrase 'the activities of an independent trade union'.

AGE DISCRIMINATION

The Employment Equality (Age) Regulations 2006 came into force on 1 October 2006. The legislation makes it unlawful to discriminate against individuals on the grounds of age. In accordance with other discrimination legislation, this applies to the full range of employment situations including recruitment, promotion, training, dismissal, etc.

The Regulations adopt a similar approach to most other discrimination legislation in that there is the concept of direct and indirect discrimination, and of harassment and victimisation.

Although a lot of reports leading up to the introduction of the legislation focused on the rights of the older worker, it is important to note that the legislation prohibits discrimination on the grounds of any age – so the younger worker is protected as well as the older worker.

Due to the recent introduction of this statute there is no case law at present to illustrate any of the points that are made, although some case law from other European countries may provide useful insights into potential rulings in the UK.

HARASSMENT

The definition of harassment fits in with other discrimination legislation. Thus, anything that violates the dignity of the person who is the subject of jokes/comments, or anything that is seen to create an intimidating, hostile, degrading, humiliating or offensive environment could potentially be unlawful harassment on the grounds of age.

DIRECT DISCRIMINATION

The legislation makes it unlawful to give less favourable treatment to a person because of his/her age. This could include situations such as:

- deciding not to employ someone because of their age
- making a redundancy selection decision on the grounds of age
- not providing training because of age.

Unlike other areas of discrimination legislation it is possible to defend direct discrimination on the grounds of objective justification (see below).

INDIRECT DISCRIMINATION

In line with other discrimination legislation, this is defined as the application of some criteria to all employees that has the effect of disadvantaging employees of a particular age, and which cannot be justified.

An issue that is likely to cause some concern is that of length of service. For example, requiring an employee to have a certain length of experience before applying for a job will make it more difficult for younger workers to be able to apply for the job. However, in line with other indirect discrimination legislation, it is allowed if it can be justified. For example, if it could be shown that the employee would be a danger to the public in a particular job if he/she did not have a certain amount of experience, it is likely that this would make the criteria justifiable.

LAWFUL DIFFERENCES

The legislation provides for limited circumstances where it is lawful to treat people differently because of their age. These are:

- where there is objective justification – such as needing to fix a maximum age for promotion because of the training requirements of the job
- in recruitment, if a person is within six months of, or is older than, the organisation's normal retirement age (or 65 years if there is no normal retirement age), when it is lawful to refuse to recruit that person
- if the act is covered by one of the specific exemptions in the legislation (see later)
- where there is a genuine occupational requirement (eg taking a role in a play where the part in question is of a specific age).

RECRUITMENT

Clearly, it is not acceptable to discriminate on the grounds of age when recruiting for employment. Many employers have all information relating to equal opportunities monitoring on a separate slip that is not given to the person carrying out the shortlisting process. Some organisations have therefore taken the decision to put the 'date of birth' section on application forms in the equal opportunities monitoring section. However, this could be perceived as somewhat artificial because a good guess at age can be made from the dates of education and the employment history.

Particular care must be taken when carrying out graduate recruitment. It is still lawful to have specific graduate recruitment and training programmes – but graduates of any age must be allowed to apply, not just those who are recently leaving university.

When recruiting people to training schemes it is not allowed to set age limits that are not justifiable. This applies to both maximum and minimum age limits.

- *Cunningham v BMS Sales Ltd* (2007) Equality Tribunal of the Republic of Ireland

  In a case ruled in the Republic of Ireland the applicant for a job was asked questions about his age at an early stage of the interview process. This included questions on the application form such as 'number of children', 'age' and 'date of birth'.

  Cunningham provided incorrect answers to the questions claiming that they were irrelevant and invasive. Despite being suitable for the job he was not offered it. At the equality tribunal it was ruled that age discrimination had occurred in the recruitment process and he received €5,000 in compensation.

RETIREMENT

During the process of consultation in relation to this legislation there was considerable discussion about the likely decision on retirement age. Despite expectations to the contrary, the government has kept the age of 65 years as the default retirement age. Prior to October 2006, employers could make an employee retire at the age of 65 years, or at a different age if the job has a different 'normal retiring age'. However, employees now have the right to request to work beyond the normal retirement age.

The concept and the process that has been put in place for requesting to work beyond the normal retirement age mirrors the concept and process for requesting flexible working (as explained in Chapter 5). The employee can make a request to work beyond retirement age, but there is no guarantee that it will be granted by the organisation. The employer has to show a legitimate business reason for refusing the request. The outline of the process is as follows:

- Between 6 and 12 months before the employee reaches the normal retirement age the employer should write to him/her informing him/her of the impending retirement and explaining the right to request to work beyond this age.

- If this is not done by two weeks before the impending retirement age and the employment is terminated at the retirement age, this will be an automatically unfair dismissal

- If the employee requests to work beyond the retirement age, the employer must hold a meeting with the employee to discuss it, give a decision, and allow the right to appeal against the decision if the employee wishes to do so.

- If the application to work beyond retirement is accepted, the work continues.

- If the employee does not request to work beyond retirement age, or if the request is refused, the employee will retire – this is termed a 'planned retirement'.

- If an employee continues to work, the employer can write to the employee at any time giving six months' notice of a planned retirement. However, the employee can then request to work beyond the new date and the whole process can start again!

This legislation adds a further potentially fair reason for dismissal to those previously listed in s98 of the Employment Rights Act 1996 – that of retirement.

As soon as the age discrimination legislation became law, Heyday (an organisation for people at or near retirement) lodged a claim against the UK Government, claiming that the interpretation of the Equality Directive was wrong, and that there should be no mandatory retirement age. This has been referred to the European Court of Justice for its judgment.

- *Felix Palacios de la Villa v Cortefiel Servicios SA* (2007) C-411/05

   In this Spanish case the Advocate General was asked to consider whether the EU Directive applied to state laws setting retirement ages. The conclusion was that it did not, and even if it did apply, such a national provision was justifiable.

Although the Advocate General's ruling is not binding on the ECJ it is unusual for it not to be followed – which might indicate that the Heyday challenge is unlikely to be successful.

BENEFITS

It is not unusual for organisations to have benefits that link in some way to length of service. This could include long-service awards, or increased sick pay entitlements as service progresses, or increased holiday allowance. Clearly, there is an obvious link between service-related benefits and age – because older people have more opportunity to have longer service. There is therefore the potential that any such benefits could be affected by indirect age discrimination.

To partly address this issue the Regulations specifically allow for service-related benefits when the length of service in question is five years or less.

Any benefits relating to longer service could be allowable if they are necessary for fulfilling a business need – such as loyalty or motivation of staff. Any benefit that mirrors the calculations for statutory benefits (eg an enhanced redundancy pay scheme that mirrors the statutory scheme) is allowable. This is a little vague – because it could be argued that any benefit is introduced to enhance loyalty and motivation, and therefore every benefit is allowable! What is allowable within this part of the statute is likely to be determined through case law.

OTHER ISSUES

As we see in Chapter 8, the process for calculating statutory redundancy pay and the basic award is based on a combination of age and length of service. In the light of that very clear link to potential age discrimination it was expected that the legislation would introduce a new calculation method for these items – but it did not.

The formula for statutory redundancy and the basic award remains the same. In justifying keeping these bands the Government explained that this approach is still justified because the job market is different for these three groups. (In other words, the Government sees it as relatively easy for someone aged up to 21 years to find work, and relatively difficult for someone aged 41+ years to find work.) There is a commitment that this will be reviewed in the future.

There are two small changes to the previous calculation process – the 'tapering' from the age of 64 years upwards is removed, and the upper and lower age limits of 65 and 18 years respectively have been removed.

Note also that employees over the age of 65 years now have rights to take claims of unfair dismissal to the employment tribunal.

In addition, the age bands that relate to the National Minimum Wage remain. The Government defends this because it does not think that employers would be willing to pay young people more – and also it thinks that the bands, set as they currently are, encourage young people to remain in education.

KEY LEARNING POINTS

- Employees are protected against discrimination on the grounds of trade union membership in recruitment, dismissal and suffering other detriments.
- Legislation related to age discrimination was introduced on 1 October 2006.
- Discrimination on the grounds of being married is prohibited within the Sex Discrimination Act 1975.
- The Race Relations Act 1976 defines 'racial grounds' as being on the grounds of 'colour, race, nationality or ethnic or national origins'. The Race Relations Act 1976 (Amendment) Regulations 2003 apply to discrimination on the grounds of 'race or ethnic or national origins'.
- A disability is defined in the Disability Discrimination Act 1995 as a 'physical or mental impairment which has a substantial and long-term adverse effect on a person's ability to carry out normal day-to-day activities'.
- It is unlawful to discriminate against an employee on the grounds of gender reassignment.
- It is unlawful to discriminate against an employee on the grounds of his/her sexual orientation.
- It is unlawful to discriminate against an employee on the grounds of his/her religion or belief.

CASE SUMMARIES

Discount Tobacco and Confectionery Ltd v Armitage (1990) IRLR 15 – Armitage consulted her trade union representative about her terms and conditions of employment, and he wrote to the employer on her behalf. As a result of this she was dismissed. This was found to be discrimination on the grounds of her trade union membership.

Scott v London Borough of Hillingdon (2001) EWCA Civ 2005 – Scott made a complaint of race discrimination against his employer, London Borough of Ealing. While this complaint was still being considered he applied for a job at the London Borough of Hillingdon. The job was offered to another applicant who refused it. It was not offered to the other applicants but was re-advertised, with a note that previous applicants need not re-apply. He took a claim of victimisation, which was dismissed by the Court of Appeal because there was no evidence that the interviewers knew about his race discrimination claim.

Reed and another v Stedman (1999) IRLR 299 – The claimant suffered a series of comments and actions that she said amounted to sexual harassment. The employer argued that none of the events was sufficient to be classed as sexual harassment. The EAT found that sexual harassment does not have to be the result of one event, but can be the cumulative effect of a series of events.

Irving and another v the Post Office (1987) IRLR 289 – An employee of the Post Office, who lived next door to the Irvings, wrote racially offensive comments on a letter addressed to them. He was given a final warning which remained on his record for 12 months. The Irvings complained that this was not sufficient punishment, but it was found that the Post Office was not vicariously liable for the act of the employee because it was an act of personal malevolence and outside the scope of his work duties.

Horsey v Dyfed County Council (1982) IRLR 395 – Horsey took a role as a social worker, and it was a condition of the appointment that she would attend a two-year training course. Her husband was appointed to a job in London and she asked to attend her course in Maidstone. Her employers refused this, because they did not believe that she would then return to work in Wales for at least two years (as was agreed in her contract) given that her husband was in London. She resigned and claimed sex discrimination. The EAT upheld her claim because the refusal was based on an assumption relating to her marital status.

Board of Governors of St Matthias Church of England School v Crizzle (1993) ICR 401 – Crizzle was of Asian ethnic origin and a non-communicant Roman Catholic: she was deputy head teacher at the school. When the head teacher resigned she applied for the job but was rejected. The reason given was that the head teacher had to be Anglican (Church of England) to guide the school in its spiritual worship. The EAT held this was justified because of the religious focus of the school.

British Gas Services Ltd v McCaull (2000) IRLR 60 – McCaull was a service engineer. Unknown to his employers he suffered from epilepsy – they found out when he had a fit. As a result of this his employers were told he was unable to drive, work at heights or work with electrical equipment. He would also need supervision. The employer was unable to adjust his work to fit with this, and so offered him a clerical job at a lower salary. He claimed this was not a reasonable adjustment – but the EAT rejected his claim.

Hutchison 3G UK Ltd v Mason (2003) EAT 0369/03 – Mason was depressed and suffering from drug addiction. He was absent for rehabilitation, assessment and treatment, but initially did not tell his employer the true reason for his absence. After he did tell them he was allowed an extended period of absence, but was eventually dismissed. Because his dismissal was due to his illness, and the depression was a disability, this amounted to discrimination.

EXAMPLES TO WORK THROUGH

1   Your organisation works a shift system. One of your employees has informed you that he does not want to work on Fridays because it is the holy day in his religion. Other employees have protested at this request, explaining that they have to work every day of the week on a rota basis and this interferes with their plans. (One employee explains he has to miss football matches every third Saturday – and he is a member of the team.) As a result, 13 employees write to you requesting not to work on certain days because of commitments that they have. How do you proceed?

2   A local church is advertising for a youth worker. One applicant for the job is homosexual, and has been refused on the basis that this does not fit with the Christian ethos. He decides to claim discrimination on the grounds of sexual orientation. Do you think he is likely to be successful? Justify your answer.

3   Following an accident one of your workers is no longer able to stand for long periods of time. The employee works as a sales assistant in a busy retail store – and has to be available on the shop floor to advise customers. The job involves standing for most of the day. How do you proceed?

4   Your organisation has experienced a lot of conflict with the trade unions over the years. As a result, the managing director has an unwritten rule that it is inappropriate for managers to be trade union members. Is this lawful?

CHAPTER 8

Termination of employment (1)

CHAPTER OBJECTIVES

The objectives of this chapter are:

- to examine the circumstances in which a dismissal might occur
- to examine the six potentially fair reasons for dismissal
- to evaluate the process of ensuring that a fair dismissal takes place
- to explain the concept of constructive dismissal
- to define and list the automatically unfair reasons for dismissal
- to examine the potential remedies for unfair dismissal.

WHEN DOES A DISMISSAL OCCUR?

Section 95 of the Employment Rights Act 1996 states that an employee is to be treated as dismissed if:

- the contract under which he/she is employed is terminated by the employer (this can be with or without notice)
- the employee is working under a fixed-term contract and the same contract is not renewed
- the employee terminates the contract of employment (with or without notice) in circumstances when he/she is entitled to terminate the contract without notice due to the employer's conduct.

There are circumstances in which a contract of employment can be terminated without a dismissal occurring:

RESIGNATION OF THE EMPLOYEE

If an employee states that he/she wishes to terminate the contract of employment, it is not a dismissal. However, if the employee considers that he/she has been forced into the resignation by the actions of the employer, there is the potential for a claim of constructive dismissal. We examine this in more detail later in the chapter.

MUTUAL AGREEMENT

If the employer and employee mutually agree to terminate the contract, a dismissal will not be deemed to have taken place. There is the possibility of an employee feeling forced into reaching a mutual agreement, and again this could lead to a potential claim for constructive dismissal.

If the employer gives an indication that the employment will terminate at 'some time' but gives no precise details about when, then it is unlikely that a dismissal will have taken place. This was determined in

- *Morton Sundour Fabrics Ltd v Shaw* (1966) ITR 84

  Shaw worked in the velvet department of the employer. He was told that the velvet department would close at some time in the future, although no precise details of dates were given. The employer offered to put him in contact with another employer. Shaw met this other employer, was offered a job, resigned from Morton Sundour and started with the new employer. He then claimed a redundancy payment from Morton Sundour. They refused to make the payment, claiming that he had resigned and had not been dismissed. The employment tribunal stated that a redundancy had taken place and instructed Morton Sundour to make the payment. However, the EAT overruled this decision, stating that the employee had only been given a warning about a possible dismissal at some time – but no actual dismissal had taken place.

This definition of dismissal was supported by the judgment in

- *Haseltine Lake & Co v Dowler* (1980) IRLR 25

  Dowler was warned that there would be no long-term role for him in the organisation, and in February 1979 was advised to start to look for alternative employment. In May he received an offer of employment elsewhere and told Haseltine Lake & Co about it. He was told that if he was not happy with this new offer of employment he did not need to leave straight away, but it was confirmed that he would need to leave eventually. It was agreed that he would leave in June 1979. Dowler claimed unfair dismissal. The employment tribunal supported Dowler's claim, but this was overturned by the EAT because the ruling of *Morton Sundour Fabrics* had not been applied. Because there had been no precise indication of when the employment was going to terminate, there could be no dismissal.

FRUSTRATION

A contract of employment is held to be 'frustrated' when some unforeseen event occurs that prevents one or both of the parties from performing the contract, or results in the performing of the contract being radically different from that which was originally envisaged. Examples of potential frustration include long-term sickness and the employee being sentenced to a term of imprisonment.

If applying the concept of frustration to a long-term sickness absence, care must be taken to determine whether the employee is suffering from a disability as defined by the Disability Discrimination Act 1995 (see last chapter). If there is a disability, it is highly possible that pursuing the route of frustration will lead to a claim for disability discrimination.

One case relating to frustration caused by imprisonment is

● *Harrington v Kent County Council* (1980) IRLR 353

Harrington was a primary school teacher who was convicted of indecency offences and sentenced to 12 months' imprisonment. Kent CC informed Harrington that his contract of employment had ended due to his inability to carry out the duties for which he was employed, for a substantial period of time. When Harrington was released from prison, he wrote to Kent CC and requested his job back – it refused. He made a claim of unfair dismissal. However, both the employment tribunal and the EAT agreed that the contract had been automatically terminated by the prison sentence, and therefore no longer existed.

In *Marshall v Harland and Wolff Ltd* (1972) WLR 899, a series of requirements were set out that should be used to determine whether a contract of employment has been frustrated.

● Marshall was a shipyard fitter and had been absent for 18 months due to angina pectoris. He expected to return to work when he had had an operation. However, the shipyard where he worked closed – and so Marshall claimed a redundancy payment. It was argued that his employment had terminated due to frustration, and he was therefore not entitled to a redundancy payment. The NIRC ruled that he was entitled to a redundancy payment because there was no certainty that the contract had terminated. It determined that the following should be taken into consideration:

● the terms of the contract

● how long the employment would have lasted if there had been no absence

● the nature of the employment

● the nature of the illness and the likelihood of recovery

● the period of past service to the employer.

Note that this case was decided before the introduction of the Disability Discrimination Act 1995. However, it still has relevance, because not every absence due to ill-health can be linked to a disability.

 EXPLORE FURTHER

To obtain a further understanding of frustration of contract read through this judgment, and the judgment in *Egg Stores v Leibovici* (1976) ICR 260 and *Four Seasons Healthcare Ltd v Maughan* (2004) EAT 0274/04. Having read the judgments, evaluate why the courts are usually reluctant to apply the approach of frustration of contract.

ELIGIBILITY TO MAKE A CLAIM OF UNFAIR DISMISSAL

Section 94 of the Employment Rights Act 1996 states that an employee has the right not to be unfairly dismissed by his employer.

There are cases where a dismissal can be judged to have occurred but the person in question cannot make a claim of unfair dismissal to the employment tribunal. These persons/situations include:

- non-employees
- those with less than one year's continuous service of employment (unless the reason for dismissal was one of those that are automatically unfair and does not require a qualifying period of service – see later in this chapter)
- where the employee is employed under an illegal contract
- persons employed in the police service.

Section 109(1) of the Employment Rights Act 1996 did prohibit any employee who had reached the normal retiring age for an employee holding that position, or was aged 65 years or more, from taking up a claim of unfair dismissal. However, that restriction was removed by the Employment Equality (Age) Regulations 2006.

POTENTIALLY FAIR REASONS FOR DISMISSAL

Section 98 of the Employment Rights Act 1996, as amended by the Employment Equality (Age) Regulations 2006, lists six potentially fair reasons for dismissal. They are:

- capability or qualifications
- conduct
- redundancy
- statutory ban
- some other substantial reason
- retirement.

CAPABILITY OR QUALIFICATIONS

The Employment Rights Act 1996 defines capability as 'skill, aptitude, health or any other physical or mental quality'. Qualifications are defined as 'any degree, diploma or other academic, technical or professional qualification relevant to the position which the employee holds'.

The employer should, at the recruitment stage and in the subsequent period of induction, make sure that the employee understands the requirements of the job. The employer should determine any training needs that exist and act upon them. The employer should also make clear to the employee the likely penalty of failing to meet the required standards. If the employee does not meet the required standards of performance, the employer would be expected to try to assist that employee through further training and education before taking disciplinary action.

If a capability issue relates to ill-health, the employer must consider the nature of the illness, the actual and potential length of the absence and the employer's situation (eg the size of the business and the impact that the absence is having on the organisation). It is also important to have due regard to the Disability Discrimination Act 1995. The need to act reasonably is illustrated by the following case:

- *Rolls-Royce Ltd v Walpole* (1980) IRLR 343

  Despite having a good attendance record for the first four years of his employment, during the next three years prior to his dismissal Walpole's attendance record averaged 50%. There was no pattern to the attendance. Rolls-Royce followed their procedures in making Walpole aware of their concerns, and could not foresee any reason that the situation would improve. They dismissed Walpole. He took a claim of unfair dismissal that was supported by the employment tribunal. The EAT overruled the employment tribunal's decision, stating that it was perverse. Dismissal was a reasonable response to an attendance record as poor as that of Walpole's.

It is important that the employer's response is reasonable in the particular circumstances of each situation. Although an absence record may be poor, the employer must consider the reasons for it in deciding how to react:

- *Kerr v Atkinson Vehicles (Scotland) Ltd* (1973) IRLR 36

  Kerr was severely disabled. He was moved from a role where his absence was interfering with his work to another role in the organisation. Although his work was satisfactory he was dismissed due to his absences. Kerr successfully claimed unfair dismissal because his employer should have anticipated the absence pattern, and taken steps to accommodate it.

In the same way, the employer must act reasonably in addressing capability issues that relate to performance in the job. The following case illustrates the need to ensure that adequate training and supervision is provided:

- *Mansfield Hosiery Mills Ltd v Bromley* (1977) IRLR 301

  Bromley responded successfully to an advertisement for a boiler service fitter. Although the advertisement stated that training would be given, he received none. He performed well and was promoted to maintenance supervisor. In this role a number of issues occurred and he was eventually dismissed. The employment tribunal found that he had been given inadequate supervision, insufficient direction and encouragement, and therefore that the dismissal was unfair. The EAT supported this finding.

If the employer has taken action to try to help the employee improve the standard of performance but capability remains an issue, then the dismissal can be potentially fair:

- *Gozdzik and Scopigno v Chlidema Carpet Co Ltd* (1979) EAT 598/78

  The two employees were employed as winders. Due to the effects of the recession the employer introduced a new bonus system aimed at improving the productivity of the winders. The two employees did not meet the new standards and were given further training by the employer. They still did not meet the new standards and they were dismissed. Their claim for unfair dismissal failed because the employer had acted reasonably in providing them with additional training before taking the decision to dismiss.

TASK

Find out what procedures your organisation, or an organisation with which you are familiar, has for addressing capability issues. (It might be useful to ask the HR department.) Do you think they are adequate in defending potential claims of unfair dismissal?

In assessing cases of dismissal on the grounds of capability, the employment tribunal will have due regard to reasonableness. What help and training should a reasonable employer give, and what is a reasonable expectation of the results of such input?

CONDUCT

Conduct – that is, misconduct – is typically divided into two categories:

- *gross misconduct*, which can result in summary dismissal (dismissal without notice): examples of gross misconduct include theft, assault, vandalism, and falsification of records

- *misconduct*, which is a less serious offence and is usually dealt with through disciplinary warnings. If the behaviour does not cease, then there is the possibility that the employee will be dismissed. Examples of this include bad language, poor time-keeping, and improper wearing of uniform.

A dismissal for misconduct is potentially fair, but the employer must show that it has acted reasonably in reaching the decision to dismiss. The role of the employment tribunal is not to determine whether the employee committed the act of misconduct, but whether the employer investigated the situation thoroughly, had a reasonable belief that the employee committed the act, and then took a reasonable course of action. This is referred to as acting within the 'range of reasonable responses'.

This test of reasonableness is illustrated in the following cases.

- An important case is that of *British Home Stores v Burchell* (1978) IRLR 379. This case demonstrates the need for the employer to have a reasonable belief in the guilt of the employee.

  Burchell was dismissed because of irregularities in staff purchases. Evidence was obtained from dockets relating to purchases of Burchell and other staff, and a statement from another employee. Burchell took a claim of unfair dismissal to the employment tribunal, which supported her claim, stating that BHS had not clearly established Burchell's guilt. The EAT overturned this decision, stating that the employment tribunal had tried to apply tests more fitting to a criminal investigation. This strict standard of proof was not required – what was required was that the employer had a reasonable belief based on a reasonable investigation. The EAT identified three key elements to this process:

- the fact underlying the belief must be established

- the belief must be held on reasonable grounds, after an appropriate investigation

- the investigation must be reasonable, in the circumstances.

It is important to note that the level of investigation and belief required in order to proceed with a dismissal is not the same level as that required in a criminal prosecution.

The reasonableness of a dismissal can also relate to the previous disciplinary record of an employee. In *Bartholomew v Post Office Telecommunications* (1981) EAT 53/81, an employee was dismissed for making a 20-minute private overseas telephone call. The employers investigated, and Bartholomew could give not explanation for the call. Because Bartholomew had already been given a number of warnings for misconduct the decision was taken to dismiss him. Both the employment tribunal and the EAT supported the decision to dismiss, in the light of Bartholomew's employment history.

However, making the decision to dismiss an employee who had made such a telephone call and had *no* record of any past disciplinary issues would probably be seen as unreasonable.

If an employee is charged with a criminal offence it can be reasonable to proceed with a dismissal, even if that employee will not co-operate with any dismissal hearings. The tests established by *BHS v Burchell* (above) are relevant here. This is demonstrated in

- *Harris and another v Courage (Eastern) Ltd* (1982) IRLR 509

    Courage believed that Harris and another employee had stolen some beer, and the police charged them both. Courage also started disciplinary proceedings. On legal advice the two employees did not attend the disciplinary hearings, and were not prepared to co-operate with any investigation by Courage. Courage carried out an investigation to the best of its ability – including the taking of witness statements. On the basis of the evidence it had obtained it dismissed the two employees. The claim for unfair dismissal was rejected because Courage had carried out a reasonable investigation, and had a reasonable belief that the employees had stolen the beer. It was found that there was no requirement to wait until after a criminal trial. (In the actual criminal trial the employees were acquitted.)

TASK

There are many cases of unfair dismissal that are regularly reported in the personnel press (for example, *People Management*). Read some recent cases and apply the 'Burchell test' to them. Try to develop an understanding of what the employment tribunal sees as a 'reasonable response' from an employer.

REDUNDANCY

We explore this issue in detail in the next chapter.

STATUTORY BAN

This is when it is unlawful to continue working because of a legal restriction or duty. An example of this is an employee who has the job of a driver within an organisation who then loses his driving licence because of motoring offences that he has committed. Clearly, he cannot continue to work in the role of driver while this ban is in place.

Again, the concept of reasonableness is central to the reaction of the employer. The employer should consider the length of time that the restriction is likely to be in place. If, to continue the use of our example, the driver has lost his licence for three months it might be possible to find him alternative duties during this period. If, however, he has lost his licence for five years, there would be the need to completely redeploy him, which might be more difficult.

This issue is illustrated in the case of

- *Roberts v Toyota (GB) Ltd* (1981) EAT 614/80

   Roberts was an area sales manager, and there was an implied term in his contract that he would have a driving licence. He was convicted of driving while over the legal alcohol limit, and lost his licence for 12 months. He offered to purchase a company car and provide a driver to drive him during this 12-month period, but the employer went ahead and dismissed him, viewing the option of using a driver as impractical. His claim of unfair dismissal was rejected because there was clear evidence that the requirement to have a driving licence was an implied term of his contract of employment.

The need to act reasonably in reaching the decision to dismiss was demonstrated in

- *Sutcliffe & Eaton Ltd v Pinney* (1977) IRLR 349

   Pinney was a hearing aid dispenser, and it was a requirement of the profession that he passed a series of examinations within a five-year period. He repeatedly failed the examinations, although he did pass the oral examination just before the five years expired. He was dismissed by the employer because it believed that he would never pass the examinations, and continuing to employ him would breach the professional requirements. The day after his dismissal he applied for an extension to the examination period, and was informed nearly three months later that an extension had been granted. He claimed unfair dismissal and this claim was supported by the employment tribunal.

   The employer, in this situation, had acted too quickly. If Pinney had not been granted the extension, we may assume that there would have been a fair dismissal. However, in not seeking an extension and waiting to hear the response to the request, the employer had acted unreasonably.

SOME OTHER SUBSTANTIAL REASON

This category allows the employment tribunal to consider any dismissal that does not fall under one of the other four headings, and to consider the reason and its fairness. Examples under this heading are:

Pressure from an external source to dismiss

In *Scott Packing and Warehousing Co Ltd v Paterson* (1978) IRLR 166, the US Naval Authorities refused to have Paterson working on their contract following alleged incidents of misconduct. This was a major part of Scott Packing's business. The employment tribunal found that Paterson had been unfairly dismissed because the employer had not investigated the issue of misconduct and established a reasonable belief in Paterson's guilt. However, the EAT overturned this decision, stating that the issue here was not one of conduct, but of 'some other substantial reason'. In this case the employer had not acted unreasonably because he had acted in accordance with the wishes of his major customer.

Although a customer might refuse to have an employee working for them, the requirement on the employer to act reasonably remains. The above case was referred back to the employment tribunal for it to consider whether there was other work to which Paterson could have been moved. Even if there is pressure from a customer to remove an employee, the employer cannot dismiss without exploring all the options for continued employment.

Reorganisation of the business

If an employer has to reorganise the business and can show that it is essential to make alterations to an employee's working pattern, there is a potentially fair reason. Again, the employer must show that all the options have been considered and that the conclusion that dismissal is the solution has been reached after reasonable consideration. This occurred in the following case:

- *Davey v Daybern Co Ltd* (1982) EAT 710/81

  Davey worked in a sweet kiosk. Business was poor, and it was decided to reorganise the working hours in order to cut wage costs. The reorganisation meant that Davey would be required to work two evenings, which she was unable to do because of family commitments. A temporary arrangement was put in place, but eventually Davey was dismissed. Her claim of unfair dismissal was unsuccessful because the employment tribunal found that the employer had acted fairly. It was able to demonstrate the commercial needs for the reorganisation, and thus the reason for the dismissal was reasonable under the heading of 'some other substantial reason'.

In a further case the EAT emphasised that the employment tribunal should not try to 'second-guess' the soundness of a business decision made by an employer:

- *Scott & Co v Richardson* (2005) EAT 0074/04

  Richardson worked as a debt collector. The employer wanted to change the hours of work to include collecting debts in the evening, when more people were at home. Richardson refused to do this unless he received overtime payments, as he had done previously for any evening work. The discussions went on for some seven months, and eventually Richardson was dismissed. The employment tribunal found that it was unfair dismissal, but the EAT overturned this decision. The EAT stated that the employment tribunal was not allowed to second-guess whether the business decision was a good one. If the employer firmly believed that the change was for the good of the business, it did not have to prove the advantages.

Mistaken belief

If an employer has a genuine belief that the reason it has for dismissing an employee is fair, the dismissal could come under the heading of 'some other substantial reason' if it is later shown that the belief was actually mistaken. This categorisation refers back to the need for an employer to carry out a reasonable investigation, which leads to a reasonable belief.

This is demonstrated in

- *Bouchaala v Trust House Forte Hotels Ltd* (1980) ICR 721

  Bouchaala was a Tunisian student who was given limited leave to enter and remain in the UK. Trust House Forte employed him as a trainee manager, but were then informed by the Department of Employment that he did not qualify for a work permit and to continue to employ him would be illegal. He was dismissed. The Department of Employment then informed the employer that Bouchaala had been given indefinite leave to remain in the UK and so a work permit was not required. Bouchaala took up a claim of unfair dismissal. This claim was not supported because the employer had a genuine belief that there was a substantial reason for the dismissal of Bouchaala. Although that belief was later shown to be mistaken, the dismissal, at the time, was still fair.

RETIREMENT

As explained in the last chapter, the law sets out a process to be followed when an employee is approaching retirement age. If this procedure is followed correctly, a resulting retirement is termination of employment – but can potentially be fair. If this procedure is not followed correctly, any retirement that results can potentially be unfair dismissal.

- *Martin v SS Photay & Associates* (2007) EAT 1100202/07

Martin was a cleaner at the employer's dental surgery. Just two days after her seventieth birthday a letter was left for her at the surgery telling her she was being dismissed due to her age, leading to her being in a high risk category for health and safety. This was found to be an unfair dismissal because the letter specifically referred to age as being a factor in the decision to dismiss. There was no doubt that the employer knew Martin's age because all employees had been invited to her birthday celebrations.

However, the employer could potentially have terminated Martin's employment fairly if it had followed the statutory retirement procedure. It was the approach to the dismissal that made it unfair.

 EXPLORE FURTHER

Read through the judgments in a variety of unfair dismissal cases (for some ideas of where to find these, look at the end of this chapter under *Case summaries*). In each one identify the test of reasonableness and how it is being applied. Build up a clear picture of what the courts consider to be reasonable behaviour on the part of both the employer and the employee. Do any clear guidelines stand out? Are there cases that do not fit in with these guidelines? How can any such anomalies be explained?

DISCIPLINARY PROCEDURE

STATUTORY DISMISSALS AND DISCIPLINARY PROCEDURE

A key part of showing that any dismissal has been reasonable is demonstrating that the procedure for carrying out the dismissal has been fair. The Employment Act 2002 introduced the statutory dismissals and disciplinary procedure (DDP) and the statutory grievance procedure. The DDP must be followed in all dismissals. Failure to do so makes the dismissal automatically unfair. (Note that to bring a claim of unfair dismissal due to the DDPs not having been followed, a minimum service of one continuous year is still required.)

The DDP has three stages:

Stage 1: The employer must write to the employee setting out the grounds on which it is considering taking disciplinary action. The letter must invite the employee to a meeting to discuss the allegations. There must be sufficient detail in this letter to allow the employee to prepare effectively for the meeting, and there must be a reasonable amount of time between the employee receiving the letter and the meeting being held to allow the employee to prepare.

Stage 2: A meeting must be held at which the allegations are formally put to the employee. The meeting must be at a time and location that is reasonable for the employee, and must give adequate opportunity for the employee to explain his/her case. After the meeting the employee must be informed of any disciplinary action that is to be taken.

Stage 3: If disciplinary action is to be taken, the employee has the right to appeal against that decision. Again, the meeting must be held at a reasonable time and location, and the employee must have adequate opportunity to put his/her case. As far as is reasonably practical, the appeal should be heard by a more senior manager than the one who took the decision to dismiss – and someone who was not involved in the original dismissal decision.

The legislation also allows for a two-stage 'modified' procedure. These two stages are:

Stage 1: The employer writes to the employee setting out the allegations that have led to a decision to dismiss that employee.

Stage 2: The employee has the right to appeal against the decision that has been communicated in writing.

This modified procedure is only likely to be applicable in rare situations of gross misconduct when the decision to dismiss is extremely unlikely to be altered by a disciplinary meeting.

As already noted, if the DDP is not followed, the dismissal is automatically unfair. If an employment tribunal finds a dismissal to be automatically unfair on these grounds, it is required to increase the compensatory award (see later in this chapter) by an amount between 10% and 50%. The employment tribunal uses its own judgment to determine the level of uplift, considering the facts of the case and the extent of the non-compliance. Similarly, if the employee has not co-operated with the DDP, any compensatory award has to be reduced by an amount between 10% and 50%.

- *Bowen v Millbank Estate Management Organisation* (2007) All ER D 143 Jul

  This case demonstrates that it is important to follow the procedure carefully. Bowen was suspended on suspicion of gross misconduct, and was invited to a disciplinary hearing. She was not given any details of the allegations or the investigations surrounding them until she attended the hearing (Stage 1 of the DDP had been omitted). The meeting was then adjourned to allow her to make further representations in writing. When the meeting reconvened the employer went on to dismiss her.

  The dismissal was held to be unfair because Stage 1 of the DDP was not complied with. Although the meeting was adjourned to allow her time to consider the allegations, it did not compensate for the procedures not being followed correctly.

STATUTORY GRIEVANCE PROCEDURE

The statutory grievance procedure also has three stages. These are:

Stage 1: The employee writes to the employer setting out the nature of the grievance. (As explained in Chapter 2, the courts have generally taken quite a relaxed approach to the definition of 'raising a grievance'.)

Stage 2: The employer arranges a meeting with the employee to discuss the grievance. This meeting must take place in a reasonable time period, and when the employer has had a chance to investigate the grievance. After considering the situation the employer must inform the employee of any action that is to be taken in response to the grievance, or explain why no action is to be taken.

Stage 3: The employee has the right to appeal against the response to the grievance. Wherever possible a more senior manager must hear the appeal. After this meeting the employee must be informed of what action, if any, is to be taken.

Again, there is in addition a 'modified' procedure. This is most likely to be used when the employee has already left the organisation.

Stage 1: The employee writes to the employer setting out the nature of the grievance.

Stage 2: The employer writes back to the employee with its response.

As noted in Chapter 2, there has been a considerable amount of case law looking at the issue of what counts as a written statement of a grievance.

If the employee takes a claim to the employment tribunal in relation to a grievance (not including a situation where the grievance is that the employee has been dismissed, or the employer is contemplating dismissing the employee) and has not raised the grievance using the statutory grievance procedure and waited at least 28 days for a response, the employment tribunal cannot hear the claim.

A claim to the employment tribunal must be made within three months of the event occuring (eg within three months of the date of dismissal, or within three months of holiday pay not being paid). Clearly, it is possible that an employee might still be waiting for a grievance procedure to be concluded when the three-month period ends. As a result of this, the employment tribunal has the discretion to extend that three-month period to six months to allow the grievance procedure to reach a conclusion.

It is important to note that the two statutory procedures are minimum standards. Organisations might have procedures that involve more stages (eg a procedure that allows for two stages of appeal against a decision to address).

The statutory procedures affected the application of the ruling in the case of *Polkey v A E Dayton* (1987) AC 344 that has been widely used. In this case Polkey was one of four van drivers working for A E Dayton. There was a need to cut costs for commercial reasons, and it was decided that the four van drivers would be replaced by three van salesmen. A E Dayton decided that Polkey was unsuitable for the role of van salesman and accordingly decided to make him redundant. The first Polkey knew about it was when he was given a letter setting out his redundancy payments and was dismissed.

On hearing his claim of unfair dismissal it was determined that the employers had not acted correctly because they had not consulted with Polkey or warned him of the possible redundancy (we explore this procedure more in the next chapter). However, they also concluded that even if the procedure had been followed, Polkey would still have been made redundant. On that basis his dismissal was found to be fair. The case was eventually referred to the House of Lords who found that the employment tribunal had taken the wrong approach. The key issue was whether the employer had acted *reasonably* in not giving any warning of the possible redundancy. This case has become a key part of determining the fairness of a dismissal. Prior to the introduction of the DDP it was potentially fair to dismiss without following a correct procedure if the actions can be shown to be reasonable.

It is important to note that there is no defence to not following the DDP – and the *Polkey* rule cannot be applied. However, if the DDP has been followed correctly but additional stages within the organisation's own policies have not been followed, then the *Polkey* rule might apply. For example, if the organisation's policy allowed for two appeals following a dismissal and the organisation had only allowed one, the DDP would have been followed (assuming that the first two stages of the procedure had also been followed). If the organisation can show that allowing the second appeal would have made no difference to the dismissal decision, it could argue the *Polkey* rule to support its non-compliance with its own procedure.

The main purpose of the statutory grievance procedure was to encourage employers and employees to resolve their disputes within the workplace, rather than bring them to the employment tribunals. It was hoped that this approach would reduce employment tribunal claims. In the same way, it was hoped that the DDP would result in dismissals being carried out fairly in the workplace, so reducing the number of unfair dismissal claims at the employment tribunal.

In March 2007 the Gibbons Report into the dispute resolution procedures was published. This Report had been commissioned by the Government to independently review dispute resolution procedures. The Report calls for an overhaul of the current procedures. Among the specific recommendations are:

- Repeal the statutory procedures.

- Provide clear and simple guidelines for employers on handling grievances and dismissals in the workplace.

- Provide incentives for complying with the guidelines through the employment tribunals' continuing to consider reasonableness of actions when making awards and cost orders.

TASK

It is extremely likely that there will be significant changes to the dispute resolution processes. Ensure that you keep up to date with this through checking on the Department for Business, Enterprise and Regulatory Reform website (www.berr.gov.uk) for the latest proposals. This is extremely important because you must be aware of any changes to the procedures.

Not all disciplinary situations warrant summary dismissal – indeed, most result in action short of this being taken. In these situations disciplinary warnings are given. The law does not set out what warnings are to be given, but it is expected that organisations will follow the guidelines set out in the Acas Code of Best Practice. This code suggests that there should be the following levels of warning:

- informal warning
- formal warning (that remains on the employee's record for six months)
- final written warning (that remains on the employee's record for 12 months)
- dismissal.

It is important to emphasise that these levels of warning, and time periods on record, are not legal requirements. Some organisations will have more levels of warning, or different time periods that warnings are kept on the record. However, in considering the reasonableness of any procedure the employment tribunal will have regard to the Acas Code of Best Practice.

If, during the period that the warning is still on the employee's record, the employee does not improve, the next level of warning can be given. It is important that any action taken is reasonable – that the employee has a reasonable amount of time to make improvements, and that any targets set are reasonable.

THE RIGHT TO BE ACCOMPANIED

Sections 10 to 15 of the Employment Relations Act 1999 give workers the right to be accompanied by a fellow worker or trade union representative to any disciplinary or grievance hearing that falls within the following definitions:

- the giving of a formal warning to a worker by the employer
- the taking of some other action to a worker in relation to a disciplinary matter
- the confirmation of a warning or other action that has been taken.

If the hearing is informal, there is no statutory right to be accompanied. It must also be emphasised that the right is to be accompanied by a fellow worker or a trade union representative – not a solicitor, member of the family or any other person who does not fall within the given definition.

CONSTRUCTIVE DISMISSAL

If the employer's conduct is such that it breaches the contract of employment, and that breach goes to the very root of the contract, the employee can terminate the contract of employment and claim constructive dismissal.

In order to show that there has been a constructive dismissal the employee must demonstrate that:

- there was a fundamental breach of the contract on the part of the employer

- the breach of the contract caused him/her to resign
- there was no significant delay in resigning.

The Court of Appeal ruled in *Western Excavating (ECC) Ltd v Sharp* (1978) QB 761 that the employer's conduct that gave rise to the claim of constructive dismissal must involve a breach of contract.

- Sharp asked for an afternoon off, and was refused. Nevertheless, he still took the afternoon off. He was dismissed, but successfully appealed. The appeal reduced the punishment to five days' suspension without payment. However, this led him into financial difficulties so he asked the employer to pay him five days' accrued holiday pay. This was refused because it was against company policy. He then asked for a loan and that was also refused. He then resigned, claiming constructive dismissal.

  The employment tribunal upheld his complaint. This finding was overturned by the Court of Appeal. They found that the employment tribunal had focused on whether the conduct of the employer was unreasonable. However, the test in a case of constructive dismissal is whether the contract of employment has been breached. In this case, they found no evidence of a breach of contract and so the complaint was dismissed.

It can be difficult to determine whether the behaviour of the employer has actually breached the employment contract. It is not important to consider what the employer *intended* to do. The employment tribunal will focus on the actual behaviour of the employer, and whether an employee cannot reasonably have been expected to tolerate such behaviour.

This is illustrated in the case of

- *Stanley Cole (Wainfleet) Ltd v Sheridan* (2003) IRLR 52

  Sheridan had been an employee for more than five years, and had no record of disciplinary action. She had a heated discussion with a colleague that upset her, and she then left the office for one and a half hours (which included her half-hour lunch break). She returned, and her line manager suggested that she go home because she was clearly still upset. She then went absent on the grounds of ill-health. Disciplinary action was taken against her for leaving the office without permission and she was issued with a final written warning (the last stage of the disciplinary procedure before dismissal). Her appeal against the decision was rejected. She resigned and claimed constructive dismissal.

  The employment tribunal found that the severe penalty of a final written warning for a first (and relatively minor) offence amounted to a breach of the contract of employment because it breached the implied term of trust and confidence and/or the implied term that the disciplinary procedure would be used fairly. Her claim for constructive dismissal was upheld.

  In this case it was judged that the behaviour of the employer, in giving such a severe penalty, was not behaviour that Sheridan could be expected to tolerate and there was thus a breach of contract.

A potential breach of employment can also relate to an employer's lack of action. This was demonstrated in the case of

- *Thanet District Council v Websper* (2002) EAT 1090/01

  Websper went on long-term sick leave claiming his illness was to do with work-related stress. The Council took advice from its medical officer, who concluded that Websper would not be able to return to his old job but might be able to return to different work in a different department. The Council told Websper they would try to find him work in the same department but in a different section. Websper refused this and resigned, claiming constructive dismissal.

The employment tribunal found that the lack of an offer of work in a different department had breached the implied contractual duty to provide the employee with a safe place of work. Therefore, this was a case of constructive dismissal.

Constructive dismissal can also be the result of a series of actions, rather than one single event:

- *Lewis v Motorworld Garages Ltd* (1986) ICR 157

  Over a period from November 1981 to August 1982 Lewis claimed that he had been subjected to a series of events which, when added together, resulted in a breach of mutual trust and confidence. These events included demotion, alteration of his pay and constant criticism of his performance (which he claimed was unjustified).

  The Court of Appeal accepted that the accumulation of the various situations could result in constructive dismissal, even if the single events on their own were not breaches of contract.

The important factor in determining whether constructive dismissal has taken place is whether the actions (or inaction) of the employer have amounted to a breach of the contract. The specific part of the contract that has been breached must be identified, and it must then be possible to show that the breach is fundamental.

AUTOMATICALLY UNFAIR REASONS FOR DISMISSAL

There are situations in which a dismissal is automatically unfair. On the following grounds dismissal is automatically unfair, and the one-year qualifying period otherwise required to bring a claim of unfair dismissal is not necessary:

- the employee's membership (or non-membership) of a trade union
- the employee's pregnancy or any maternity-related issue
- a transfer of employment (see next chapter for further explanation)
- the refusal of a retail employee to work on a Sunday
- activities carried out in the role of health and safety representative
- asserting a statutory right
- making a protected disclosure under the Public Disclosure Act (see Chapter 10)
- asserting the right to be paid in accordance with the National Minimum Wage Act 1998
- disclosing fraud or corruption.

There are three situations in which a dismissal is automatically unfair, but the one-year qualifying period is still required. These are:

- not complying with the statutory dismissals and disciplinary procedure

- dismissal because of a spent conviction
- dismissal where there is a transfer of the undertaking.

REMEDIES FOR UNFAIR DISMISSAL

If the employment tribunal finds that an employee has been unfairly dismissed, it has to decide on the remedy. As explained in Chapter 2, there are three possible remedies:

- re-engagement
- re-instatement
- compensation.

RE-ENGAGEMENT AND RE-INSTATEMENT

Although re-engagement and re-instatement are by far the least common remedies, the employment tribunal has a duty to explain these options and to ask the employee whether he/she wants the tribunal to make such an order. In reality, the employee rarely wants such an order, either because he/she has already obtained alternative employment or because the relationship with the employer is sufficiently poor after bringing the claim that future employment would seem to be untenable.

If the employee is re-instated, he/she returns to the job previously held and the employer must treat the employee as if he/she had not been dismissed. This means that all monies that would have been paid to the employee (salary and any benefits) during the time between the dismissal and the order to re-instate must be paid. All rights and privileges that the employee previously enjoyed must be re-instated.

If the employee is re-engaged, he/she returns to the employer but in a different role. The employment tribunal must state the nature of the employment, and the benefits that accompany the role. Again, the employee must be treated as if he/she had not been dismissed, and any monies he/she would have earned during the period between dismissal and the order to re-engage must be paid.

If the employment tribunal makes an order for re-instatement or re-engagement and it is not carried out by the employer, the tribunal will then award compensation to the employee in the way we outline later in this section. In addition, there will be an additional award of not less than 26 weeks', and not more than 52 weeks', pay.

COMPENSATION

If compensation is awarded, it will consist of two parts (according to section 118 of the Employment Rights Act 1996). These two parts are the basic award and the compensatory award.

The *basic award* is calculated by determining the employee's period of continuous service with the employer (up to a maximum of 20 years). The following amounts are awarded:

- 1½ weeks' pay for each year when the employee was between the ages of 41 and 64 years

- 1 week's pay for each year when the employee was between the ages of 22 and 40

- half a week's pay for each year of employment when the employee was aged under 21 years.

The statutory definition of the maximum limit on a week's pay is reviewed each year by the Government. It is currently £330 (as of February 2008). If an employee is paid more than this, the figure of £330 will be used for all calculations.

If the employee has been unfairly dismissed for a reason relating to health and safety, being a trustee of an occupational pension scheme or an elected employee representative, there is a minimum basic award of £4,400 (as of February 2008).

(Note that the figures quoted are reviewed every February. The recent figures can be found at www.berr.gov.uk.)

If the dismissal is unfair because the statutory dismissals and disciplinary procedure has not been followed, there is a minimum basic award of four weeks' pay. The employment tribunal has the discretion to waive this minimum if it judges that it would cause injustice to the employer.

If an employee is judged to have unreasonably refused an offer of re-instatement by the employer, the amount of the basic award can be reduced. An employment tribunal can also decide to reduce the basic award on the basis of conduct before the dismissal that makes such a reduction fair.

The *compensatory award* is that which the employment tribunal sees as fair given all of the circumstances and the loss that the employee has suffered. The aim is to compensate the employee for the loss he/she has suffered, not to punish the employer. The items that are taken into consideration when determining the compensatory award are:

- loss of earnings from the date of dismissal to the date of the employment tribunal hearing

- potential future loss of earnings (the tribunal will give consideration to the degree of difficulty the employee might encounter in getting alternative employment, and the likelihood of obtaining employment at a similar level of remuneration to the role from which he/she was dismissed)

- loss of statutory industrial rights (the employee has lost the continuous service he/she had accrued with the previous employer, and will have to start the process of accrual anew with a new employer – this item aims to compensate the employee for that loss)

- loss of pension rights

- loss of benefits (eg health insurance, company car)

- expenses incurred in seeking alternative employment

- damages for injury to feelings.

There is a maximum level for any compensatory award, which is also reviewed each year. At the last review (February 2008) it was increased to £63,000.

INJURY TO FEELINGS

The issue of damages for injury to feelings has been contentious. In section 123 of the Employment Rights Act 1996 the compensatory award in unfair dismissal cases is defined as that which is 'such amount as the tribunal considers just and equitable in all the circumstances having regard to the loss sustained by the complainant in consequence of the dismissal'.

In determining the amount of compensation in the case of *Norton Tool Co Ltd v Tewson* (1972) ICR 501, a clear statement was made that the compensatory award for unfair dismissal could only reflect economic loss.

This interpretation of section 123 of the ERA 1996 remained unchallenged until a ruling in the case of *Johnson v Unisys Ltd* (2001) ICR 480.

- In this case Johnson claimed he had suffered psychological problems due to the nature of his dismissal. He won a claim for unfair dismissal, but the compensatory award did not include any damages for injury to feelings. He tried to pursue a claim for breach of contract in the County Court, on the basis that the nature of the dismissal had breached the term of mutual trust and confidence. However, it was ruled that such a claim could not be made because the term of mutual trust and confidence applied to the preserving the relationship, and not terminating it.

  In making the House of Lords judgment specific reference was made by one of the judges to the *Norton Tool* case. It was commented that the interpretation of the compensatory award was too narrow, and the definition of compensatory award should include damages for distress, humiliation, damage to reputation or family life and psychiatric injury when appropriate. (Note that in the *Johnson* case the House of Lords did not go on to review the unfair dismissal compensatory award because they were hearing an appeal relating to a breach of contract claim.)

This judgment was then tested in the case of

- *Dunnachie v Kingston upon Hull City Council* (2004) EWCA Civ 84

  Dunnachie worked for the Council and had been subjected to a long campaign of bullying and undermining by his colleague and former line manager. The Council failed to resolve the situation and eventually Dunnachie resigned and successfully claimed constructive dismissal.

  Although there was no evidence of Dunnachie suffering from a recognised psychiatric disorder, he had been reduced to a 'state of overt despair'. In light of the ruling in the *Johnson v Unisys* case the employment tribunal included a £10,000 award within the compensatory award for injury to feelings flowing from the dismissal.

  Although the EAT overturned the tribunal's decision the Court of Appeal supported the £10,000 award, and thus supported the tribunal's calculation of the compensatory award.

  The Court of Appeal decision was later overturned by the House of Lords who determined that damages for non-economic loss (which would include injury to feelings) are *not* recoverable in the situation of unfair dismissal.

REDUCTIONS

The amount of compensation can be reduced due to the employee's contribution to the dismissal. For example, in *Parker Foundry Ltd v Slack* (1991) IRLR 11, Slack was dismissed following a fight with a fellow employee. The employment tribunal found that Slack had been unfairly dismissed because of procedural irregularities relating to the way that the claim had been handled. However, they reduced his compensation by 50% because they believed that his conduct had made him 50% to blame for the dismissal.

There is also the possibility to make a reduction to the compensatory award when the procedure for dismissal has not been followed fairly but the employment tribunal judges that (even if the procedure had been followed) the employee would still have been dismissed. This approach refers back to the case of *Polkey v A E Dayton* (1988) that we examined earlier in this chapter. However, it is important to note that this does not apply to the non-compliance with the statutory dismissals and disciplinary procedure, which is automatically unfair.

The employment tribunal can apply the *Polkey* reduction when the employer can show that there was a potentially fair reason for dismissal although the correct procedure (that goes beyond the requirements of the statutory DDP) was not followed. The tribunal can then assess what chance the employee would have had of keeping his/her job if a correct procedure had been followed, and that percentage chance can be applied to reduce the compensation awarded.

MITIGATION

The employee also has a duty to take reasonable steps to mitigate his/her loss (by making serious efforts to find alternative employment). The basic rule of mitigation is that the employee must take all reasonable steps to mitigate the loss to him/her resulting from the employer's actions, and he/she cannot recover compensation for any such loss that he/she could have avoided but failed to avoid through unreasonable action or inaction. The duty is to act *reasonably*, although the level of requirement on the employee is not high – given that the employer is the wrongdoer.

The level of mitigation expected is illustrated in

● *Fyfe v Scientific Furnishings Ltd* (1989) IRLR 331

Fyfe was dismissed on the grounds of redundancy, but was offered the alternative of taking early retirement. Although the financial package offered as part of the early retirement was more advantageous than the redundancy payment, Fyfe chose not to take early retirement. He claimed unfair dismissal, and his claim was upheld by the employment tribunal. However, it determined that he had failed to mitigate his loss by not taking the offer of early retirement, and hence reduced his compensation by 100%. The EAT overruled this decision. They found that the circumstances in which Fyfe had been made the offer of early retirement, and the time he was given to consider the option, were not adequate. Given the relatively low level of expectation on the employee to mitigate the loss, the EAT found that he had not failed in the requirement to act reasonably, and should be entitled to the full amount of compensation.

KEY LEARNING POINTS

- A contract of employment can be terminated without a dismissal taking place,

- There are six potentially fair reasons for dismissal – capability, conduct, redundancy, statutory ban, some other substantial reason and age.

- There are some employees who are unable to take up a claim of unfair dismissal – these include employees with less than one year's continuous service of employment.

- For a dismissal to be fair, a correct procedure must be followed. Following the Employment Act 2002 statutory disciplinary and dismissals procedures have been introduced.

- Employees have the right to be accompanied at a disciplinary hearing.

- Constructive dismissal occurs where the conduct of the employer breaches the contract of employment, making it intolerable for the employee to continue working according to that contract.

- There are a number of situations in which it is automatically unfair to dismiss an employee.

- The remedy for unfair dismissal is re-instatement, re-engagement or compensation.

- Compensation consists of a basic award and a compensatory award.

- Compensation can be reduced on the basis of the employee's contribution to the dismissal, or the failure of the employee to mitigate his/her loss.

FURTHER READING

CASE SUMMARIES

Hare v Murphy Brothers Ltd (1974) ICR 603 – Hare was imprisoned for 12 months following his involvement in a fight (unconnected with work). When he was released from prison he was told his job was no longer available, and he claimed unfair dismissal or, alternatively, redundancy. The Court of Appeal ruled that his contract had been frustrated, due to the length of the prison term.

Horkulak v Cantor Fitzgerald International (2003) EWHC 1918 (QB) – Horkulak was subjected to a series of bullying behaviour from his line manager. He eventually resigned in response to this. It was held that the behaviour had breached the mutual trust and confidence, and Horkulak was therefore successful in his claim of constructive dismissal.

Ogilvie v Neyrfor-Weir Ltd (2003) EAT 0054/02 – The employee was asked to go abroad for work purposes over a Bank Holiday weekend when he was due to attend his sister-in-law's engagement party. When he refused his manager swore at him and used abusive language. Ogilvie resigned and the EAT held that this was constructive dismissal.

YMCA Training v Stewart (2007) IRLR 185 – The employee was dismissed following allegations of misconduct. The employee argued that the dismissal was automatically unfair because the correct procedures had not been followed. However, the EAT ruled that the statutory DDP had been complied with – although some details of the YMCA Training procedure which went beyond the statutory DDP had not been complied with. Because the basic requirements of the statutory DDP had been followed, the dismissal was not automatically unfair.

Sahatciu v DPP Restaurants Ltd (2007) EAT 0177/06 – The employee allowed a student to work hours in breach of immigration rules. He was warned, but continued to do it. He was dismissed and lost his appeal. He claimed the dismissal was unfair because the statutory DDP had not been complied with – primarily that the Stage 1 letter did not set out sufficient detail of the allegations. However, the EAT found that he had confirmed he was aware of the allegations at the Stage 2 meeting, and so the claim failed.

There are many cases relating to conduct that you might want to read. All the following are of potential interest:

John Lewis plc v Coyne (2000) IRLR 139

Morgan v Electrolux Ltd (1990) IRLR 89

Lock v Cardiff Railway Company Ltd (1998) IRLR 358

Panama v London Borough of Hackney (2003) IRLR 278

Carr v Alexandra Russell Ltd (1976) IRLR 220

McDonagh v Johnson & Nephew (Manchester) Ltd (1978) EAT 140/78

EXAMPLES TO WORK THROUGH

1   Jenny, a long-serving employee, has recently been making a lot of errors. Some of these errors have resulted in a financial loss to the organisation. The problems seem to have started when a new computer system was installed. Jenny was given full training, and says she has no problems with using the system. Today she has made an error that has resulted in a customer complaint and her line manager is demanding that action should be taken. What is your advice?

2   Bill and Fred were fighting in the office. Bill says that Fred started it by taunting him about a recent disciplinary warning that he had received for poor performance. Fred says that Bill is just too sensitive, and everyone laughs and jokes in the office. What action should you take?

3   Today you have received a letter of resignation from Judy. She has a new job to go to. She has also informed you that she is taking a claim of constructive dismissal to the employment tribunal due to the ongoing bullying that she has received from a number of colleagues. This is the first time she has raised any allegations of bullying. What action should you take?

4   It is alleged that Julia has been stealing from the organisation. She was issued with a letter inviting her to a disciplinary meeting, setting out the detail of what she was alleged to have stolen and when. When she attended the disciplinary meeting she gave evidence that showed it was unlikely to be her that was responsible for the thefts. However, her evidence demonstrated that she had been breaching a number of health and safety rules – and she has now been dismissed for that reason. Is the dismissal potentially fair?

CHAPTER 9

Termination of employment (2)

CHAPTER OBJECTIVES

The objectives of this chapter are:

- to explain the concept of wrongful dismissal and the associated remedies
- to outline the differences between wrongful and unfair dismissal
- to analyse the concept of termination by summary dismissal
- to outline the procedures required to ensure that a redundancy is a fair dismissal
- to explain the transfer of undertaking regulations.

WRONGFUL DISMISSAL

Wrongful dismissal occurs when the employer terminates the contract of employment, and in doing so breaches the contract of employment. The breach of contract can be:

- giving no notice of termination, or insufficient notice (assuming that a summary dismissal was not justified – see next section)
- where the dismissal is in breach of a contractual disciplinary procedure
- where the dismissal is in breach of a contractual redundancy procedure
- the termination of a fixed-term contract before the date it is due to expire.

If the employee is claiming that a wrongful dismissal has taken place, he/she must be able to show that the employer has terminated the contract of employment, and that such termination has been a breach of the contract. To defend the action of termination the employer must demonstrate that the employee had conducted himself/herself in such a way as to show no intention to be bound by the contract of employment.

If an employee successfully shows that wrongful dismissal has taken place, he/she is entitled to compensation for the breach of the contract. This will usually be equal to the loss of salary between the date of the termination and the date of the hearing when wrongful dismissal is determined.

Alternatively, the employee can ask for an injunction against the dismissal being carried out, or a declaration by the court that the dismissal is invalid. In most cases the remedy given is that of damages.

Although injunctions are not common, the granting of one was allowed in the case of

- *Irani v Southampton and SW Hampshire Health Authority* (1984) IRLR 203

  Irani was a part-time ophthalmologist working in a clinic within the Health Authority. Irreconcilable differences developed between Irani and the consultant in charge of the clinic. The Health Authority decided that the only solution was for one of the employees to leave the clinic. Because Irani was the junior employee, and worked part-time, he was dismissed. The Health Authority did not determine that there was any particular fault with Irani.

  Irani successfully obtained an injunction against the dismissal because the correct procedures had not been followed. The injunction meant that the dismissal was suspended until the issues had been correctly considered. Irani did not work during this period.

The salary lost during the period between the termination and the hearing determining wrongful dismissal will include any pay awards agreed during that period, or agreed at a later date and back-dated. Compensation for share options, discretionary bonuses and enhanced pension rights has also been awarded by the courts.

- *Clark v Nomura plc* (2000) IRLR 766

  Clark was dismissed and was not paid his discretionary bonus (which he would have expected to amount to around £1.5 million) although he had been in employment at the time that annual bonuses were paid. He had earned significant profits for his employer, and argued that he should have received the bonus.

  The employer argued that the 'performance' that the bonus depended on was much more widely defined than achieving financial success. They cited a number of aspects about Clark's performance (eg his dress and appearance, erratic time-keeping and attendance and not attending management meetings) that gave cause for concern, and claimed that these had resulted in his bonus being assessed as 'nil'.

  The High Court held that these issues had not been the subject of any warnings, and it was not convinced that the employer would have assessed the bonus as 'nil' if Clark had not been dismissed. It therefore upheld that the bonus should be paid.

If an employee is wrongfully dismissed because the employer did not follow the correct disciplinary procedure, the employee is entitled to damages reflecting the time that it would have taken for the procedure to operate.

This is illustrated in the case of

- *Gunton v London Borough of Richmond-upon-Thames* (1980) IRLR 321

Gunton was dismissed and given one month's notice. The dismissal did not follow the correct procedure, and so Gunton claimed wrongful dismissal. He was successful in his claim and on outlining his damages, claimed loss of earnings up to retirement age, stating that he would have remained with the employer until that time unless he were made redundant or dismissed in accordance with the disciplinary procedure. The employers appealed against this assessment of the damages.

> The Court of Appeal supported the finding that he had been wrongfully dismissed, but stated that the damages should be limited to the period from when the dismissal took place until the contract could have been properly brought to an end. In this case it would have been when the disciplinary procedure had been properly carried out plus the one-month notice period.

If an employee has lost the right to claim unfair dismissal because of the wrongful dismissal, there is the possibility that extra damages can be received. This could occur, for example, when an employee with 10 months' service with a three-month contractual notice period is wrongfully dismissed by reason that the contract was terminated without notice. If the correct notice period had been given, the employee would have had 13 months' service at the time of termination, and thus would have been eligible to bring a claim of unfair dismissal.

This was shown in

- *Raspin v United News Shops Ltd* (1998) IRLR 9

> Raspin was dismissed because her employers suspected that she had stolen money from them. Raspin successfully claimed wrongful dismissal because she was dismissed without notice, and the employment tribunal found no evidence that she had been stealing the money. In awarding compensation for the wrongful dismissal, an additional three weeks' pay was considered that would reflect the time it would have taken to reach the decision to dismiss if the correct procedure had been followed. This additional three weeks would have increased Raspin's service to an extent that she would have been eligible to make a claim for unfair dismissal.

> The employment tribunal rejected this claim, relying on case law that suggested that a tribunal must restrict its deliberations to what has happened, and not consider what might have happened. However, this decision was overturned by the EAT and the claim for damages relating to the lost opportunity of claiming unfair dismissal was allowed.

It should be noted that if there is a clause in the contract of employment allowing the employer to pay in lieu of notice (see Chapter 5), such a claim would not be allowed. This would be because the ending of the contract without the employee working through the period of notice is expressly allowed by the contract.

It should also be noted that the damages allowed for wrongful dismissal do not include an amount for injury to feelings. This was ruled in the case of *Addis v Gramaphone Company Ltd* (1909) AC 488, and has not been overruled since.

- In this particular case Addis was wrongfully dismissed. In assessing his damages Addis claimed loss of earnings, and also sought damages for injury to feelings, distress caused by the manner of his dismissal and the difficulty in finding alternative employment. The additional damages were not allowed, and similar claims since this case have also failed.

THE DIFFERENCES BETWEEN UNFAIR AND WRONGFUL DISMISSAL

In studying both unfair and wrongful dismissal many of the differences will have already become apparent. A summary of the main differences is:

	Wrongful dismissal	**Unfair dismissal**
Basis	Based on breach of contract	Based on statute and the concept of fairness
Right to claim	No qualifying period required to make a claim	Unless the reason for dismissal is automatically unfair, one year's continuous service is required to make a claim
Time limit	Claim must be made within six years of the dismissal	Claim must be made within three months of the dismissal
Damages	No limit to damages that can be awarded	Maximum compensatory award currently (as of February 2008) £63,000
Court	Only dismissal claims for damages less than £25,000 are heard in the employment tribunal; other claims are heard in the County Court or the High Court – although an employee claiming for damages less than £25,000 can be heard at these courts if he/she so elects	All claims heard in the employment tribunal
Future loss	Future loss is not considered	Future loss may be considered when compensation is being calculated
Remedy	The remedy is damages	The remedy can be re-instatement, re-engagement or compensation

TERMINATION BY SUMMARY DISMISSAL

TASK

If your organisation, or an organisation with which you are familiar, has a dismissal procedure, look to see if it has a part of the procedure dealing with summary dismissal. If it does, read it, and then read this section to gain a better understanding of the legal requirements of such a procedure.

A termination by summary dismissal occurs where the employer terminates the contract of employment without giving the employee a period of notice. The contract is terminated because the employee has breached the contract of employment. This is not the same as an instant dismissal where the employer has acted unlawfully because he has chosen not to follow a correct procedure (and, as already noted, if the statutory procedure was not followed, the dismissal would be automatically unfair). If the employer can show that the employee has breached the contract of employment, then the act of summary dismissal can be lawful.

The nature of the behaviour that causes the breach of contract can be varied. As a general principle, the behaviour must be shown to have disregard for the essential conditions of the contract. For example, if the employee has stolen from the employer, there is a potential breach of mutual trust and confidence (the employer can no longer trust the employee because of his/her actions) and summary dismissal results because of this breach of contract.

In determining whether the employee has breached the contract of employment the employment tribunal will consider whether the act is one isolated incident or indicative of a pattern of behaviour.

This is illustrated in

● *Pepper v Webb* (1969) WLR 514

Pepper was employed as head gardener by the Webbs. After a period of time both his standard of work and his attitude deteriorated. One day he refused to carry out their instructions, and used foul language to them. He was summarily dismissed. In considering his claim for wrongful dismissal the Court of Appeal found that his manner and his standard of work showed that he had no intention to be bound by the fundamental aspect of service within a contract of employment. By taking such a stance he had breached the contract of employment, and so summary dismissal was justified.

In another case of a gardener, the courts found that an isolated incidence of foul language and not obeying an instruction did not amount to a breach of contract, and summary dismissal was therefore unfair:

● *Wilson v Racher* (1974) ICR 428

Wilson was the head gardener employed by Racher. One afternoon he was cutting the hedges using an electric hedge-cutter when it started to rain. He stopped the hedge-cutting and busied himself with other jobs. Two days later Racher accused him of stopping work early when he stopped cutting the hedge. There followed a heated exchange during which Wilson used a range of foul language. He was summarily dismissed.

Although the summary dismissal of Wilson was unfair, there can be occasions where an isolated incident is sufficient to be classed as a breach of contract. Consideration must be given to the nature of the incident, and the impact it has.

This is shown in

● *Jupiter General Insurance Company Ltd v Shroff* (1937) ER 67

Shroff worked in insurance and recommended that an endowment policy be issued upon a life that a senior employee had refused to reinsure a few days earlier. The Privy Council concluded that the seriousness of making such an error in the insurance business could lead to a serious loss. For that reason, the summary dismissal was justified.

EXPLORE FURTHER

Students who wish to explore this area in more detail should consider the relationship of wrongful and summary dismissal. In one the employer breaches the contract of employment; in the other the breach is by the employee. Compare and contrast the cases cited here, and referenced in the *Case summaries* section. In each case identify which part of the contract of employment has been breached. Are there any cases where the breach of the contract seems to be carried out by both the employer and the employee?

REDUNDANCY

DEFINITION OF REDUNDANCY

As we saw in the last chapter, redundancy is one of the six potentially unfair reasons for dismissal – as listed in the Employment Rights Act 1996. According to section 139(1) of this Act employees are regarded as redundant if their dismissals are attributed, primarily or partly, to any one of three reasons:

The fact that the employer has ceased, or intends to cease, to carry on the business for the purposes for which the employee was employed

This is illustrated in the case of

- *Hindle v Percival Boats* (1969) WLR 174

  Hindle was employed as a boat-builder. Percival Boats moved from their traditional methods of making boats from wood to making them from fibreglass. Hindle was unable to adapt to the new methods of working, and was made redundant on the grounds that the employer had ceased to carry on the business for which Percival had been employed.

  However, it was ruled that Hindle was not in fact redundant. He was employed to make boats, and Percival Boats were continuing as boat-builders. Therefore, there was no redundancy.

 TASK

If Hindle was unable to make boats out of fibreglass and could not be lawfully made redundant, what action could Percival Boats take? Would a dismissal on the grounds of capability be potentially fair?

The fact that the employer has ceased, or intends to cease, to carry on that business in the place where the employees were employed

If the employee has a clause in their contract of employment requiring them to be 'mobile', it is possible that a redundancy will not occur if the location where the employee works is closed but other locations remain open. The mobility clause may allow the employer to move the employee to a different location. The employer would have to show that such a request was reasonable.

This is demonstrated in

- *Bass Leisure Ltd v Thomas* (1994) IRLR 104

  Thomas worked at the employer's Coventry depot that closed. She was asked to move to another depot that was 20 miles away, and refused because of family commitments. There was a mobility clause in her contract, which the employer relied on in requesting her to make the move. After a trial period she left employment and claimed a redundancy payment. The EAT ruled that she should be paid a redundancy payment because, given her family commitments, travelling 20 miles was an unreasonable request.

The fact that the requirement of that business for employees to carry out work of a particular kind, or for employees to carry out work of a particular kind in the place where they were employed, has ceased or diminished or is expected to cease or diminish

In the case of *Safeway Stores plc v Burrell* (1997) IRLR 200, the EAT gave a clear approach to follow in determining whether there has been a reduction in the need for employees.

In this case Burrell was employed as a petrol station manager. Following a reorganisation the role of manager disappeared and was replaced with the role of filling station controller, at a lower salary and lower level of status. Burrell decided that he did not want this role and he was dismissed with a redundancy payment. He claimed the dismissal was unfair, because there was no diminution in the duties that he had been carrying out – they were being carried out by someone else. The employment tribunal supported his claim.

In considering the appeal made by Safeway against the decision, the EAT laid out the following approach to determining whether someone has been dismissed for redundancy:

- Has the employee been dismissed?
- Has the requirements of the employer's business ceased or diminished, or are they expected to do so?
- If so, is the dismissal the whole or primary result of the cessation or diminution?

In applying this test the EAT found that the dismissal of Burrell was due to redundancy and was fair. His duties as a manager had diminished, because not all the duties would be carried out by someone of a lower status – so applying this test there is a redundancy situation.

CONSULTATION

TASK

Look back at a dispute that has occurred in recent years (British Airways catering staff in 2004/5 is a good example). See how the redundancy selection was applied, and also how the consultation took place.

If no consultation takes place prior to employees being made redundant, the redundancy will usually be unfair. If the employer can show that any consultation would have been a futile exercise, it could be found that consultation was not necessary – however, this would be an unusual finding.

The length of time that must be spent in consultation is laid down in the Trade Union and Labour Relations (Consolidation) Act 1992:

- If the proposed redundancies involve more than 100 employees, the consultation must take place over at least 90 days.

- If the proposed redundancies involve more than 20, but fewer than 100 employees, the consultation must take place over at least 30 days.

- If fewer than 20 employees are to be made redundant, the redundancy is not covered by the above legislation relating to collective redundancies. However, case law has demonstrated a clear requirement on the employer to consult with the individual who is potentially affected by the proposed redundancy. This consultation must take place over a 'reasonable' period of time.

The consultation over collective redundancies must be with trade union representatives, or with elected employee representatives if the organisation is not unionised.

It should be noted that any employer intending to make more than 20 employees redundant at one establishment is required to inform the Secretary of State for Trade and Industry in writing at the time that the intention is announced, using the form HR1.

Some key requirements of the consultation period were laid down in the Court of Session's ruling in *King and others v Eaton Ltd* (1995) IRLR 199:

Eaton Ltd announced a redundancy, and consultation took place with the trade union representatives. During this consultation period the issues relating to selection were not addressed. The employment tribunal found that the redundancies were unfair because there had been insufficient consultation. The EAT disagreed with this view, but it was supported by the Court of Session. In making the decision they laid down the following guidelines:

- The consultation must take place when the proposals are still at a formative stage (ie starting the consultation when all decisions have already been made does not lead to a meaningful consultation).

- The employer must give adequate information and give adequate time for a response to be given.

- The employer must give 'conscientious consideration' to the points made during the consultation process.

This was further supported in the case of *Junk v Kuhnel* (2005) IRLR 310, where the ECJ ruled on when, in the consultation period, notices of dismissal can be issued. Consultation must be concluded before any dismissal notices are given. (Clearly, if dismissal notices had actually been issued, any further consultation is probably meaningless anyway.) If consultation has concluded, actual dismissal notices can be issued within the 30-/90-day periods described above. However, no dismissals should actually take place within the consultation period.

Consultation must, however, be taken before the decision to dismiss has been made.

- In *Leicestershire County Council v Unison* (2005) IRLR 920, an officer of the Council made a recommendation to the Employment Committee on 18 November that following a job evaluation exercise, redundancies should occur. The formal decision to proceed with the dismissals took place at a meeting of the committee on 12 December. The trade union, Unison, was informed of the decision on 18 December and there was then total failure to consult.

The EAT ruled that the actual decision to proceed with dismissals was taken on 18 November, and that consultation should have commenced at this point. Consultation should have commenced before decisions on dismissals had been reached.

Section 188(4) of the Trade Union and Labour Relations (Consolidation) Act 1992 also determines that certain information must be given in writing by the employer at the start of the consultation:

- the reason for the proposed redundancies
- the number and description (ie the types of jobs involved) of the employees who it proposes to make redundant
- the total number of employees at the establishment who are to be affected
- the proposed method of selection
- the procedure to be followed in dealing with the redundancies
- the method of calculating the redundancy payment, if it differs from the statutory payment.

A meaningful period of consultation cannot start until the employees (or employee representatives) have been supplied with all the required information regarding the redundancy. In *Green and Son (Castings) Ltd and others v ASTMS and AUEW* (1983) IRLR 135, a redundancy was announced but details of the proposed selection methods were given to the trade unions only eight days before the dismissals took effect. In this case it was ruled that there was insufficient time for meaningful consultation to take place regarding the selection criteria.

If the employer fails to consult, the dismissal will not be automatically unfair, although that is a possible conclusion. However, a protective award will be made when the appropriate length of consultation has not been observed. The protective award is the wages that the employer would have earned during either the 30- or 90-day consultation period, if that period of consultation had taken place.

SELECTION FOR REDUNDANCY

Although an employer might have a situation that classifies as a redundancy under the definition we have just considered, it is still possible for the dismissal to be unfair if the selection of the redundant employee(s) is unfair.

It is important to emphasise that it is the job that is made redundant. Therefore, if there is more than one person carrying out similar jobs and only some of those jobs are to be made redundant, there must be a fair way of determining who is to be selected for redundancy.

The first step is to determine the selection 'pool'. These are the employees that all carry out a similar job, and so are all potentially at risk from the redundancy. In some cases this is quite straightforward. For example, assume that a company operating a call centre needs, for economic reasons, to make 10 call centre operators redundant. The call centre has 50 call centre operators who all do broadly similar work. The call centre has no other operations. In this case the selection of 10 redundant employees must be made from the 50 call centre operators.

However, consider the example of another call centre that handles three separate contracts. One is for a car breakdown company, one is for a home shopping company, and one is for a tourism information company. The home shopping company's business has reduced and there is therefore a need to make five employees redundant. Should the selection be made from only those call centre operators working on the home shopping company? Would your decision change if you were told that the employees working on each contract do move around when necessary to cover absence?

The general rule gleaned from case law is that the employer should err on the side of including employees in a pool.

This is illustrated in

- *Bristow and Roberts v Pinewood Studios Ltd* (1982) EAT 600/81–601/81

  Bristow and Roberts were two of 14 drivers employed by Pinewood. The drivers were employed in four different sections of the business. Bristow and Roberts were employed in the Commercial section, along with two other drivers. Pinewood announced the need to make two drivers redundant, and following consultation with the trade union it was agreed that the selection would be made solely from the Commercial section. As a result Bristow and Roberts were selected for redundancy. The EAT ruled that the redundancy had been an unfair dismissal because no good reason had been given for the restriction of the selection pool.

Having determined the correct selection pool, the method of selection must then be agreed. The process of selection must be fair and must be as objective as possible.

In the past the most common method of selection has been LIFO (last in, first out). It is often preferred because it is a clearly objective method of making selection. However, the courts have increasingly been unhappy with LIFO as the only method of selection. In addition, it is likely to be indirect discrimination under the Employment Equality (Age) Regulations 2006, because young people cannot have longer periods of service.

The approach of LIFO was challenged in the case of

- *Blatchfords Solicitors v Berger and others* (2001) EAT 25/4/01

  Blatchfords announced that it was going to close two of its three offices. The cashier at one of the offices that was to close was put in a selection pool for redundancy with two other cashiers working in the other offices. The selection of the cashier to be made redundant was made solely on the length of service.

  The employment tribunal found that the employer was unable to give any reason for LIFO being the only criterion that was considered in the selection process and the selection pool was also unexplained. The tribunal's view was that no reasonable employer would use LIFO as the sole reason for selection. The EAT rejected that opinion because the tribunal was imposing its own view of the best selection criteria to be used, and it was a perverse finding that LIFO could never be a reasonable criterion.

However, in looking wider than length of a service as a selection tool the employer must choose appropriate criteria.

Guidelines for this were laid down in

- *Williams v Compair Maxam* (1982) IRLR 83

In this case employees were selected for redundancy by the three departmental managers listing those they felt should be retained for the best long-term viability of their departments and the company. The employer justified this approach because the reasons for the redundancy were that business was struggling, and long-term viability was a real issue.

However, the EAT found that the selection criteria were completely subjective. There had been no attempt to agree objective criteria with the trade union representatives, and the selection was therefore unfair. In making the ruling on this case a number of points were made that should be followed to ensure a fair redundancy:

- As much warning as possible should be given of any impending redundancies.

- Consultation must take place over the selection criteria, with a view to agreeing those criteria.

- The criteria chosen must be able to be checked objectively (eg against attendance records or records of performance).

- The criteria must be applied fairly in carrying out the selection.

- If possible, alternative employment must be offered in preference to making an employee redundant.

- Any selection that is carried out must be completed by assessors who know all the employees in the selection pool, and are able to assess each of the criteria correctly.

There have been various challenges relating to the right to see a selection assessment that has been made. The ruling in *British Aerospace v Green and others* (1995) IRLR 433 is of relevance here.

British Aerospace announced the need to make 530 of its 7,000 employees redundant. They used agreed selection criteria in identifying the employees to be made redundant. Of the employees made redundant 235 claimed unfair dismissal. In preparing for their claims at the employment tribunal the employees asked for sight of their own assessments (which were provided) and the assessments of those employees who had not been made redundant – so the reason for selecting the redundant employees could be examined. This disclosure was refused.

There are occasions, however, when a ruling has been made that such assessments should be revealed for specific reasons:

- *Eaton Ltd v King and others* (1996) EAT 1353/96 – because the employer was unable to explain how the selection criteria had been applied

- *British Sugar plc v Kirker* (1998) IRLR 624 – because the employee alleged that a disability had been taken into account when making the assessment, and it was important to see how the criteria had been applied to employees who were not disabled.

It should be noted that any employee wanting to see their own assessment criteria would have the right to do so under the Data Protection Act 1998. Similarly, the employer might fall foul of the Act if they allow employees to see assessments made of other employees (see Chapter 11).

In devising selection criteria it is important to note that no criteria must be directly or indirectly discriminatory (see Chapters 6 and 7).

EXPLORE FURTHER

Consider the impact of discrimination legislation on redundancy selection criteria. Think broadly about the type of criteria that an employer might want to use. Consider whether there are any circumstances in which indirect discrimination might possibly occur. How can the need to make a fair selection be balanced with the requirements of this legislation?

DISMISSAL

Once the collective consultation is over and the selection has been completed, there will be individual employees whose jobs have been identified as potentially being redundant. At this stage the employer must consult with the individual employees before making a final decision to dismiss.

It is very important to note that the statutory dismissals and disciplinary procedure (see last chapter) must be followed. The employer must write to the employee informing him/her that the organisation is considering making him/her redundant, and detailing the reasons for it. The employee must then be invited to a meeting to discuss it.

It is very likely that one meeting with the employee will not be sufficient for proper consultation to take place. It will largely depend on the response from the employee, and any evidence that the employee might bring. If the employee does raise information that requires exploration, the meeting will have to be adjourned and then reconvened when the necessary investigations have taken place.

When the decision to dismiss has been communicated, the third stage of the statutory DDP still applies – ie the employee has the right to appeal against the decision.

REDUNDANCY COMPENSATION

An employee is entitled to a statutory redundancy payment if he/she has been employed for more than two continuous years at the time of the dismissal.

The statutory redundancy payment is calculated in the same way as the basic award (see last chapter).

If an employee is offered suitable alternative employment and refuses it unjustifiably, he/she loses the entitlement to a redundancy payment.

SUITABLE ALTERNATIVE EMPLOYMENT

Section 141 of the Employment Rights Act 1996 provides that:

- If the employer makes an offer to renew the contract of employment, or to re-engage the redundant employee under a new contract which is to take place when the old contract expires, or within four weeks of the contract expiring:
  - if the capacity and place of employment, and the other terms and conditions of employment do not differ from the previous contract, *or*

- the terms and conditions of the proposed contract differ, but the proposal constitutes an offer of suitable employment, *and*

- in either case the employee unreasonably refuses that offer,

● the employee will not be entitled to a redundancy payment.

The employer has the burden of showing that the offer of employment was a suitable alternative, and that the refusal of it was unreasonable. In assessing these points consideration has to be given to the extent that any terms and conditions might vary, and the impact that this might have upon the individual employees concerned:

● *Universal Fisher Engineering Ltd v Stratton* (1971) ITR 66

When Stratton was recruited it was agreed that he would only work four night shifts per week. The employer then told him he would need to work five nights a week. He refused and was dismissed. The employer claimed that the job working five shifts was a reasonable alternative, but this was not supported because it had been clearly agreed that no more than four shifts would be worked when Stratton was recruited.

● *Allied Ironfounders Ltd v Macken* (1971) ITR 109

Macken was made redundant and was offered an alternative that involved working double day shifts. He refused this because he had a sick wife whom he looked after. His claim that this, and the drop in salary, made the alternative unsuitable, was supported by the employment tribunal.

● *Little v Beare & Son Ltd* (1980) EAT 130/80

Little was employed at Rathbone Place in central London, when his job was moved to Barnet (an additional 30 miles). Beare & Son bought him a van to assist in the travelling. There was then a further move to Hemel Hempstead that involved an additional 70 miles of travel – the cost of which his employers agreed to pay. He refused the second move, but the employment tribunal found he had refused a suitable offer of alternative employment.

It should be noted that in considering such issues, consideration will normally be given to the mode of transport available to the employee and any impact that the extra travelling time might have.

If the employee accepts an offer of alternative employment, he/she is entitled to a statutory minimum trial period of four weeks. That four-week period can only be extended if retraining is required. If, during that period, the employee finds the job to be unsuitable, he/she can resign and claim a redundancy payment. However, if the employer does not agree that the job is unsuitable, it could refuse to make the payment. If the employer determines that the job is not suitable during, or at the end of, the trial period, the employee is still entitled to a redundancy payment.

TRANSFERS OF UNDERTAKINGS

The Transfer of Undertakings (Protection of Employment) Regulations 1991 (known as TUPE) were introduced as a result of the Acquired Rights Directive 77/187/EEC. These Regulations were further revised by the Transfer of Undertakings (Protection of Employment) Regulations 2006.

The rights protect employees who work in an organisation that is transferred to a new owner. When a transfer of an undertaking takes place all the contractual rights of an employee are transferred from the old owner to the new owner. This includes continuity of service, contracts of employment, trade union recognition, collective agreements and all rights and obligations contained within the contract of employment.

- *Taylor v Connex South Eastern Ltd* (2000) EAT 1243/99

  In this case the employer sought to change the employee's terms and conditions of employment two years after the transfer had taken place. The proposed change was minor, but the employee refused to agree to it. As a result the employee was dismissed. The EAT ruled that this was an unfair dismissal because it related to the transfer, even though two years had passed since the transfer had taken place.

An occupational pension scheme does not transfer. However, if the transferor has a contractual obligation to pay an amount into a pension scheme of the employee's choice (a non-occupational scheme), that obligation will transfer.

In studying this area we will be referring to the 'transferor' – the old employer who is selling the business – and the 'transferee' – the new employer who is buying the business.

DEFINITION OF A TRANSFER

The Acquired Rights Directive and the TUPE Regulations 1991 gave unclear definitions of a transfer. It therefore took a great deal of case law to build up a picture of what actually defines a transfer of undertaking.

The 2006 TUPE Regulations aimed to address that confusion by giving clearer definitions. A transfer can be of two kinds (although they are not mutually exclusive). These are:

1 The transfer of an economic entity that retains its identity.

For example, a national transport company decides to sell 'South West Buses' to another transport company. The routes run by 'South West Buses' remain the same, the actual buses transfer to the new company and the customers and suppliers remain the same. This would be the transfer of an economic entity that retained its identity.

2 A change of service provision in which:

i)   activities are currently carried out by one person on his/her own behalf, and transfer to another person on the client's behalf

For example, if an organisation carried out its own catering, and then decided to offer the catering contract to a catering organisation.

ii) activities are currently carried out by one contractor and are then transferred to another contractor

For example, if 123 Catering currently ran the catering within an organisation, and the contract was transferred to 456 Catering.

iii) an organisation decides to carry out activities itself that are currently carried out by a contractor.

For example, 123 Catering currently runs the catering within an organisation, but that organisation decides to employ its own catering and run the operation itself.

In all the three situations listed here there must, immediately before the transfer, be an organised group of employees whose principal purpose is carrying out the activity – and it is intended that the activities will be carried out by the transferee after the transfer.

Note that this does not apply to one specific event. For example, if our organisation currently ran its own catering but for one major conference decided to use a catering contractor, this would not amount to a transfer.

Cases that relate to the definition of a transfer include:

- *Berg and Busschers v Besselsen* (1988) IRLR 447

   This case is a ruling by the ECJ. Berg was the manager of a bar/disco in the Netherlands. His employer decided to transfer the ownership of the bar/disco to a commercial partnership under a lease-purchase agreement. The new ownership was ultimately unsuccessful and the business was transferred back to the original owner. Berg claimed for loss of wages during the period of the transfer. In making its ruling the ECJ referred back to the Acquired Rights Directive that states that the TUPE Regulations apply when there is a change in the legal or natural owner of the entity. In this case there had been a clear change of ownership, and thus there was a transfer.

- *Brookes and others v Borough Care Services Ltd and others* (1998) IRLR 636

   In this case the running of a number of care homes for the elderly was to be transferred to the voluntary sector. This was achieved by the directors of the voluntary company becoming directors of Borough Care Services and the shares being transferred – there was no change in legal ownership, and so no transfer took place.

- *Spijkers v Gebroeders Benedik Abattoir CV and another* (1986) CMLR 296

   In this case a slaughterhouse was sold to a new owner, who kept all the existing employees apart from Spijkers and one other. At the time of the sale the existing owner had ceased trading. The buildings and equipment were transferred to the new owner, but the question posed to the ECJ was whether the transfer of assets was sufficient to determine that a transfer had taken place, and whether the fact that the business had ceased trading before the change of ownership preclude a transfer taking place.

   Because a clearly defined economic entity had not been transferred there was not a transfer of undertaking. In making this judgment the ECJ determined that all the factors of the situation had to be considered in deciding whether a transfer had taken place. These included such things as the transfer of tangible assets (eg buildings and equipment), the similarity of activities before and after the transfer, the period of time for which the business is interrupted (if it is) before and after the transfer, and the value of any intangible assets.

An important case that caused considerable confusion in the interpretation of the 1981 Regulations was

- *Süzen v Zehnacker Gebäudereinigung GMBH Krankenhaus Service and Lefarth GMBH* (1997) IRLR 255

   Süzen was a cleaner employed by a contract cleaning company to work in a school. The contract ended and one month later was taken over by a new contractor – Süzen was not offered work with the new contractor. Süzen claimed her employment should have been protected by the Transfer of Undertaking Regulations. The ECJ ruled that in this case a transfer of an entity did not take place. There was no transfer of assets or taking over of the majority of the workforce: all that happened was a transfer of an activity.

This case caused confusion because it seemed to be contrary to judgments in other similar cases. It is noted here because it is a good example of how the 2006 Regulations have aided the courts by being specific about the definition of a transfer. The *Süzen* case would now be seen as a transfer of an undertaking because there was a change of service provision in which an activity performed by one contractor was transferred to another contractor.

TASK

Try to find an example of a transfer of an undertaking in an organisation with which you are familiar. Take time to understand why the events that took place were defined as a transfer.

EXPLORE FURTHER

At the time of writing, there have been very few rulings under the 2006 Transfer of Undertaking Regulations, and none that is of particular note. Students are advised to keep abreast of any developments by reading the HR press.

PROTECTION BY THE TUPE REGULATIONS

The Regulations give protection to employees of the company being transferred at the time of the transfer. If employees are unfairly dismissed for a reason relating to the transfer immediately prior to the transfer, they will still be covered by the transfer Regulations.

An employee can refuse to transfer to the new employer. This right does not prejudice the employee's right to resign and claim constructive dismissal. If the employee objects, the transfer goes ahead and the employee does not resign, the contract will be treated as being frustrated.

Any dismissal relating to the transfer of undertaking will potentially be unfair. Any employee with one year's continuous service will be able to take up a claim of unfair dismissal. As already stated, the new employer is not entitled to make any changes to the employee's contract of employment.

The only exception to these rules is where the employer can show an 'economic, technical or organisational' (ETO) reason for its actions. An example of the use of the ETO defence is found in *Whitehouse v Chas A Blatchford & Sons Ltd* (1999) IRLR 492.

- In this case the contract provision of certain hospital supplies was transferred to the new employer. A condition of the contract was that the costs of running the contract would be reduced, in line with the reduction of the hospital's budget. In order to make the required cost savings the new employer had to make an employee redundant. The employee claimed that this redundancy was an unfair dismissal because it resulted from a transfer of the undertaking. The employer successfully argued the ETO defence, showing that the dismissal was essential in order to fulfil the economic requirements of the contract.

CONSULTATION

The Regulations specify that consultation must take place with the relevant employee representatives. These representatives may be trade union representatives or elected employee representatives. The following information must be supplied to the representatives:

- that a transfer is to take place
- the reason for the transfer and when it is expected to take place
- the implications for the employees (legal, social and economic)
- the measures that the employer expects to take in relation to the employees
- the measures that the transferee expects to take in relation to the employees.

If the consultation does not take place, or is ruled to be inadequate, the liability for this is jointly the responsibility of the transferee and the transferor. Up to 13 weeks' pay may be awarded as compensation to each of the employees affected by the transfer.

EXCHANGE OF INFORMATION

The transferor is legally required to provide the transferee with certain information. This includes:

- the names of the employees who will transfer, and their ages
- the details of the employee's statement of employment particulars
- details of any applicable collective agreements
- details of any disciplinary action taken against any of the employees in the past two years in which the statutory dismissals and disciplinary procedure applied
- details of any grievances raised by any of the employees in the past two years where the statutory grievance procedure applied
- details of any legal action against the transferor taken by any of the employees in the past two years.

If this information is not provided, the employment tribunal can award the transferee up to £500 per employee affected by the information.

KEY LEARNING POINTS

- Wrongful dismissal is when the employer terminates the contract of employment, and in doing so breaches that contract.

- A wrongful dismissal can relate to a dismissal that does not follow the correct procedure, a dismissal without appropriate notice being given, or the termination of a fixed-term contract before the agreed date.

- Summary dismissal is where the employee breaches the contract of employment and as a result the contract is terminated without notice.

- Redundancy is one of the six potentially fair reasons for dismissal.

- If an employer is proposing to make more than 20 employees redundant, it must follow clear guidelines on the length of the consultation period.

- The consultation period must be meaningful, and employees must be supplied with certain minimum information in writing.

- Statutory redundancy payments are calculated in accordance with the basic award.

- An employee who refuses an offer of suitable alternative employment forgoes the right to a redundancy payment.

- A transfer of undertaking takes place when there is a transfer of an economic entity, or a change of service provision.

- An employee transfers to a new organisation with no change to his/her contract of employment.

- Any changes to the contract, or dismissals associated with the transfer, can only be allowed if they can be supported by the 'economic, technical or organisational' (ETO) defence.

FURTHER READING

CASE SUMMARIES

Silvey v Pendragon plc (2001) IRLR 685 – The employee was dismissed and accepted payment in lieu of notice, although there was no contractual provision to pay in lieu. He subsequently took a claim for wrongful dismissal within which he sought damages for loss of pension rights. Although he had accepted the payment in lieu of notice, it was ruled that it did not stop him from pursuing other losses.

Levett v Biotrace International Ltd (1999) IRLR 375 – Levett was dismissed after disciplinary proceedings. The rules of the share option scheme were that the ability to exercise the options was removed if the employee was dismissed on disciplinary grounds. However, Levett argued that the dismissal was in breach of contract, and if

he had received the correct notice period he could have exercised his right during this period. This was upheld.

Murray and another v Foyle Meats Ltd (1999) IRLR 562 – Murray worked in a slaughterhouse, where there was a downturn in business. He was made redundant as a result of this downturn and this was held to be a fair dismissal.

Mugford v Midland Bank plc (1997) IRLR 208 – The employer was proposing 3,000 redundancies and collective consultation took place. Mugford was selected for redundancy and a number of individual meetings took place with him regarding redeployment – but these discussions came to nothing. Although the individual consultation was not thorough, it was seen as adequate in the circumstances.

High Table Ltd v Horst and others (1998) ICR 409 – The employees worked as waitresses for a contract catering company. They primarily worked at one location, although there was a clause in their contract requiring them to work at other locations if the needs of the business changed. Due to a reduction in the contract at their usual place of work, they were made redundant. They argued that this was unfair dismissal because there should have been regard to the clause requiring mobility. The Court of Appeal ruled that it was of primary importance to look at what happened in the job. Because they usually worked in one location, a downturn in business at that location could result in a fair redundancy dismissal.

Cambridge and District Co-operative Society Ltd v Ruse (1993) IRLR 156 – Ruse was the manager of a butcher's shop, and when it closed down was offered the position of butchery department manager in a supermarket. He refused this because he did not see it as suitable alternative employment, on the grounds of diminished status (he had to report to the supermarket manager, did not have his own key and no longer had responsibility for banking money). This was found not to be suitable alternative employment.

EXAMPLES TO WORK THROUGH

1 Peter was dismissed on the grounds of capability, without notice, on 31 August 2007. He joined the company on 1 October 2006 and his contract allowed for a three-month notice period. Following a High Court hearing it has been ruled that he was wrongfully dismissed. What impact does this have on Peter and potential future hearings?

2 There is a redundancy taking place in your organisation and your managing director has drawn up potential criteria for selection. He has asked for your views on whether these are acceptable criteria. If you judge any to be unsatisfactory, suggest alternatives:

Length of service

Willingness to work from other locations within the region

Performance

Physical strength (because the work requires a lot of manual lifting)

Absence.

3 Following collective consultation regarding redundancies you have now identified the individuals who are at risk of redundancy. You have written to all of these employees asking them to come to individual meetings to discuss the situation. One employee has written back immediately stating that he does not want to 'waste his time at such a meeting – management won't change their mind'. How should you react?

4 Upon hearing the news of a possible transfer of undertaking three employees started a petition against it. The transferor was furious about this lack of co-operation and summarily dismissed all of them. They have now taken up claims of unfair dismissal. What will be the liabilities of both the transferee and the transferor in this situation?

CHAPTER 10

Trade union legislation

CHAPTER OBJECTIVES

The objectives of this chapter are:

- to define and describe a trade union
- to explain the role of the Certification Officer and the Central Arbitration Committee
- to outline the legislation relating to the recognition and derecognition of a trade union
- to analyse the legislation relating to collective bargaining
- to explain the legislation relating to industrial action
- to analyse the legislation relating to consultation.

TRADE UNIONS

TASK

Before studying this chapter about trade union legislation, find out if your organisation, or an organisation with which you are familiar, recognises a trade union. Try to understand the reasons behind the recognition or lack of it and the impact it has on the relationships between the employer and employees.

Section 1 of the Trade Union and Labour Relations (Consolidation) Act 1992 (TULRCA) defines a trade union as:

> an organisation consisting wholly or mainly of workers of one or more descriptions and whose principal purposes include the regulation of relations between workers of that description or those descriptions and employers or employee associations.

This definition shows us that the group of people wishing to be defined as a trade union must be workers who are concerned with relations with employers. This was demonstrated in the case of

- *Midland Cold Storage v Turner* (1972) ICR 230

  In this case the employees took industrial action against the employer, instructed by the Joint Shop Stewards Committee (JSSC – the employee representative body within the organisation). The company tried to sue the JSCC because of its actions in threatening drivers who attempted to cross picket lines set up to deter anyone from working during the industrial action. Section 10 of TULRCA allows for a trade union to be sued. The courts held that the JSSC was not a trade union – rather it was a pressure group, because it was not primarily concerned with the relationships between workers and employers – and so it could not be sued.

A list of trade unions is kept by the Certification Officer. The post of Certification Officer was established under section 7 of the Employment Protection Act 1975. The Certification Officer (www.certoffice.org) is an independent statutory authority appointed by the President of the Board of Trade.

A trade union can be included on this list by paying the appropriate fee and submitting a copy of its rules, officers, address, and the name under which it is known. The list of trade unions is available for public inspection. If a trade union wants to apply for a certificate of independence, it must be on this list held by the Certification Officer.

There are clear advantages to a trade union in receiving a certificate of independence. If it is successful its members can:

- appoint safety representatives (see Chapter 12)

- receive information for bargaining purposes (see later in this chapter)

- be consulted in the situation of redundancies and transfers of undertakings (see Chapter 9)

- take time off for trade union activities (see later in this chapter).

In addition, its members cannot have action taken against them because of their membership or trade union activities.

The Certification Officer determines whether the trade union is independent or not. In making that decision the Certification Officer must consider the definition of independence given in section 5 of TULRCA:

- The trade union is not controlled or dominated by an employer or a group of employers.

- The trade union cannot be interfered with by an employer or group as a result of the giving of financial or material support or by any other means which could tend towards control.

The process of determining whether a trade union is truly independent was laid down by the EAT in the case of *Blue Circle Staff Association v Certification Officer* (1977) ICR 224.

- The Blue Circle group of companies formed a staff consultative organisation. Initially it was under the control of the management, and received financial support from the company. The organisation wanted to move away from this control and instituted a new set of rules, and agreed a negotiating procedure with the management in a bid to achieve this independence. Five months after agreeing the rules it applied to the Certification Officer for a certificate of independence. This was refused on the grounds that there had been no clear move away from the former dependence on the employer.

In giving its judgment the EAT gave some clear guidelines in what issues should be considered when assessing independence. These were:

finance – If the organisation is getting any financial help from an employer, it is clearly not independent.

other assistance – Being given assistance such as free premises from which to operate is likely to rule out independence, although the extent of the support has to be considered.

employer interference – If the organisation gets considerable help from the employer, it is unlikely to be independent.

history – It is quite possible for an organisation to start as dependent, and then to grow into independence. However, the recency of this will be relevant. In the case of Blue Circle the dependence was still very recent.

rules – Is there anything in the rule-book of the organisation that allows the employer to interfere or control it? If so, this is likely to contradict independence.

single company unions – Although it is possible to have an independent trade union within and of a single company, it is more likely to be interfered with than a trade union that represents workers across a range of organisations.

organisation – Who is in charge of the group that wants it to be recognised as an independent trade union? If it is the senior management of the employer, it is likely to have more interference.

attitude – Is there a record of a robust attitude to negotiation, giving a sign of genuine independence?

 EXPLORE FURTHER

In considering the important issue of independence, students should examine the status of a range of trade unions. Start by looking at some of the larger and well-known trade unions and understand why they are clearly independent (eg Unite, USDAW, Unison). Then look at some smaller trade unions – maybe those that are specifically focused on an industry. Do these have a certificate of independence? Why/why not? Information about this can be found on the Certification Officer website.

RECOGNITION AND DERECOGNITION

Recognition of a trade union means that the employer is required to negotiate with the trade union on matters covered by collective bargaining such as redundancies or pay negotiations. It is possible for an employer to agree to negotiate on a limited range of issues (maybe just disciplinary and grievance matters). In such a case the trade union is not defined as a recognised trade union.

There are four routes to recognition:

- voluntary – when the agreement is made voluntarily between the employer and the trade union
- semi-voluntary – when the trade union makes a formal approach to the employer in writing, which the employer then agrees to

- automatic recognition

- recognition by ballot.

The last two routes can be a result of the statutory recognition procedure. This applies only when the employer has at least 21 employees (although the employees potentially represented by the trade union can be of a smaller number). For the statutory recognition procedure to be invoked, the trade union making the request must have a certificate of independence.

The statutory recognition process is as follows.

The trade union seeking recognition makes a written request to the employer for recognition. This must identify the trade union and the bargaining unit.

The bargaining unit is the group of workers that the trade union is seeking to represent. This might be all employees, or it could be a specific group within the organisation.

If the employer and the trade union cannot agree on the definition of the bargaining group, the Central Arbitration Committee (CAC) will decide. The CAC can only become involved in the discussions if there are at least 10% of trade union members in the proposed unit and the majority of workers in the unit are likely to favour recognition.

The CAC is an independent body that has statutory powers, the main one being the adjudication on decisions relating to recognition or derecognition of trade unions. Although the body is independent, the committee members are appointed by the Department for Trade and Industry following discussions with Acas.

 EXPLORE FURTHER

Students who want to know more about the work of the CAC and recent judgments it has made should look at its website: www.cac.gov.uk.

The Employment Relations Act 2004 determined the process that must be followed if the employer and trade union have been unable to agree on an appropriate bargaining unit. At this stage the CAC becomes involved, and must start by considering the bargaining unit that has been proposed by the trade union. If the CAC does not consider that this bargaining unit is appropriate, it must make an alternative proposal taking account of the need for the unit to work within the current management and bargaining arrangements. The CAC must try to avoid small, fragmented bargaining units within an organisation.

Once the bargaining unit has been decided the next question is whether the trade union should be recognised as representing the workers. If the CAC is satisfied that at least 50% of the workers in the unit are union members, the CAC will issue a declaration that the trade union is recognised for the purpose of collective bargaining. This is the route of automatic recognition.

However, the CAC can decide to proceed with the route of a ballot if one of three qualifying conditions are fulfilled. These are:

- The CAC determines that a ballot is the best way of proceeding for the purpose of good employee relations.

- A significant number of the members of the trade union within the bargaining unit tell the CAC that they do not want the trade union to carry out collective bargaining on their behalf.
- The CAC has evidence that leads to doubts that a significant number of trade union members do want the union to represent them.

In addition, if fewer than 50% of the workers are union members, a ballot of the workers in the bargaining unit will be held.

If the CAC decides to proceed with a ballot, it will appoint an independent person to carry it out. The ballot must take place within 20 days of the appointment, unless there are good reasons for an extension to that period of time.

If the result of the ballot is such that

- a majority of those who voted supported recognition, *and*
- at least 40% of the workers within the bargaining unit supported recognition,

the CAC will issue a declaration that the union is recognised.

Once the declaration of recognition has been given, the two parties have 30 days to agree a process for conducting collective bargaining. They can agree an extension to this period of time if required. If the two parties are unable to reach an agreement, the CAC may be asked to assist. The CAC has 20 days in which to help the parties reach agreement, although this period of time may be extended by agreement. If the parties are unable to reach agreement, the CAC will specify the method of collective bargaining that is to be used.

Once an agreement is reached it is a legally enforceable contract.

If there are significant changes to the original bargaining unit, either party may apply to the CAC asking for a decision on the appropriate bargaining unit. If the CAC accepts that the bargaining unit has changed, it can issue a declaration ending the current bargaining arrangements or making a declaration on a more appropriate bargaining unit.

An application for derecognition of the trade union can only be made after a minimum of three years after the declaration of recognition. The application can only be made if

- the size of the workforce is now less than 21
- there is no longer majority support for the collective bargaining arrangements
- the original declaration was made on the basis of 50% union membership and the rate of membership has now fallen below this level.

TIME OFF FOR TRADE UNION DUTIES

Employers must allow official representatives of independent trade unions that they recognise a reasonable amount of paid time off during working hours. The allowed time should be for the purpose of:

- carrying out duties relating to negotiations with the employer
- carrying out duties connected with their role (specifically listed in section 178(2) of

TULRCA) and duties that the employer has agreed they may carry out – the most likely examples are representing their members at disciplinary and grievance hearings

- receiving information from the employer
- undergoing training relevant to their trade union duties, which is approved by their trade union or the TUC (Trades Union Congress).

A trade union representative is not required to have a minimum length of service before these entitlements apply.

COLLECTIVE BARGAINING: DISCLOSURE OF INFORMATION

As we saw in the last section, a recognised trade union negotiates with the employer on issues covered by collective bargaining. Examples of such issues are terms and conditions of employment, disciplinary matters and grievances. Sections 181 to 185 of TULRCA give the regulations relating to information that the employer is required to disclose in order for the bargaining process to proceed effectively.

Information should be disclosed which:

- is information without which the union would be impeded to a material degree in carrying out collective bargaining with the employer
- it would be good industrial relations practice to disclose.

Clearly, there could be a range of interpretations of these two definitions. The Code of Practice produced by Acas (*Disclosure of Information by Trade Unions for Collective Bargaining Purposes*) gives useful additional guidance. Some important guidelines to consider are:

- Any information that is requested must be relevant to the issue being addressed through the collective bargaining.
- The information must be of importance to the negotiations.
- The level at which the negotiations are taking place must be considered.
- The relevance of the type and size of the organisation must be taken into account.

TASK

Students are recommended to read the Acas code of practice to gain a fuller outline of the disclosure process. This can be accessed from the Acas website: www.acas.org.uk.

The need for the requested information to relate to the matters being discussed in the collective bargaining is illustrated in the case of *R v Central Arbitration Committee ex parte BTP Tioxide Ltd* (1981) IRLR 60.

- In this case BTP Tioxide entered into a limited bargaining agreement with the trade union ASTMS. ASTMS thereafter asked the employer to disclose information regarding a job evaluation process that was not part of the area covered by the bargaining agreement. BTP Tioxide refused to disclose the information and ASTMS took a complaint to the CAC. The CAC ordered BTP Tioxide to disclose the information, and they appealed to the High Court.

The appeal was upheld – the High Court stated that the CAC had been misdirected because the information did not relate to the representational function of the trade union.

There are certain classifications of information that the employer is not required to disclose. These include:

- information that might affect national security
- information that can only be disclosed by contravening other legislation (maybe the Data Protection Act 1998 – see next chapter)
- information that has been given to the employer in confidence
- information relating specifically to an individual, unless he/she gives consent
- information that could significantly damage the employer's undertaking
- information obtained by the employer for the purpose of defending or bringing legal proceedings.

Any information that is disclosed by the employer can be used only for the purposes of collective bargaining.

If the trade union considers that the employer is failing to comply with the requirement to disclose information, it can make a complaint to the CAC. If the CAC considers the complaint can be resolved by conciliation, it must refer the case to Acas. If the case is not referred to Acas, or if any conciliation is unsuccessful, the CAC must hear the complaint. If the complaint is upheld, the CAC can require the employer to release the information, specifying a period in which the disclosure must be made.

INDUSTRIAL CONFLICT

TASK

In understanding the legislation relating to industrial conflict it would be useful to consider occurrences within recent employment disputes. Find articles relating to disputes in newspapers, magazines or relevant websites to broaden your understanding of the processes of such disputes.

Within the law there is a right to organise strikes and other industrial action. This right is supported by giving statutory immunity from liability at common law for civil wrongs or torts provided that certain conditions are met.

Whenever workers strike, or take some other form of industrial action they are acting in breach of their contract of employment. So when a trade union calls for organised industrial action, it is inducing its members to take action in breach of their contracts.

Under common law it is unlawful to induce people to act in breach of a contract, and so trade union officials would face legal action each time they called for strike action if there were not special immunities granted. The immunity from legal action only applies to actions that are in preparation for, or in the activities, of a trade dispute. The immunities relate to:

- inducing a breach of contract

- intimidation

- conspiracy

- interference with a business by unlawful means

- inducing a breach of a statutory duty.

A trade union's immunity from any legal action only applies to actions that are in contemplation or furtherance of a trade dispute. This immunity is known as the 'golden formula'. To understand the immunity in more detail we will look at the first three of those listed above, because they are most commonly encountered.

INDUCING A BREACH OF CONTRACT

Direct inducement is when pressure is put on a person to break a contract. A tort (wrong) is committed if the person putting the pressure on knows that the result of the pressure will be a breach of the contract.

Indirect inducement is where pressure is put on a person to do an unlawful act to another body, which then results in that other body breaching a contract.

Section 219 of TULRCA gives immunity from any legal action in relation to the tort of inducing a breach of contract, presuming that the inducement relates to the contemplation of furtherance of a trade dispute.

The issue of inducement is illustrated in

- *Timeplan Education Group Ltd v National Union of Teachers* (1997) IRLR 457

  In this case Timeplan (a recruitment agency for teachers) had agreed to place a series of advertisements in a magazine run by a teachers' union in New Zealand (NZEI). However, the NUT was in dispute with Timeplan at this time, regarding terms and conditions of the teachers that it supplied. Because the NZEI was a sister organisation of the NUT, the NUT contacted it to inform it of the ongoing dispute with Timeplan and to request that the advertisements cease. After some correspondence NZEI agreed to withdraw the advertisements. Timeplan then took action against the NUT claiming that it had unlawfully interfered with the contract between Timeplan and NZEI.

  The Court of Appeal held that the NUT had not been aware of any contract that existed between NZEI and Timeplan and so could not be found guilty of persuading, procuring or inducing the NZEI to breach a contract. The NUT had therefore not committed the tort of inducement to breach a contract.

INTIMIDATION

This tort is committed when a person is threatened. For example, Fred is convicted of stealing the funds of the local football club. He is also an employee at Bloggs Ltd. A number of the employees at Bloggs Ltd are also members of the football club. They are no longer prepared to work with Fred and their trade union representative tells the management of Bloggs Ltd that the employees will take industrial action unless Fred is dismissed. If such a threat is made in contemplation or furtherance of a trade dispute, section 219 of TULRCA gives immunity from any legal action.

CONSPIRACY

This occurs when two or more people combine to damage the employer by unlawful means with intent to damage the employer (for example, gathering together to take industrial action to protect jobs). Clearly, any industrial action is likely to damage the employer. Alternatively, it can be when two or more people combine together to harm the employer by using unlawful means.

Section 219 of TULRCA gives immunity if the action is taken in contemplation or furtherance of a trade dispute, unless the act would be subject to legal action if it had been carried out by one person (eg criminal action).

If a trade union is involved in action without the support of a ballot, unlawful picketing, secondary action or action to enforce union membership, it forfeits statutory immunity.

LAWFUL INDUSTRIAL ACTION

Sections 226 to 235 of TULRCA 1992, further altered by the Employment Relations Acts of 1991 and 2004, explain the process that must take place for any industrial action to be lawful.

At least seven days before any ballot is held, the trade unions must inform the employers (in writing) of all employees involved in the ballot. They must tell the employers that a ballot is to be held, when the ballot will take place, and give the employer information that the trade union holds that will help the employer to make plans and bring information to the attention of those employees who are to be balloted. This requirement does not mean that the trade union must supply the names of all those who are to be involved in the ballot, but the numbers, categories of employees and workplaces are to be disclosed. If the trade union intends to organise industrial action at more than one place of work, it must carry out separate ballots at each of those places of work. An independent scrutineer must be appointed to oversee the ballot process, and the counting of the votes.

It has been shown that a trade union is not deprived of its immunity from the tort of inducing a breach of contract if additional members join the trade union after the ballot has taken place.

- In *London Underground v National Union of Rail, Maritime and Transport Workers* (1995) IRLR 636, the RMT Union held a ballot of members receiving a clear majority in favour of strike action (over a number of one- and two-day periods). After the ballot a further 20 members joined the trade union, which the London Underground was prepared to accept.

  However, around one month later notice was given of further industrial action, and this time a further 672 new members had joined the RMT. London Underground claimed that the action could no longer be supported by the original ballot, and a further ballot was required. However, the RMT argued that the original ballot still held because a clear majority had voted for industrial action.

  The Court of Appeal ruled that the industrial action is supported by the view of the majority of those who are eligible to vote in a ballot, and that this ballot was not rendered invalid if new members joined the trade union, because the ballot is still relevant to the dispute in question. The industrial action was therefore still lawful and the RMT still had immunity from the tort of inducing breach of contract.

All those who are entitled to vote must be given a reasonable opportunity to vote. This includes giving the opportunity for a postal vote when it is appropriate. The voting paper must clearly state the name of the independent scrutineer, the address to which the ballot paper is to be returned (assuming there is the option of a postal vote) and the date by which it must be returned. It must be marked with a number which is one of a series of consecutive numbering, must allow the voter to clearly indicate a 'yes' or 'no' response to the willingness to participate in strike action, and identify the person authorised to call industrial action.

- In *Connex South Eastern Ltd v National Union of Rail, Maritime and Transport Workers* (1998) IRLR 249, the issue of the definition of a strike was addressed. The members of the RMT were balloted for industrial action that was to include an overtime ban and refusal to work on rest days. On the ballot paper they were asked to vote 'yes' or 'no' for strike action, with no mention of action short of a strike. Following a majority vote the RMT informed Connex of a subsequent overtime ban and refusal to work on rest days. Connex immediately applied for an injunction, claiming that such action had not been addressed by the ballot paper.

  The Court of Appeal refused the injunction. It agreed that the definition of a strike used by the RMT in this situation was not the usual definition. However, 'strike' is defined in TULRCA 1992 as any concerted stoppage of work. Clearly, the proposed action of the RMT fell into this definition, and thus lawful industrial action was being proposed.

The voting paper must also contain a clear statement as follows:

> If you take part in a strike or other industrial action, you may be in breach of your contract of employment. However, if you are dismissed for taking part in a strike or other industrial action which is called officially and is otherwise lawful, the dismissal will be unfair if it takes place fewer than 12 weeks after you started taking part in the action, and depending on the circumstances may be unfair if it takes place later.

The voting must be secret and the ballot papers must be fairly and accurately counted, and the counting must be overseen by an independent scrutineer. As soon as reasonably possible the trade union must inform all those concerned of the result of the ballot. If the result is in favour of industrial action, the trade union must give the employer seven days' notice of the industrial action. Any industrial action must commence within an agreed period. This is usually four weeks, but could be longer if agreed between the employer and the trade union. If the industrial action does not commence within the agreed period, a new ballot must take place.

The notice to take industrial action must give the employer sufficient information to make plans and to bring information to the attention of those who are likely to be involved in the action. The trade union must explain whether the industrial action is intended to be continuous or on specific days or at specific times (and explain what days and times those are to be). If the action is to be continuous, the date it will start must be given.

If this procedure is not followed in any significant way the ballot can be declared void.

UNLAWFUL INDUSTRIAL ACTION

If unlawful industrial action is taken (which could be action following a void ballot, or could be action taken without a ballot – known as a 'wildcat strike'), the employer can apply for an injunction to stop any further action being taken.

Given the immediacy of the situation (ie the desire to stop unlawful action that is already occurring) it is usual for an employer to start by trying to obtain an interim injunction. This gives an order for the unlawful action to cease until a particular date. It is hoped that by the given date the matter will have been considered at a full hearing and either the application will have been refused or a permanent injunction will have been granted.

In deciding whether to grant an interim injunction the courts will consider firstly whether there is a serious issue to address. The courts will then have to consider the balance of convenience – in other words, is the granting of an interim injunction in the interests of both parties (and is there any relevant public interest)? The court also has to consider the likelihood of the trade union being able to give a defence under the immunities that we examined earlier in this chapter. If it can be shown that a person has suffered loss as a result of unlawful industrial action, he/she can bring an action for damages. Claims are usually brought against trade unions, although they can be brought against individual participants.

In August 2007 the Prison Officers Association (POA) called an unofficial strike over their pay dispute. Without warning, all prison officers took industrial action from 7am on 29 August. The Government went to the High Court to seek an injunction which would demand that the prison officers returned to work. The injunction was granted, but the prison officers did not return to work immediately. However, as a few hours passed they started to return to work. If they had ignored the court order, they could have faced prison or unlimited fines. In addition, the Government (as the employer) could have sued the POA as outlined below.

The level of damages against a trade union that can be awarded by the court is subject to limits imposed by section 22 of TULRCA. The limits vary according to the size of the union:

£10,000 if the union has fewer than 5,000 members

£50,000 for 5,000 to 25,000 members

£125,000 for 25,000 to 100,000 members

£250,000 for 100,000+ members.

PICKETING

Section 220 of TULRCA 1992 allows for a person who is contemplating or acting to further a trade dispute to attend at or near his/her place of work or (if he/she is a trade union official) at or near the place of work of a member of the trade union he/she is representing for the purpose of peacefully communicating information or peacefully persuading a person to abstain from working.

Picketing is therefore not unlawful in itself, although there are situations in which actions taken in relation to picketing may be deemed to be unlawful. It should be noted that mass picketing is likely to be unlawful because it may no longer be picketing for the purposes of 'peaceful persuasion'. This is illustrated in the case of *Thomas v National Union of Miners (South Wales)* (1985) IRLR 136.

- This case took place during the miners' strike of 1984/5. When a number of miners started to return to work, although the dispute continued, large groups of pickets assembled at the entrances to the mines. Although there were only six official picket groups, 60 to 70 miners would gather, shouting abuse at those who crossed the picket lines. It was found that this was no longer 'peaceful persuasion' and was also restricting the miners from using the highway to get to work. An injunction was placed on the NUM restricting it to the placing of just six pickets at the mine gates.

There are other civil and criminal offences that could potentially be committed in the process of picketing:

Civil

- Inducing a breach of contract. This could occur if a driver from another organisation is persuaded not to cross a picket line. In this situation the driver is being induced to breach his/her contract of employment.
- Trespass to the highway. This could occur if the regular passage along the highway is disrupted.
- Private nuisance. This could be interference with a person's use of nearby land or premises. It could also be action that makes it unpleasant for a person to access premises, such as using foul language or beating on cars as they drive through.

Criminal

- Obstruction of the highway
- Causing a breach of the peace
- Obstruction of a police officer in the execution of his/her duty
- Riot, affray, violent disorder
- Public nuisance
- Criminal damage to property
- Harassment.

EXPLORE FURTHER

Students who wish to consider the issue of industrial action in more detail would be well advised to look at any current employment disputes and note what is occurring. Although there are not always high-profile disputes happening, a careful reading of any newspaper over a number of days usually uncovers some dispute. Alternatively, read about recent disputes such as with British Airways (2005 and 2007), the Royal Mail (2007), London Underground (2007), prison officers (2007) and Central Trains (2005 and 2007).

Read the summaries of the actions taken and the reasons for them. Then apply the relevant legislation. In applying legislation try to understand any limitations that were placed on either the employers or the trade unions in their activities.

DISMISSAL OF EMPLOYEES

The Employment Relations Act 1999 provided that it is unfair to dismiss those involved in strike action for the first eight weeks of any strike. This period was extended to 12 weeks by the Employment Relations Act 2004. After that time the dismissal is fair if the CAC judges that all reasonable action has been taken by the employer to end the strike.

This 12-week period does not include any period of 'lock-out'. Lock-out occurs when an employer closes the place of employment or suspends all work or refuses to continue to employ the employees because of a dispute. The action is taken with a view to compelling the employees to accept the terms and conditions that are the focus of the dispute.

If an employer unreasonably refuses to use conciliation or mediation services, the 12-week period of protection against dismissal can be extended. This was inserted by the Employment Relations Act 2004 with the aim of encouraging employers to resolve disputes.

If an employer dismisses all employees involved in industrial action and then re-engages a selection of those employees within a three-month period, the dismissal of those who are not re-engaged is likely to be unfair.

It is automatically unfair to dismiss an employee because he/she is a member (or proposes to become a member) of an independent trade union, or has taken part (or proposes to take part) in activities of an independent trade union or refuses to join, or proposes to resign from, a trade union.

CONSULTATION

THE TRANSNATIONAL INFORMATION AND CONSULTATION OF EMPLOYEES REGULATIONS 1999

The European Works Council Directive was implemented in the UK by the Transnational Information and Consultation of Employees Regulations 1999, which came into force on 15 January 2000.

The Regulations require that a European Works Council (EWC), or an alternative process for consulting and informing employees, is set up for 'community-style undertakings' if a valid request to do so is received. A valid request must include at least 100 employees from at least two member states. A 'community-style undertaking' is defined as an undertaking with at least 1,000 employees within the member states, with at least 150 members in each of at least two of the states.

From 15 January 2000 any undertaking that has not already set up a voluntary EWC had to start negotiations about setting up an EWC within six months of receiving a request to do so. If the undertaking refuses to commence negotiations, it can be ordered by the EAT to set up a statutory EWC as defined in the Regulations.

The purpose of the EWC is for the employees to receive information on, and to be consulted about, matters that concern the company as a whole. These include issues such as business structure, economic and financial situation, mergers, cut-backs, redundancies, production and sales.

There should be a minimum of three members of an EWC and a maximum of 30. The EWC is required to meet at least once every year. The organisation is required to pay the costs of the EWC, which can include costs relating to travel, accommodation, interpretation and any resources required for members to carry out their duties.

Members of the EWC are entitled to paid time off for the carrying out of their duties. Any dismissal or detriment relating to membership of an EWC is automatically unfair.

THE INFORMATION AND CONSULTATION OF EMPLOYEES REGULATIONS 2004

Clearly, the EWC regulations apply only to multinational companies. The Information and Consultation of Employees Regulations 2004 address the need to establish a general framework for the rights to information and consultation of employees in undertakings within the European Community. As with works councils there is only the requirement to take action if a valid request is made. In this case to be valid the request must come from at least 10% of the employees (or at least 15 employees if the workforce comprises fewer than 150 staff, or at least 2,500 employees if it comprises more than 25,000 staff).

The Regulations were introduced in April 2005 and initially applied only to businesses with 150 or more employees. The Regulations were extended to businesses with 100 or more employees in April 2007, and to all businesses with 50 or more employees in April 2008.

The rights given to employees within the Directive are to receive information relating to such issues as activities within the organisation, economic position, the development of employment (particularly when this might involve a threat to employment) and any proposed substantial changes in work organisation or contractual relations. The information must be given in sufficient time to allow the employees to prepare for consultation.

Consultation must then be carried out with appropriate timing and content at the relevant level of management. The consultation must involve the employees' representatives having ample opportunity to express their opinions, and take place with a view to reaching agreement.

If there are already existing agreements about information-giving and consultation, the employer may hold a ballot to seek the endorsement of the employees for these agreements. A pre-existing agreement must:

- be in writing

- cover all employees

- have been approved by the employees

- set out how the employer is to give information to employees, and how the employer will seek their views on this information.

- *Stewart v Moray Council* (2006) IRLR 592

   This case centred on the definition of a pre-existing arrangement. Stewart, on behalf of 500 colleagues, submitted a request to Moray Council asking for negotiations to be held on an information and consultation agreement. The Council took the view that it already had a number of existing agreements with employees, and so it would hold a ballot for those agreements to be endorsed.

   Stewart argued that the agreements had been made with trade union representatives, and therefore just covered employees who were trade union members, and had not been approved by non-union members.

   The CAC, later supported by the EAT, held that the agreements did cover all employees, and were not restricted to trade union members only. However, it was upheld that the existing agreements did not clearly set out how the Council as employer was to give information and to seek views of employees on the information. The agreements in place thus did not meet all the requirements of pre-existing agreements, and the Council was ordered to negotiate on that point.

COLLECTIVE REDUNDANCIES, HEALTH AND SAFETY, AND TRANSFERS OF UNDERTAKING

It should also be noted that employers have specific requirements to consult with employees (elected employee representatives if there are no trade union representatives in place) in the situations of collective redundancies and transfers of undertaking (see Chapter 9) and health and safety (see Chapter 12).

KEY LEARNING POINTS

- A trade union is a group of workers who are concerned with the relationship between the workers and employers.

- A certificate of independence is issued to a trade union by the Certification Officer.

- Recognition of a trade union means that the employer and trade union negotiate on issues covered by collective bargaining.

- There are four routes to recognition – voluntary, semi-voluntary, automatic and by ballot.

- If the employer and trade union cannot agree on the definition of a bargaining unit, they can ask the Central Arbitration Committee for assistance.

- The Central Arbitration Committee (CAC) is an independent body with statutory powers.

- An application for derecognition of a trade union can only be made three years or more after the declaration of recognition.

- A trade union representative is allowed a reasonable period of paid time off work to carry out his/her duties.

- An employer is required to disclose to the trade union any information without which the trade union would be impeded in the process of collective bargaining, or information which should be disclosed in accordance with good employee relations.

- If a trade union takes lawful industrial action, it has immunity from certain torts, as long as the relevant actions are taken in contemplation or furtherance of a trade dispute.

- For lawful action to take place a process must be followed that involves notifying the employer of a ballot, holding a ballot and giving notice of any industrial action.

- If unlawful action takes place, the employer may seek an injunction to halt the action.

- Picketing is lawful as long as it is done with the aim of 'peaceful persuasion'.

- Although picketing is lawful, certain actions that might take place during picketing could breach civil or criminal legislation.

- An organisation that has at least 1,000 employees within the member states of the European Community, and at least 150 employees in each of at least two of the states, is required to establish a European Works Council.

- The information and consultation of Employees Regulations 2004 give further requirements for consultation arrangements within all organisations within the European Community.

FURTHER READING

CASE SUMMARIES

Amicus and Solent & Pratt (2002) TUR 1/168 – Union membership amounted to 68%, but the employers wanted a ballot due to concerns about union recognition that had been expressed by one worker (who stated that many of his colleagues felt similarly). There was also concern about some level of misrepresentation of the company's position on a range of issues. The CAC ruled that a ballot was not in the best interests of employee relations because of the high level of union membership.

TGWU and Economic Skips Ltd (2002) TUR 1/121 – The CAC ordered that a ballot be carried out although 55% of the bargaining unit were union members. The union and

the company had carried out their own surveys, which gave greatly differing figures of support for recognition (73% and 10%).

UNIFI and Bank Tejerat (2002) TUR 1/144 – 54% of the bargaining unit were union members. The employer argued that it was inappropriate to proceed with the recognition process because of an impending merger. The CAC ruled that the process could continue and, indeed, no ballot was necessary. If the bargaining unit changed significantly as a result of the merger, there could be an application for a review.

Camellia Tanker Ltd SA v International Transport Workers Federation and another (1976) ICR 274 – A tanker was moored in the Manchester Ship Canal, and the ITF made claims including increases in wages, back pay and other concessions. It told tug men and lock operators about the dispute, and asked them to support the dispute in not co-operating in the sailing of the ship. The employer applied for an injunction stopping the tug men and lock operators from becoming involved. It was ruled that their involvement was allowed because the induced breach of contract was protected.

Post Office v Union of Communication Workers (1990) IRLR 143 – The Union of Communication Workers balloted its members, asking if they supported 'industrial action up to and including strike action'. They received a majority vote, and strike action followed. After a lull for a publicity campaign, further industrial action took place. However, the Post Office successfully argued that the trade union had not sought a vote on 'action short of strike action' and therefore could not rely on the existing ballot for taking such action. Separate questions must be asked for each type of action.

News Group Newspapers Ltd v SOGAT '82 (1986) IRLR 227 – During a dispute the trade union refused to handle any titles published by the employer, not just those relevant to the dispute. The employer successfully sought an injunction, but the trade union refused to comply with the order. The trade union was found to be in contempt of court.

EXAMPLES TO WORK THROUGH

1 Your organisation has received an application from a trade union asking for recognition. It claims that 65% of the workforce are asking for trade union recognition. Your managing director does not want to have a unionised workforce, and suggests that an agreement be set up under the Information and Consultation of Employees Regulations 2004. What is your response?

2 For several weeks you have been carrying out pay negotiations in your organisation, and the negotiations have not been going very well. At the end of a meeting with the trade union representatives this morning they reported back to their members that they did not think they would succeed in reaching a good settlement. After lunch around 75% of your employees refused to return to work. They have said they will not return until management agree to their pay claim. What should you do?

3 Over recent years trade union recognition in your organisation has decreased from 76% to 34%. A number of employees have now claimed that the trade union is not relevant in the organisation, and so they want to agree a process for information-giving and consultation that is not part of the current union agreement. How should you proceed?

4 You are the HR manager. The employees at your organisation are currently taking strike action. When you drove into work this morning, passing the picket line, your wing mirror was damaged by one of the pickets. What action can you take?

CHAPTER 11

Privacy and confidential information

CHAPTER OBJECTIVES

The objectives of this chapter are:

- to outline the provisions of the Human Rights Act that are relevant to employment law
- to analyse the provisions of the Data Protection Act
- to outline the requirements imposed by the Access to Medical Reports Act
- to outline the main issues relating to patents, inventions and copyright
- to explain the importance of restraints of trade
- to explain the relevance of public interest disclosures.

THE HUMAN RIGHTS ACT 1988

Of the 14 articles within the Human Rights Act (HRA) there are six that have potential relevance to employment law. It is those six articles that we examine below. The Act, which came into effect in England and Wales on 2 October 2000, incorporates the provisions of the European Convention on Human Rights (ECHR) into UK law. It is important to note that the Human Rights Act applies only to those employed by public bodies – those working in the private sector have no rights under the HRA.

ARTICLE 6(1): THE RIGHT TO A FAIR TRIAL

This article states that everyone is entitled to a fair and public hearing in the determination of civil rights and obligations within a reasonable time by an independent and impartial tribunal established by law.

This article is of particular relevance to the employment tribunals system. As we noted in Chapter 2, Employment Judges do have the power to 'strike out' cases that have very little chance of success. When this happens, the applicant is not allowed to bring the case before the tribunal, and there is the possibility that the claimant could argue that his rights under Article 6 have been ignored.

It is also important to note the requirement the article places to hear any case within a 'reasonable period of time'. This was challenged in the case of *Somjee v United Kingdom* (2002) IRLR 886.

● Somjee was a doctor who worked for a hospital in Merseyside. She brought cases against the hospital relating to race discrimination and unfair dismissal. The applications went through a series of hearings and appeals, and there were a number of delays in the proceedings. The cases were reasonably complex, and the reasons for the delays were varied. Somjee took a complaint to the ECHR relating to the length of time taken to hear the cases. There were three claims she had brought: the first took eight years and nine months to reach a conclusion, the second took seven years and eleven months, and the third took eight years and eight months. The ECHR ruled that there had been unreasonable delays, although they did note that some of the reasons for the delays were the fault of Somjee.

These delays were unusually long, but it should be noted that Article 6 does bring in the requirement to deal with claims in a timely manner.

 EXPLORE FURTHER

The reasons for the many delays in the *Somjee* case were complex. Students who wish to understand the requirements of Article 6(1) in more detail are advised to read a full synopsis of the case to obtain further insight.

ARTICLE 8: THE RIGHT TO RESPECT FOR PRIVATE AND FAMILY LIFE

The first part of this article determines that everyone has the right to respect for his/her family life, home and correspondence. However, this first part of the article is subject to the provisos included in the second part, which allow for there to be 'interference' with this right when it is necessary for reasons of public safety, national security, the economic well-being of the country, the prevention of crime or disorder, the protection of health or morals, or the protection of the rights and freedom of others.

● *Whitefield v General Medical Council* (2003) IRLR 39

Whitefield was a doctor (working as a general practitioner) and suffered from a depressive illness and excessive use of alcohol. The problems were affecting his work and the General Medical Council imposed three conditions in order for his registration as a doctor to continue – he was to abstain completely from alcohol, was to submit to random blood and urine tests, and had to attend Alcoholics Anonymous.

Whitefield challenged these requirements under Article 8 of the Human Rights Act. He argued that not being allowed to drink alcohol socially, and having to take random blood and urine tests, was an infringement of his right to a private life.

This claim was not upheld. It was stated that he could still enjoy a social life, drinking non-alcoholic drinks – and that the justification for asking for random blood and urine tests was proportionate to the reasons (ensuring that he was practising safely as a doctor).

The issue of surveillance and monitoring of employees has been debated in some detail in recent years, partly because of the increased ability to carry out sophisticated surveillance. The use of CCTV (closed-circuit television) is becoming increasingly common. In addition, the use of emails and the Internet has become widespread and some employers do have concerns about the use that employees might be making of such tools.

There has been specific legislation to address these issues. The Regulation of Investigatory Powers Act 2000 made it a civil wrong to intercept communications on private and public systems. Section 3 of this Act does allow for interception if the parties to the communication have consented to it. This emphasises the need for organisations to have clear policies on email and Internet use, and to make it very clear that the employer reserves the right to monitor such use.

This right does appear to be a direct breach of Article 8. However, it has not been tested in court at the time of writing.

The Telecommunications (Lawful Business Practice)(Interception of Communications) Regulations 2000 nonetheless allowed exceptions for 'legitimate business purposes'. There is considerable breadth to the legitimate business purposes allowed, which include monitoring quality, investigating unauthorised use and ensuring compliance with internal procedures. There is the concern that employers can apply the concept of legitimate business purposes to almost anything – but they still must have regard to the Data Protection Act, which we examine later in this chapter.

Two cases in this general area are well worth noting.

- *Copland v United Kingdom* (2007) ECHR 62617/00

  The events in this case took place before the Regulation of Investigatory Powers Act 2000 was enacted – the outcome of the case therefore does not address the application of this Act.

  In this case the European Court of Human Rights ruled that the college at which Copland worked had breached her right to privacy. Over a prolonged period the college monitored her phonecalls, emails and Internet use. The college argued that it merely kept a log of the use, and did not actually intercept any communications.

  However, the ECHR ruled that it was a breach of Copland's privacy because she was not informed that any monitoring was taking place. She thus had a reasonable expectation that all her communications were private.

- *Long and others v SP Dataserve Ltd* (2005) ET 103200/05

  In this case Long and others were dismissed by the company for sending and receiving an excessive number of personal emails. Over three days one employee had received or sent 537 personal emails, and another employee had sent or received 745 personal emails over six days. There was a company email policy in place, which allowed 'limited and reasonable' Internet/email use for personal reasons. However, the organisation argued that the use by these employees fell outside the definition of 'limited and reasonable'.

  The employees successfully argued that the definition of 'limited and reasonable' was not clear, and so the dismissal was unfair.

The important message from both these cases is that employers must have a clear Internet and email usage policy that is clearly communicated to all employees.

TASK

Find out if your organisation, or an organisation with which you are familiar, has a policy relating to privacy in the workplace. If there is a policy, do you think it adequately addresses all the issues? If there is no policy, what problems might the organisation face in addressing any issues relating to privacy?

EXPLORE FURTHER

In the light of the current relevance of the topic students might find it interesting to explore the issue of privacy relating to emails, Internet use, etc in more detail. An interesting publication is *Computer Use in the Workplace*, IDS Brief 822 (2007). Contact IDS on www.idsbrief.co.uk.

ARTICLE 9: FREEDOM OF THOUGHT, CONSCIENCE AND RELIGION

This article gives the freedom of thought, conscience and religion, and the freedom to manifest the religion or belief. This freedom is subject to limitations prescribed by law, and those limitations necessary for public safety, public order, health or morals, and the protection of the rights and freedom of others.

There is some overlap between the provisions of this article and the legislation relating to discrimination on the grounds of religion or belief that was introduced in December 2003.

An interesting aspect of this article is the issue of 'manifesting' the religion or belief, particularly where this clashes with work obligations.

This is illustrated in the case of

● *Ahmad v United Kingdom* (1982) EHRR 126

Ahmad was a schoolteacher and a devout Muslim. He worked under a contract of employment that required full-time service, but also allowed time off with pay on special religious days, when his religion determined that no work should be done. He was refused permission for a 45-minute absence every Friday to attend the mosque. He resigned and claimed unfair dismissal. The case was referred to the ECHR, which found that there was no breach of Article 9 because Ahmad had known the terms of the contract of employment when he commenced work.

The issues to be considered here are similar to those examined in Chapter 7 in relation to discrimination on the grounds of religion or belief. The ruling in this case (and in the case of *Stedman v United Kingdom* – see *Case summaries*) seem to suggest that the ECHR is not sympathetic to the employee when the request to worship clashes with reasonable work obligations.

This case seems to suggest that the employer is not required to allow time off during regular work commitments for the purpose of regular worship. Do you think that this conclusion contradicts the Employment Equality (Religion and Belief) Regulations 2003 in any way? Take note of any cases that are brought under the 2003 legislation and contrast them with the *Ahmad* and *Stedman* cases.

Sunday working

Certain retail workers are protected for refusing to work on Sundays. 'Protected shop workers' cannot be required to work on Sundays, and cannot be dismissed or suffer any detriment for refusing to work on Sundays. Those who fall into this category are those who were employed as shop workers when the Sunday Trading Act 1994 came into force (25 August 1994). They lose this protection if they agree to work on a Sunday, or by giving written agreement to the employer to work on Sundays.

Workers who commenced after 25 August 1994, or who have lost this protection, are known as 'opted-out shop workers'. They can give their employer notice that they object to working on a Sunday. Three months after this notice is given they receive the same protection as protected shop workers.

These provisions do not apply to any employee who has specifically agreed to work on a Sunday.

ARTICLE 10: FREEDOM OF EXPRESSION

This article allows everyone the freedom of expression including the right to hold opinions and to give and receive information relating to these opinions without interference. Again, there are restrictions given in the second part of the article relating to the interests of such things as national security, public safety, the prevention of disorder or crime and the protection of health, morals and the reputations of others.

The ECHR has determined that freedom of expression can relate to the way the employee dresses – because dress can be a form of expression. However, there may be circumstances in which an employer can show that a dress code at work is reasonable because of the nature of the work. This could include the need to tie back long hair for hygiene reasons. Less clear could be a dress code that the employer justifies on the grounds of the 'reputations of others' – ie the employer's reputation is related to the appearance of the employees.

Freedom of expression can also relate to the employee's interests outside of work. This is shown in the case of *Pay v Lancashire Probation Service* (2003) ICR 1138.

- Pay was employed as a probation officer specialising in the treatment of sex offenders. His employers became aware that he was involved in an organisation that promoted the sale of items relating to sado-masochism and also that he performed acts in hedonist and fetish clubs. The employers decided to dismiss Pay, because they considered that these outside activities were inconsistent with his role as a probation officer, particularly in the light of his work with sex offenders. Pay applied to the employment tribunals claiming unfair dismissal and contravention of Articles 8 and 10 of the Human Rights Act.

It was ruled that the dismissal was fair. In specific relation to Article 10 it was agreed that the continuing employment of Pay, given his outside interests, was not justified in the light of the need to protect the reputation of others – in this case the reputation of the Probation Service.

In considering the case it is important to note the relevance of the nature of Pay's job. If his employment had not involved work with sex offenders, it might well be that any dismissal would have been found to be unfair.

ARTICLE 11: FREEDOM OF ASSEMBLY AND ASSOCIATION

This article gives everyone the right to peaceful assembly and association with others, and includes the right to form and join trade unions for the protection of one's interests. Again, there are provisos that include potential restrictions on the grounds of national security or public safety interests, the protection of health or morals and the rights and freedoms of others and the prevention of disorder or crime.

The restrictions that can be imposed on this article are clearly illustrated by the decision in the case of *Government Communications Staff Federation v Certification Officer and the Council of Civil Service Unions* (1992) ICR 163, which was later referred to the ECHR for its judgment.

- In 1984 the rights of employees of the Government Communications headquarters (GCHQ) to join a trade union were withdrawn. The employees were allowed to join a staff association which was set up at GCHQ, known as the Government Communications Staff Federation. In 1989 the Federation applied for a certificate of independence (as explained in the last chapter) but was refused because it was not truly independent – the GCHQ Director could 'interfere' with its operation, and indeed its existence was subject to the approval of the GCHQ Director.

  The UK Government argued that the refusal to allow GCHQ employees to join an independent trade union was justified because the employees were involved with matters of national security. Their rights to freedom of association under Article 11 were therefore restricted by the interests of national security. This case was referred to the ECHR, which ruled in favour of the UK Government.

An interesting question occurs when the rights of different groups, under the Human Rights Act, seem to clash.

- In the case of *ASLEF v United Kingdom* (2007) ECHR 110022/05, the trade union ASLEF expelled a member who was also a member of the British National Party (BNP). It argued that it did not support the values of the BNP and under Article 11 had the freedom of association – which included the freedom to choose who it associated with.

  The ECHR found that the right of ASLEF to choose its members outweighed the right to freedom of expression of the BNP members, and so ASLEF did not have to accept them into membership.

EXPLORE FURTHER

The impact of Article 11 on trade union recognition and activities is potentially wide-ranging. Exploring this matter further the student should consider the impact on:

– the right to picket
– the unlawfulness of the closed shop
– the right to strike
– the refusal to recognise a trade union.

(See the last chapter for some relevant case law to start the exploration.)

ARTICLE 14: PROHIBITION OF DISCRIMINATION

Article 14 specifically relates to discrimination relating to one of the articles within the HRA. It does not, therefore, give protection against discrimination in any circumstance. The areas of discrimination covered in the article are sex, race, colour, language, religion, political or other opinion, national or social origin, association with a national minority, property, birth or other status.

To illustrate the essential relationship between the discrimination and an article within the Human Rights Act, consider this example.

If an organisation introduced random drug-testing for all employees aged over 50 years, this would be discrimination in contravention of Article 14. This is because the random drug-testing relates to Article 8 – the right to privacy – and discrimination on the grounds of age is specifically listed within Article 14.

However, if the organisation introduced the requirement that all employees aged over 50 years who applied for promotion had to give a presentation to the senior management, this would not be in contravention of Article 14 because the issue of giving a presentation does not fall under any article of the Human Rights Act.

EXPLORE FURTHER

Students who wish to explore the issues of the Human Rights Act and the work of the European Court of Human Rights in more detail are advised to start by looking at the ECHR website – www. echr.coe.int. This website gives summaries of recent judgments and advice on further reading.

THE DATA PROTECTION ACT 1998

As already mentioned, the Data Protection Act (DPA) has some relevance to Article 8 of the HRA – the right to privacy. The DPA is specifically concerned with the safe handling and use of personal data that is held about individuals.

In UK legislation, issues relating to the safe handling of the data were initially addressed in the Data Protection Act 1994. Subsequent to this the UK Government was required to implement the Directive on the Protection of Personal Data 1995. This has resulted in the Data Protection Act 1998.

The Directive applies to a wider remit than employment, although we concentrate on employment in this chapter. The Directive widened the definition of data that was previously held in the DPA 1984. This addressed automated data. The definition of data in the Directive, and therefore in the DPA 1998, is much broader and includes:

- any information that is processed by equipment operating automatically in response to instructions given for that purpose
- any information that is recorded with the intention that it should be processed by means of such equipment
- any information that is recorded as part of a relevant filing system, or that is intended to form part of a relevant filing system
- any information that forms part of an accessible record, but is not covered in the earlier definitions (bullet points 1 to 3).

It is clear from this definition, therefore, that the Act covers information that is held manually as well as electronically.

TASK

Find out if your organisation, or an organisation with which you are familiar, has a data protection policy. If there is such a policy, read it and consider whether it meets the requirements of the Data Protection Act 1998.

For any processing of data to be lawful *one* of the following criteria must be met:

- The subject of the data has unambiguously given his/her consent.
- The processing of the data is necessary for the performance of a contract or in order to enter into a contract requested by the subject of the data.
- The processing is required by law.
- The processing is necessary to protect a vital interest of the data subject.
- The processing is necessary in the performance of tasks carried out in the public interest or by official authorities.
- The data can be processed where the employer has a legitimate interest to do so, and this is not overridden by the interest of protecting rights of the subject, such as the right to privacy.

Within the DPA 1998 is a list of *eight data protection principles*. The Act requires each data controller (in the case of employment this corresponds to the employer) to abide by these principles in all keeping and processing of personal data. The eight principles are:

- All personal data must be processed lawfully and fairly. To achieve this, the processing of the data must be necessary for the reasons already listed, or the data subject (the employee) must give permission for the data to be processed. The employee should be made aware of the processing of the data that is to take place. Without this knowledge the employee cannot give informed consent, and so the processing is unlikely to be fair.
- The personal data must be obtained only for specific and lawful purposes. The Act does allow an employer to list such purposes in a note to employees.

- The personal data must be adequate, relevant and not excessive in relation to the purpose for which it is required.

- The personal data should be accurate, and be kept up to date. The employer must keep an accurate record of the information provided by the employee. There should be opportunity for the employee to advise the employer of any changes, but the employer is not necessarily at fault if the information is inaccurate due to the employee not notifying the employer of changes. It is important that the employer takes 'reasonable steps' to ensure the ongoing accuracy of the data.

- Personal data should not be kept for longer than is necessary. This is particularly relevant to employees who have left employment. Some information must be kept in case an employee makes a claim against an employer, and in case there is a need to supply references. The employer must consider what information to keep – it might not be necessary to keep all information for an extended period of time.

- The personal data must be processed in accordance with the rights of the employee (which are listed below).

- The employer must take reasonable steps against unauthorised or unlawful processing of data and loss of or damage to data. This will include considering who needs to have access to the data and including some sort of protection against unauthorised access such as password protection.

- Personal data should not be transferred outside the European Economic Area unless the country in question can ensure adequate levels of protection for the data.

As well as abiding by these eight principles the employer is required to inform the Data Protection Registrar of the type of records it holds which contain personal data. The employer is also required to inform the Data Protection Registrar of the use that is made of these records.

The main *rights of the data subjects* are:

- to have access to personal data. The employee is allowed to ask the employer to inspect all records held about him/her, and the employer may charge a small fee (not usually greater than £10) for allowing this. Some information is exempt from inspection, such as any references that have been given in confidence by the employer

- to correct any data that is inaccurate.

It should be noted that there are additional restrictions relating to the holding and processing of 'sensitive personal data'. This is data relating to such things as racial or ethnic origin, political opinions, religious belief, trade union membership, health, sexuality and committing a criminal offence. Before any such data can be processed specific consent must be obtained from the employee.

In determining the restrictions placed by the Data Protection Act, the reasons for processing the data must be considered. This is shown in *Blackpool and the Fylde College v National Association of Teachers in Further and Higher Education* (1994) IRLR 227.

- In this case the trade union (NATFHE) had informed the College of the intention of its members to take industrial action. However, the College argued that it did not know the full list of the teachers that were members of NATFHE and the trade union had thus not met its obligations under TULRCA 1992 – see last chapter. The College successfully applied for an injunction against the industrial action. NATFHE challenged the injunction, claiming that to disclose the names of its members would contravene the Data Protection Act. NATFHE were unsuccessful in its challenge because although it was trying to adhere to the Data Protection Act, in doing so its actions had breached the legislation relating to industrial action and ballots. It was noted that the union could ask members to give their permission for their names to be given to the College because this detail was required by law when giving notice of proposed industrial action.

Another example of the correct use of information is illustrated in

- *Dalgleish v Lothian and Borders Police Board* (1991) IRLR 422

In this case the local authority asked the employer to provide details of employees' names and addresses to help them trace those who were in arrears with their community charge payments. The employees applied for an injunction stopping the employer from complying with this request. It was ruled that the information held by the employer was for the sole purpose of employment-related issues and was not information that was generally available to the public. The employer therefore had no right to disclose the information to the local authority.

 EXPLORE FURTHER

Any student who wishes to examine the legislation relating to data protection in more detail, or wants to understand further the role of the Data Protection Registrar, is recommended to refer to the website www.dataprotection.gov.uk.

THE ACCESS TO MEDICAL RECORDS ACT 1998

This Act covers any medical report which is supplied before employment commences or during employment by a medical practitioner who is or has been responsible for the clinical care of the individual.

The Act thus covers any information sought from an employee's GP because that medical practitioner is responsible for the clinical care of the individual. However, if the employer asks an independent doctor for a report on an employee (for example, if the employee has had long periods of absence due to illness), the report is not covered by this Act, unless the doctor is going to be involved in treating the employee in some way.

If an employer wants to apply for a medical report that is covered by the Act, the employer must seek the consent of the employee and specifically inform the employee that:

- he/she has the right to refuse consent for the application for the medical report
- he/she can request access to the medical report before the employer sees the report.
- he/she can request that the report is amended or is allowed to record, in writing, a difference of opinion over any details within the report
- he/she can refuse consent for the report to be disclosed to the employer.

An employee can be denied access to a medical report if the medical practitioner considers that the disclosure would be likely to:

- cause serious physical or mental harm to the employee
- reveal information about another individual
- reveal the intentions of the practitioner in relation to the individual
- reveal the identity of another person (non-medical) who has supplied information to the medical practitioner.

If the medical practitioner decides to withhold part or all of a report, he/she must inform the employee. The employee then has the right to refuse consent to the report being disclosed if he/she wishes.

PATENTS, INVENTIONS AND COPYRIGHT

Section 39 of the Patents Act 1977 provides that an invention made by an employee shall belong to the employer if *one* of the following conditions is met:

- The invention was made in the course of the employee's normal duties and an invention might reasonably be expected to result.
- The employee had a special obligation to further the interests of the employer's undertaking because of his duties and the particular responsibilities arising from those duties.
- Although the invention was not made in the normal course of duties, it was made in the course of duties specifically assigned to the employee so that an invention would be expected to result.

In every other situation the patent will lie with the employee.

The issue of 'normal duties' was examined in the case of *Reiss Engineering v Harris* (1985) IRLR 23 that we looked at briefly in Chapter 1.

- Harris was manager of a department within a company that sold and assembled valves. It provided an after-sales and advice service for its customers, but it had never designed a valve or a modification to a valve.

  Harris was given six months' notice of his impending redundancy. During this time he invented a new valve that overcame some of the problems that existed with valves currently sold by Reiss Engineering. There then was a dispute over who owned the patent to the valve. Reiss Engineering argued that Harris had developed the valve in the course of his 'normal duties' and in addition that he had a special obligation to further the interests of his employer. The patent should therefore belong to them. Harris challenged this.

  The High Court ruled that the patent should belong to Harris. Because Reiss Engineering was not involved in any way with the design or modification of valves, it was not correct to claim that Harris had developed the valve in the course of his normal duties.

  In addressing the issue of his responsibility the Court held that this requirement had to relate to some extent to the employee's status and responsibilities within the organisation. Harris was not employed in a senior role, and it was also noted that he was actually under notice of redundancy when he made his invention. On this basis, Harris had no special obligation placed upon him.

Clearly, it can be difficult to determine exactly what might result from an employee's normal duties. However, it is unlikely to be found that an invention belongs to an employer for this reason if the employer does not design and develop similar products to the invention.

If it is found that a patent does belong to an employer, the employee can still apply to the Controller of Patents for compensation on the grounds that the invention is of 'outstanding benefit' to the employer. The Controller can then consider whether the employee is entitled to a share of the benefits, giving regard to the nature of the employee's duties, the effort and skill involved in making the invention, the effort and skill of any third party, and the significance of any contribution made by the employer towards the invention.

If an employee produces any literary, musical, dramatic or artistic work in the course of employment, the copyright is owned by the employer unless there is any agreement to the contrary (section 11 of the Copyright Designs and Patents Act 1988).

RESTRICTIVE COVENANTS

There are situations in which an employer might wish to restrict the activities of an employee. This is normally after the employee has left the employer's employment, but it might refer to the desire to restrict an employee from engaging in certain other work. If the employer wishes to restrain the employer in some way, a restrictive covenant may be put in place within the contract of employment.

However, a restrictive covenant must be reasonable; otherwise, it will be deemed to be void. To be reasonable the covenant must be in the interests of both parties and the public. There must be a clearly enforceable interest to protect. This could include the knowledge of trade secrets, particular influence over customers, or situations in which the employee might entice other employees away from the employer after his/her employment has terminated. If a restrictive covenant simply seeks to restrict competition, it will not be deemed to be reasonable.

An example of a restraint that was not reasonable is shown in the case of

- *Greer v Sketchley Ltd* (1978) IRLR 445

  Greer was a director of Sketchley's dry-cleaning business. At the time of this case Sketchley operated only in the Midlands and the south of England. After Sketchley was taken under new management, Greer proposed to leave and join a competitor. Sketchley tried to stop him because there was a restrictive covenant in his contract of employment. This covenant restricted Greer from working in any organisation where his knowledge of trade secrets/special processes was of relevance. The restriction was in place for 12 months and geographically the restriction applied to the whole of the UK.

  Greer successfully applied for a declaration that the restriction was invalid. The Court of Appeal ruled that the geographical restriction was unreasonably valid (primarily because Sketchley did not operate throughout the UK) and thus the restraint was void.

It is important to note that the whole restrictive covenant was ruled invalid because of the unreasonableness of one aspect of the restraint.

Although this restraint was declared void, because of its unreasonable scope, there are many occasions where restraints are successfully used:

- *Bullivant Ltd and others v Ellis* (1987) IRLR 491

  Bullivant was the managing director of an organisation, and left to set up a competing business. He used information relating to the customers of his old organisation to assist him in setting up his own business. Within his contract of employment there was a restraint of trade clause that prohibited him from carrying out any business with any organisation or person with whom he had carried out business activities during his time working for Bullivant. This restraint was for a period of 12 months following the end of his employment. Bullivant successfully sought an injunction enforcing the restraint. It was found to be a reasonable restraint, protecting the business of Bullivant for a reasonable period of time.

Some useful guidelines for restraints of trade were set out in the following case:

- *TFS Derivatives Ltd v Morgan* (2004) EWHC 3181

  In this case the High Court set out that for a restraint including a non-competition clause to be valid:

  - There must be a legitimate business interest that needs protecting.

  - The clause must be no wider than that required to protect that interest.

  - The reasonableness of issues such as geographical location, time and other issues will depend on the extent and nature of the threat to the employer's business.

Recent rulings have also suggested that the seniority of the employee within the organisation might be relevant:

- *Thomas v Farr plc and Hanover Park Commercial Ltd* (2007) EWCA Civ 118

  Thomas, who was a former managing director, appealed against a non-competition clause that lasted for 12 months. However, the court upheld the restraint due to the seniority of Thomas's position and with it the likelihood that he would know confidential information that would be of interest to a competitor.

TASK

Find out if your organisation, or an organisation with which you are familiar, uses restrictive covenants. If possible, read one. Do you think that the provisions within the covenant would be judged to be reasonable by a court? If not, what problems do you foresee?

CONFIDENTIAL INFORMATION

A restraint of trade often refers to confidential information, and all employees (whether they have a restraint clause or not) have a duty of fidelity to their employer – which includes an obligation not to disclose or misuse confidential information. However, it is not always clear what information is to be classed as 'confidential'. The guidelines to addressing this were set out in the case of *Faccenda Chicken Ltd v Fowler* (1986) IRLR 69.

- Faccenda Chicken Ltd prepared and sold chickens to a range of customers. Fowler was the sales manager. He left Faccenda and set up an organisation in competition – selling chickens to customers in the same area. His eight recruits included five salesmen from Faccenda. In setting up his business he used information which he had gained from Faccenda, including names and addresses of customers, their usual requirements, and the prices they were charged. Faccenda brought an action for damages against Fowler.

Faccenda Chicken was unsuccessful in its application. In making its judgment the Court of Appeal gave some clear guidelines about the use and misuse of confidential information:

– When assessing what is confidential information it is first important to consider the express terms of the contract of employment. In this case there were no express terms clearly stating what was to be considered to be confidential information.

– When the employment ends, the requirement to keep information confidential only applies to information that can be clearly defined as a trade secret.

– In determining what is a trade secret, regard must be given to the nature of the employment, the nature of the information and whether the employee was clearly told that the information was confidential. In this case the sales information was freely available to a wide range of employees and they had never been told that it was classed as confidential information.

The case demonstrates, therefore, that the employer must address the issue of confidentiality by an express term within the contract of employment. This can relate back to the introduction of a restrictive covenant, as described in the previous section. Again, it is important to be specific and reasonable – and this can be difficult for employers because it is difficult to consider the varied range of information to which the employee might be exposed during employment.

PUBLIC INTEREST DISCLOSURES

The Public Disclosure Act (PDA) 1998 makes additions to the protection already offered to employees in sections 43 and 47 of the Employment Rights Act 1996. The Act specifically addresses situations when the employee knows of (or suspects) some wrongdoing within the organisation.

In order to gain the protection offered by the Act disclosures must be made in good faith. The employee must reasonably believe that the information and any allegations being made are true. The employee must not make the disclosure for any personal gain and must have already disclosed very similar information to his/her employer. If the employee believes that the employer might disrupt evidence if made aware of the disclosure, or is concerned about any potential detriment, the employee does not have to make such a disclosure to the employer.

The employee must act reasonably in making the disclosure. In determining this reasonableness regard will be given to issues such as the identity of the person to whom the disclosure has been made (if the employee has gone straight to the media it is quite likely that the disclosure will not be protected), the seriousness of the matter, the likelihood of the issue recurring (and the number of times it has already occurred) and whether the disclosure results in a breach of a duty of confidence.

If the disclosure deals with a failure of an exceptionally serious nature, the employee is not obliged to work through any existing internal procedures. In this case the employee can go straight to an appropriate body.

The type of disclosures that are protected include those where the employee has a reasonable belief that a criminal offence has been committed, where there has been a failure to comply with a legal obligation, where health and safety is endangered, and where a miscarriage of justice has occurred.

The need for an employee to have a reasonable belief in the truth of his/her allegations was illustrated in the case of *Babula v Waltham Forest College* (2007) EWCA Civ 174:

- Babula was a college lecturer, and he was concerned that remarks made by one of his colleagues amounted to racial hatred. The college did not seem to react to his concerns, and so he reported the concerns to the police. It was eventually determined that no criminal offence had taken place, but Babula felt that the College reacted sufficiently badly to his making the disclosure to give him no option other than to resign.

  He resigned and made a claim for unfair constructive dismissal on the basis that he had been treated unfairly under the Public Disclosure Act. The employer argued that he did not merit protection under the Act because the disclosure he had made was not shown to be true (ie there was no criminal act of racial hatred).

  However, the Court of Appeal ruled that the test was whether he reasonably believed, at the time that he made the disclosure, that a criminal activity was being committed. Because the events did allow for him to reach this conclusion they ruled that he was protected under the Act.

An employee should not be subjected to any detriment as the result of making a protected disclosure. Any dismissal as a result of making a disclosure is automatically unfair. However, for the detriment to be unfair it must relate specifically to the disclosure:

- *Bolton School v Evans* (2006) IRLR 500

  Evans, a schoolteacher, was concerned that the school computer system was insufficiently secure. The school did not take his concerns seriously, and he therefore hacked into the system to prove what he was saying.

  He was given a written warning and resigned in protest. He claimed unfair constructive dismissal, claiming that he had suffered detriment because of making a protected disclosure.

  However, the EAT dismissed his claim, finding that the warning was a reaction to the hacking – not to the making of the disclosure.

- *Kuzel v Roche Products Ltd* (2007) EAT 0576/06/CEA

  Kuzel claimed she was dismissed for making a protected disclosure – the employer claimed she was dismissed because of very poor relationships with other staff. The EAT held that the correct approach for determining the burden of proof in 'whistleblowing' cases is:

  – Has the claimant shown that the reasons for the dismissal given by the respondent might not be the true reason?

  – If so, has the respondent proved the reason for dismissal?

  – If not, has the respondent disproved that the reason was a protected disclosure?

  – If not, dismissal is because of the protected disclosure.

KEY LEARNING POINTS

- Article 6(1) of the Human Rights Act determines the right to a fair trial.
- Article 8 of the HRA determines the right to respect for private and family life.
- Article 9 of the HRA determines the right to freedom of thought, conscience and religion.
- Article 10 of the HRA determines the right to freedom of expression.
- Article 11 of the HRA determines the right to freedom of assembly and association.
- Article 14 of the HRA prohibits discrimination.
- The Data Protection Act 1998 defines what information can be kept about an individual, and how it should be processed and stored.
- The Access to Medical Reports Act 1998 covers medical reports made by a medical practitioner who is responsible for the clinical care of the employee.
- The Patents Act 1977 specifies when an invention will belong to an employer.
- A restrictive covenant can protect an employer against certain activities of an employee once that employee has left employment – but all aspects of the restriction must be reasonable.
- An employer must determine what information is confidential as an express term within the contract of employment.
- An employee must suffer no detriment from making a public interest disclosure, as long as the disclosure is protected and is made in good faith.

FURTHER READING

CASE SUMMARIES

Halford v United Kingdom (1997) IRLR 471 – The Assistant Chief Constable of the Merseyside police force claimed that there was an invasion of her privacy during investigations into allegations that had been made against her – which included alleged bugging of her phones – contrary to Article 8 of the HRA. The ECHR upheld her claim.

Stedman v United Kingdom (1977) 23 EHRR CD 168 – An employee claimed she was dismissed for refusing to work on Sundays, and this dismissal was contrary to Article 9 of the HRA. However, the ECHR ruled that the dismissal was made because she refused to work on Sundays, rather than because of her freedom of thought, conscience or religion.

Aspinall v MSI Mech Forge Ltd (2002) EAT 891/01 – Aspinall asked a colleague to take a video of production processes to demonstrate how he had been injured at work. The employer was concerned about this because of the secrecy of the production processes. Aspinall was asked to name the person who made the video, but refused. He resigned – but was asked to reconsider. He claimed he had suffered detriment because he had made a public disclosure. However, the EAT ruled that he had resigned of his own accord.

EXAMPLES TO WORK THROUGH

1   There have recently been a number of thefts from the warehouse where you work. The managing director has decided to install CCTV, partly as a security measure – and he says it is also to protect employees. A number of employees have signed a petition stating that the CCTV is a violation of their human rights. Advise the managing director of how to proceed.

2   One of the sales team in an organisation that designs, manufactures and sells cosmetics has invented a new face-cream which he claims will be better than anything else on the market. He is trying to register the patent as his own. The organisation states that the patent should belong to it – because he works for it selling cosmetics. Advise the two parties.

3   You have concerns that the accounts in the small organisation where you work are incorrect. In particular, you think you have evidence that shows that some customers are paying cash and the transactions are not being recorded – in a bid to avoid VAT payments. What should you do to ensure that any action you take is covered by the Public Disclosure Act 1998?

CHAPTER 12

Health and safety legislation

CHAPTER OBJECTIVES

The objectives of this chapter are:

- to provide an overview of current health and safety legislation
- to list the duties of the employer in relation to health and safety
- to list the duties of the employee in relation to health and safety
- to explore the issues relating to stress in the workplace
- to list the potential penalties for breaching health and safety legislation
- to outline the legislation to support good health and safety practices.

HEALTH AND SAFETY LEGISLATION

In this chapter we examine a range of issues relating to health and safety. The legislation underpinning all that we look at may be summarised as follows:

Health and Safety at Work Act (HASAWA) 1974

This is the main statute relating to health and safety. It sets out the main duties of the employer and the employee. It also provides for a variety of means of enforcement of the legislation, which are wide-ranging and can include criminal action.

Workplace (Health, Safety and Welfare) Regulations 1992

The Regulations impose a duty on employers to maintain places of work, equipment and systems in an efficient state of good order and repair.

Personal Protective Equipment Regulations 1992

An employer must identify the protective equipment that is needed by the employee, provide that equipment, and ensure that it is kept in a good state of repair. The employee must be trained in the correct and appropriate use of the equipment.

Health and Safety (Display Screen Equipment) Regulations 1992

These Regulations focus on the specific risks associated with the use of display screens. They specify the need for regular breaks when using display screens, the optimal layout of work-stations, and provision regular eye examinations where appropriate.

Reporting of Injuries, Diseases and Dangerous Occurrences Regulations (RIDDOR) 1995

These Regulations set out the need to report events arising from events at work ranging from injury requiring hospital treatment to the death of the person involved in the incident. There is also the requirement to report the occurrence of certain diseases at work.

Manual Handling Operations Regulations 1998

The Regulations require an employer to examine all work involving lifting and manual handling, looking at ways to eliminate the amount of lifting and handling involved, and ensuring that all employees are trained in the correct ways to lift and move heavy objects.

Provision and Use of Work Equipment Regulations 1998

These Regulations specify the need to supply appropriate equipment for use at work with special emphasis on particular dangers such as fires and explosions. There is a duty to give employees information and training with regard to the equipment.

Management of Health and Safety at Work Regulations 1999

The main object of these Regulations is to use risk assessments to improve health and safety at work. Employers are required to look at each activity within the organisation, consider the potential risks, and look at ways to reduce or to eliminate those risks.

Control of Substances Hazardous to Health (COSHH) Regulations (amended 2002)

These Regulations set out the requirements for the storage, use and risk assessments of materials that can be hazardous if incorrectly used.

From this list you will note that whereas the HASAWA addresses a full range of general issues associated with health and safety, the other legislation focuses on specific areas of health and safety activity.

It should also be noted that the Working Time Regulations 1998 might also have been included in this list. As we noted when we examined these Regulations in Chapter 5, their basis is in health and safety concerns.

TASK

Talk to the person responsible for health and safety in your organisation, or an organisation with which you are familiar. Find out what processes the organisation has in place to ensure that it meets the requirements of health and safety legislation.

DUTIES OF THE EMPLOYER

The HASAWA (section 2(1)) clearly states that the employer has a duty to ensure, as far as is reasonably practicable, the health, safety and welfare at work of all employees. This requirement includes the following aspects of work:

Safe and adequate plant and equipment

- In *BAC Ltd v Austin* (1978) IRLR 332, Austin's job required the wearing of eye goggles. She had to wear these over her own spectacles which resulted in the goggles becoming misted up and light reflecting. She complained, but her employers did nothing. She was left with the option of dropping her complaint, not wearing the goggles and risking an eye injury, or leaving her job. She chose to leave her job and took up a claim of constructive dismissal. Her claim was successful because her employers had breached the implied contractual requirement to provide safe equipment for her use at work.

Safe premises and/or place of work

- The case of *Latimer v AEC Ltd* (1953) AC 643 illustrates this point, with emphasis on the requirement to act as far as is 'reasonably practicable'. Here, Latimer slipped on an area of floor where oil had become mixed with water. The employer was aware that this had happened, and had put sawdust across the floor to make the place of work safe. However, it had not had enough sawdust to cover the whole floor. Latimer argued that AEC had breached the requirement to provide a safe place of work. However, it was ruled that the employer had acted as far as was practicable because the only alternative would have been closing the factory.

Competent and safe fellow employees

- In *Hudson v Ridge Manufacturing Co Ltd* (1957) QB 348, an employee had carried out practical jokes for many years, which included tripping up fellow employees. He had been warned against such behaviour by his foreman, but no further action had been taken. He tripped up Hudson, who was disabled, and Hudson sustained an injury. It was found that the employers had breached the requirement to provide safe fellow employees because they were aware of the employee's behaviour and had not stopped it.

A safe system of work

- In *Jagdeo v Smiths Industries Ltd* (1981) ICR 47, Jagdeo was transferred to work in the soldering area, following a reduction of work in her usual department. She soon became ill and had a period of sickness absence. On her return to work she was soon taken ill again. When she returned to work she refused to work in the soldering area, and the employer was advised that it was possible to be allergic to soldering fumes. After some time of discussion and trial of protective equipment, Jagdeo was dismissed. The EAT found that her dismissal was unfair because the employer had breached the requirement to provide a safe system of work.

In addition to these primary requirements, there have been two specific requirements that have attracted a significant amount of attention in recent years:

Employee's health damaged by smoking in the workplace

It is an implied term of the contract of employment that the employer will provide a workplace which, as far is reasonably practicable, is suitable for the employee to perform his/her contractual duties. If the employee is subjected to poor quality of air because of the smoking habits of colleagues, the employer could be in breach of this implied term.

- In *Waltons & Morse v Dorrington* (1997) IRLR 488, Dorrington worked as a secretary in a firm of solicitors. She worked in an open-plan area with other secretaries, some of whom smoked. She also worked near the offices of solicitors who smoked, and their smoke drifted to her place of work. After her complaint the solicitors decided to ban smoking in open-plan areas, but solicitors were still allowed to smoke in their offices and a smoking area was set up for other smokers. Unfortunately, Dorrington had to work near one of these smoking areas. She asked to be moved, but her request was refused – and when she moved her own desk she was instructed to move back. Eventually, she resigned and claimed constructive dismissal.

    The employment tribunal, supported by the EAT, upheld Dorrington's claim. They decided that there was a requirement to provide a suitable place of work in comparison with other similar places (ie other offices based in London). They decided it was not enough to consider how the needs of non-smokers could be balanced with smokers, because the choice of an employee not to smoke had no adverse impact on smokers, whereas the choice to smoke did have an adverse impact on non-smokers. They found, therefore, that the employer had breached the contract of employment and thus that there had been a constructive dismissal.

It is interesting to note the way the courts defined a suitable workplace in this case. They compared the situation Dorrington was working in with what could generally be expected of offices in London. Clearly, different workplaces have different levels of noise, smells and other potentially irritating factors. This case suggests we have to consider what might be reasonable, given the type of workplace in which the employee is operating.

This case will largely be taken over now by the banning of smoking in public places (as a result of the Health Act 2006). However, the effects of being in such an environment can have an effect on health that is not evident until some years later, and so it cannot be presumed that the Health Act 2006 will see the immediate end of any claims similar to the one outlined above.

Employee has suffered from repetitive strain injury, also known as work-related upper limb disorder (WRULD)

If the employee is involved in highly repetitive work that results in damage to one or both upper limbs, it is possible that the employer has breached the requirement to provide a safe system of work. The issue of proof has been key in the cases that have been brought in this area.

- In *Pickford v ICI* (1998) WLR 1189, a secretary brought a claim for WRULD on the basis that her employer had failed to ensure that she took regular breaks from prolonged spells of typing. However, she was unable to prove that she was actually suffering from WRULD and that the problem was not 'in her mind'. Her claim therefore failed.

- In contrast, a successful claim for damages resulting from WRULD was made in *Alexander and another v Midland Bank plc* (2000) ICR 464. The employees were encoders working in the Bank. They were required to input data at great speeds, which was emphasised by the league tables run by the Bank. The employees complained of damage to their necks, arms and hands. In this case the employees were able to prove that the most likely probability was that the work regime had caused the damage, and so the claim was successful.

TASK

Earlier in this chapter we considered the use of risk assessments. How could they be used to reduce the potential number of claims of WRULD from employees?

DUTIES OF THE EMPLOYEE

Section 7 of the HASAWA states that employees have a duty to:

- take reasonable care for the health and safety of themselves and others who may be adversely affected by their acts or omissions at work
- co-operate with their employer as is necessary to enable health and safety requirements to be met.

More specific duties on employees are laid down in other health and safety legislation that was cited at the start of this section. Examples include:

- the requirement to use any personal protective equipment that is provided, to ensure it is stored correctly, and to report any loss or obvious defect of the equipment (from the Personal Protective Equipment at Work Regulations 1992)
- the requirement to follow appropriate systems of work laid down by the employer to ensure safety during manual handling operations (from the Manual Handling Operation Regulations 1992)
- the requirement to inform the employer of any serious and imminent dangers to health and safety, and to inform the employer of any shortcomings in the employer's protection arrangements for health and safety (from the Management of Health and Safety at Work Regulations 1999).

An employer is expected to bring the attention of employees to the requirements that are placed upon them. The Health and Safety Information for Employees (Modifications and Repeals) Regulations 1995 require employers to inform employees of what is expected of them through the distribution of leaflets or the displaying of posters giving the appropriate information.

Although any prosecutions relating to health and safety are more typically brought against the employer, employees can be prosecuted for not complying with certain safety laws. In a Magistrate's court there can be a fine of up to £50,000, and claims in the Crown Court can bring the penalty of an unlimited fine.

Work-related stress is an area of health and safety that has attracted a number of high-profile claims in recent years. Claims for stress have been based on the tort (wrong) of negligence – that the employer's duty of care to the employee has been breached. Most of the claims have related to the duty to provide a safe system of work.

One of the first, and often quoted, claims relating to stress (which we looked at briefly in Chapter 1) was *Walker v Northumberland County Council* (1994) IRLR 35.

- Walker was a social worker. There was a heavy workload in the area that he worked, largely because of the increased reporting of child abuse cases. On a number of occasions Walker discussed the workload with his employer, expressing his concern at the pressure he was under. No solution was found. In November 1986 Walker suffered a nervous breakdown, and he was absent due to this breakdown until March 1987. During his period of absence he discussed the workload with his employers again, and certain support mechanisms (including the temporary assignment of extra staff to help with the work) were agreed. When Walker returned to work most of this support mechanism did not materialise, and any that did was withdrawn within a month. Walker suffered a second breakdown, and in February 1988 was dismissed on the grounds of permanent ill-health.

  He claimed that the employers had been negligent in not providing him with a safe system of work. The High Court ruled that the employers were not liable for Walker's first breakdown because it was not reasonably foreseeable that it would occur. However, they were liable for the second breakdown because he had already suffered the first breakdown, and the agreed support mechanisms had been withdrawn. An out-of-court settlement of £175,000 was eventually agreed.

The fact that the damages were awarded for the second breakdown only is very significant. For an employer to be liable for damages resulting from the stress of an employee, the illness resulting from the stress must have been reasonably foreseeable.

This point was emphasised further in a judgment given by the Court of Appeal when considering appeals on four cases which were grouped together (*Sutherland v Hatton and three other cases* (2002) IRLR 263).

In this appeal, damages had been awarded in four unrelated cases, and in each one the employer was appealing against the decision:

- *Hatton* had been awarded £90,766. She was a teacher who had suffered stress and depression and had eventually retired early on the grounds of ill-health. Her workload had not been exceptionally heavy, and she had not told the school she was struggling. The history of events included her being attacked in the street in January 1994, and suffering the anxiety of her son being hospitalised in April 1994 for a considerable period. Neither of these events related to her work. In August 1994 she first saw a stress counsellor, but did not tell the school. In October 1995 she went absent due to sickness, and never returned to work. She eventually took ill-health early retirement in August 1996. The appeal of the employer succeeded, and the award of damages was withdrawn. There could be no liability because the illness relating to stress was not foreseeable, because the school had not been made aware that she was struggling.

- *Barber* was also a teacher. He worked at a difficult school, but did not have a particularly heavy workload in comparison to other teachers. He became depressed in August 1995, and did not tell his employers at that time. In October 1995 he talked to the deputy headteacher and told him he was struggling, and he helped Barber to prioritise and delegate some work. He continued to experience symptoms of stress and in May 1996 was absent for three weeks due to stress and depression. On his return he discussed his problems with the headteacher and two deputy headteachers, but no real help was forthcoming. He eventually collapsed in November 1996. In March 1997 he took early retirement on the grounds of ill-health. He took up a claim for damages relating to stress-induced injury and was awarded £101,042. In the Court of Appeal the employers won the appeal. However, this was later overturned by the House of Lords (2004). They concluded that Barber had given the employer sufficient indication that he was struggling, and that the employer had been negligent by not offering any assistance to Barber.

- *Jones* worked as an administration assistant. Hers was a unique job in the organisation that involved working very long hours. The employer commented that it was a gamble to expect one person to do the job, which was really two or three people's work. She complained of the workload and was offered extra help – but that never happened. She then wrote a five-page document explaining the problems in detail and invoked the formal grievance procedure. She was threatened with the loss of her job if she continued to complain. In January 1995 she became ill with anxiety and depression and never returned to work. Towards the end of 1996 the centre where she worked closed, and she was therefore made redundant. She was awarded £157,541 upon her claim for damages relating to stress-induced illness on the grounds of the employer's negligence.

  The employers lost this appeal. The outcome was clearly foreseeable – Jones had complained in detail about the problems, and the employer had accepted that the workload was too great.

- *Bishop* was a factory worker. His organisation was bought by another, and there was a reorganisation. He had to move to a new job, and found it hard to adjust. He complained and asked for his old job back, but it no longer existed. The pressures in the new job were not seen to be excessive, but Bishop could not cope with the changes. He saw his GP due to symptoms of depression, but did not tell his employer. His employer knew he was unhappy, but was not aware of any medical impact it was having on him. In February 1997 he had a breakdown and attempted suicide. In 1998 his employment was terminated. He brought a claim for damages relating to a stress-induced illness, and was awarded £7,000 plus loss of earnings.

  The employer won the appeal. At no time had the employer been made aware that the difficulties at work were having any impact on Bishop's health, and so the outcome was not foreseeable.

These rulings are important because they result in some clear guidelines for dealing with claims of negligence relating to stress. The key points to note are:

- The ordinary principles of employer's liability apply to any psychiatric injury, in the same way as they apply to any physical injury.

- An essential question is whether the harm was reasonably foreseeable – in particular, was an injury to health attributable to stress at work (as opposed to stress from personal difficulties)?

- Foreseeability has to depend on what the employer knows (or ought to know – the employer cannot decide to ignore obvious signs, and then claim ignorance). If the employer is not aware of any problems, it is entitled to assume that there aren't any.

- In deciding whether an event was reasonably foreseeable consideration must be given to the type of work being carried out, and the demands placed upon an employee in comparison to other employees in similar work.

- *Intel v Daw* (2007) IRLR 346

Daw complained of excessive work in emails, and had been found in tears by one of her managers, but no urgent action had been put in place to address the issue. She suffered a breakdown and took up a claim of negligence against her employer.

The employer argued that there were confidential counselling services in place which she had not opted to use. However, the Court of Appeal held that this could not have addressed the underlying problem – which was the excessive workload. It also held that having a counselling service in place did not absolve the employer of its duty of care to the employee.

TASK

Find out what safeguards your organisation, or an organisation with which you are familiar, has put in place to guard against claims of work-related stress. Do you think that sufficient has been done?

EXPLORE FURTHER

Read about other cases concerning stress-induced illness and damages sought for the employer's negligence. Apply the guidelines given by the Court of Appeal in the four appeals grouped together. Try to understand what the courts see as 'reasonably foreseeable' when dealing with these cases. Cases that might be of interest can be found in the *Case summaries* section at the end of this chapter.

PENALTIES FOR BREACHES OF HEALTH AND SAFETY

THE TORT OF NEGLIGENCE

We have seen from the cases that we have examined so far that the focus in determining the outcome of a claim has been on the breach of the employer's duty of care. As explained at the start of the second section, the employer's duty of care extends to a range of different aspects of health and safety (eg a safe system of work, a safe place of work).

These claims are based on the tort (wrong) of negligence. In order to demonstrate that the tort of negligence has occurred, and so succeed in a claim for damages, the employee must be able to show that:

- the employer owed the employee a duty of care
- the employer breached that duty through negligence
- the employee suffered damage as a result of that negligence.

Having established that the employer has been negligent in some way, the courts will consider any contribution that the employee has made to the situation before determining what damages should be awarded. This is known as contributory negligence.

The Law Reform (Contributory Negligence) Act 1945 provides that where an employee has contributed to his/her injuries by his/her own negligence, his/her damages may be reduced by the percentage by which he/she is to blame. An example of this is not wearing the protective equipment that has been provided by the employer.

In addition, the courts will give consideration to any consent the employee has given to the act concerned. This is known as 'volenti non fit injuria' – the employee was aware of the risk associated with a particular act and voluntarily consented to continue. In reality, there are difficulties with this defence because it can be argued that an employee never gives completely 'voluntary' consent to anything. However, if this defence is successfully argued, any compensation will be reduced to nil.

A claim for damages for negligence is brought in the County Court if the amount claimed is less than £50,000, and in the County or the High Court if the amount claimed is greater than £50,000.

CONTRACTUAL CLAIMS

As we have also seen in the cases we have looked at in this chapter, there is the possibility of bringing a claim of constructive dismissal if the employee has resigned as a result of the employer's breach of the duty of care. As we determined in Chapter 8, the employer's breach must go to the root of the contract and the employee's resignation must be as a result of that breach.

CRIMINAL ACTION

If the employer is successfully prosecuted under the HASAWA, the penalty is either a fine or imprisonment. The severity of the penalty will depend on the actual breach of the legislation that has been proved.

In deciding on the level of fine to be imposed the courts will consider the penalty that the offence merits. However, the fine is not usually so large as to create a risk that the organisation might itself collapse – unless the breach is so serious that the organisation should not be trading. The courts will also consider such things as whether any warnings had been given (and if so, whether any action was taken), any profit the employer made from the failure to take adequate health and safety measures, prompt admission of guilt, the action that has since been taken to remedy the problem, and the previous safety record.

In April 2008 the Corporate Manslaughter and Corporate Homicide Act 2007 came into force. This Act introduces the offence of 'corporate manslaughter' in England, Wales and Northern Ireland and 'corporate homicide' in Scotland.

An organisation will be guilty of the offence if the way in which senior management have organised or managed the activities amounted to a gross breach of the duty of care that the employer has to employees, the public or others, and if that gross breach resulted in a fatality. Companies and public bodies will face prosecution if a death results from health and safety failings. The penalties will include an unlimited fine, a remedial order and a publicity order (making it public that the organisation has been convicted and giving details of any remedial order and fine that has been imposed).

ENFORCING GOOD STANDARDS OF HEALTH AND SAFETY

Much of the health and safety legislation is focused on putting systems in place to ensure that employers are providing a healthy and safe place of work. Within that legislation there are specific requirements placed on the employer.

WRITTEN STATEMENTS

Section 2(3) of the HASAWA requires every employer who employs more than five people to prepare (and revise as often as required) a written statement of the general policy with respect to the health and safety at work of the employees, and the process in force for carrying out that policy. The statement, and any revisions of it, must be brought to the attention of all employees.

No guidance is given in the HASWA as to what the statement should include, or how it should be brought to the attention of employees. However, advice is available from the Health and Safety Executive (HSE – see later in this section). Generally, the statement should include the responsibilities of all employees in relation to health and safety, and general safety precautions.

SAFETY REPRESENTATIVES

Section 2(4) of the HASAWA refers to the appointment by recognised trade unions (see Chapter 10) of safety representatives. The safety representatives must be employees, and may be elected or appointed. The employer has a duty to consult with these representatives about all measures to ensure the health and safety of employees at work.

The main duties of the safety representatives are to investigate potential hazards and dangerous occurrences, investigate complaints by their colleagues about health- and safety-related issues, make general representations regarding health and safety to their employer, carry out inspections, and attend safety committees.

A trade union safety representative is allowed paid time off to carry out his/her duties during normal working hours. The safety representative is also allowed paid time off for relevant training.

SAFETY COMMITTEES

If at least two trade union safety representatives submit a written request, employers must establish a safety committee. This must be formed after consulting with those who made the request, and any other representatives of recognised trade unions, and within three months of the request being made. The function of the committee is to review measures being taken to ensure the health and safety at work of employees.

TASK

Find out if your organisation has a safety committee. If it has, ask if you can attend a meeting to see what issues are discussed and the decisions that are made.

CONSULTATION WITH EMPLOYEES

The Health and Safety (Consultation with Employees) Regulations 1996 require that employees or their representatives are given sufficient information to enable them to participate effectively in consultation about health and safety matters. Employers are required to consult with employees and/or their representatives about all questions relating to health and safety at work.

THE HEALTH AND SAFETY EXECUTIVE (HSE) AND THE HEALTH AND SAFETY COMMISSION (HSC)

The HSE (www.hse.gov.uk) and the HSC were set up by the HASAWA to help enforce the requirements of the Act.

The role of the HSC is to carry out research into health- and safety-related issues, to provide information and training, to advise employers and employees with regard to health and safety issues, and to develop and submit proposed regulations.

The HSE's role is to enforce the HASAWA. The HSE appoints inspectors who have the right to enter an employer's premises at any reasonable time and to carry out any necessary investigations. If there has been an incident that requires investigation, they have the authority to demand that premises are left undisturbed for as long as it takes them to carry out any investigation and to take any necessary evidence. They also have the right to see any documents or books that contain information relating to the issue under investigation.

If an inspector is concerned that a practice is contravening a statutory requirement, such that the contravention is likely to continue, the inspector can serve an Improvement Notice. The Notice must specify the area of concern and the reasons that the inspector has the concerns, and must give a time period within which action must be taken to address the issue. The period must not be less than 21 days. (If the employer wishes to appeal against the Notice, it must also do so within 21 days.)

If the inspector believes that the contravention of the statutory requirement is such that there is a risk of serious personal injury, he/she may serve a Prohibition Notice. Again, the Notice must specify the issue and the reasons for the concerns. This Notice usually takes immediate effect – and the activity cannot continue until the problems have been remedied.

An employer who has received an Improvement Notice or a Prohibition Notice can appeal to the employment tribunal – who can cancel the Notice, affirm the Notice or modify it. If an appeal is made against an Improvement Order, it is suspended until the appeal is heard. If an appeal is made against a Prohibition Order, it is only suspended if the employment tribunal specifically directs that this be so. Failure to comply with either order is an offence under the HASAWA, and could lead to a fine or imprisonment.

EXPLORE FURTHER

Read the annual reports of the HSC and the HSE (both on the website address given at the start of this sub-section). Study some of the incidents that they cite. What legislation has been breached, or could be breached, in these incidents?

KEY LEARNING POINTS

- The main duties of the employer and employee, with relation to health and safety at work, are set out in the Health and Safety At Work Act (HASAWA) 1974.

- In addition to the HASAWA there are a number of pieces of legislation concentrating on specific aspects of health and safety at work.

- The employer has a duty of care to the employee that includes the duty to provide a safe place of work, a safe system of work, safe equipment and safe fellow employees.

- The employee has a duty to take reasonable care of his/her own health and safety, and to co-operate with the employer in all matters relating to health and safety.

- In assessing the employer's liability in cases of alleged work induced stress a key is whether the psychiatric illness caused by the stress was foreseeable.

- Potential claims relating to the breach of health and safety legislation include damages under the tort of negligence, claims for breach of contract (eg constructive dismissal) and prosecution.

- Processes to enforce good standards of health and safety include written statements, safety representatives, safety committees and the support of the HSE and HSC.

FURTHER READING

CASE SUMMARIES

Thanet District Council v Websper (2002) EAT 1090/01 – Websper was absent from work for 12 months with stress that was found to be related to his job. His employer offered him alternative work, but within the same division, which Websper held would not help address his problems. The employer offered him no other work and he resigned. The EAT held that by not offering an alternative job the employer had not provided a safe system of work.

Barlow v Borough of Broxbourne (2003) EWHC 50 (QB) – Barlow broke down in tears at work, left, and did not return. It became apparent that he had been suffering from stress and depression – but he had not told his employers this. His claim for damages relating to the employer's negligence failed because he had not given any indication that he was struggling, and his situation was therefore not reasonably foreseeable.

Morland v London Borough of Tower Hamlets (2003) High Court 1.5.03 – Morland was a school inspector, and had complained about the amount of work he had. However, his work was interspersed with quieter periods – and he had an annual holiday entitlement of seven weeks per year. The High Court did not think that his overall workload was excessive. He did have a breakdown and took up a claim for damages against his employer. However, he also had a range of personal problems. The High Court rejected his claims on the basis that his breakdown had not been reasonably foreseeable, and the injury was not solely caused by his work.

Johnstone v Bloomsbury Health Authority (1992) QB 333 – Johnstone was a junior doctor who was contracted to work 40 hours per week, plus up to a further 48 hours overtime. He successfully claimed that the hours he was required to work were damaging to his health.

EXAMPLES TO WORK THROUGH

1   In a factory guards are in place against all the saws – large industrial saws that are used to cut through metal. However, some of the employees find that the guards slow down the processes and routinely tie them back. The supervisors are aware that this practice takes place, and insist that the ties are removed from time to time. An employee, working on a machine with the guard tied back, cuts off three of his fingers. He takes up a claim against the organisation for negligence. What is the likely result?

2   You work in a busy call centre where staff turnover and absence is high. As a result of this, employees regularly work overtime and extra shifts. Employees moan about this all the time, but there have been no formal complaints. One employee has been absent for three months, and today has submitted a claim for damages in relation to a stress-induced illness. What will she have to show to be successful?

3   The trade union-appointed safety representative has attended two training courses on his duties recently. He has now requested that he be allowed to attend a further four-day course. The employer does not believe that this is necessary and has refused the request. What is the likely outcome?

CHAPTER 13

Study skills in employment law

CHAPTER OBJECTIVES

The objectives of this chapter are:

- to explain the skills required for studying employment law
- to suggest sources that can be used when studying and writing about employment law
- to consider specific skills required when writing assignments
- to consider specific skills required when preparing for examinations.

Many students have studied a range of different business- or HR-related topics when they start an Employment Law module. They soon find there are some very specific skills required when studying and preparing assessed work for employment law. In this chapter we look at some of those skills.

FINDING INFORMATION

Employment law is an ever-changing area of study. New laws are introduced, and new judgments are made in important cases on a regular basis. It is very important, therefore, to ensure that the work that you present is correct and up to date. To achieve this there is the need to access a range of sources to check the accuracy of the information that you are presenting.

There are a large number of employment law websites that should provide you with detailed information. However, many of these require an annual subscription to access them – and they can be quite expensive. Before deciding to make any subscription consider the following:

- If you are working, talk to the head of your HR department. A lot of organisations – particularly larger ones – already subscribe to some information sites. Find out if your organisation subscribes to anything that is of use to you and ask if you might be able to access this during the period of your study.

- Talk to your tutor/lecturer or the librarian at the place where you are studying. Again, a lot of larger organisations already subscribe to useful information sites. If you are a student registered with a college or university, you are likely to be able to access sites relevant to your studies.

- If you have no access to any sites through these two routes, look to see if any of the subscription sites have special group rates. Maybe you could group together with some of your fellow students to have group access to a site.

However, before you actually make any subscriptions, make sure that you need to do so. There is a lot of information available that is accessible to everyone.

CASE LAW

If you know the name of a case but just want to find out more about the details or the ruling, then put the name of the case in your Internet search engine. You are likely to end up with a list of sources from which you can access details. It is certainly true that some of these will relate to subscription-based websites, but there is likely to be a summary in one of the sources which you can access free of charge.

In addition, you can access the full judgment in many cases. (Most of the websites will not keep judgments beyond around ten years.)

- If you want to read the full judgment in a case that has gone to the Employment Appeals Tribunal, these can be accessed at: www.employmentappeals.gov.uk/judgments/judgments.htm.
- Full judgments from the House of Lords can be found at: www.hmcourts-service.gov.uk/judgments.htm.
- Full judgments from the European Court of Justice can be found at: www.curia.eu.int.
- Judgments from the European Court of Human Rights can be accessed at: www.echr.coe.int.
- Full judgments from the employment tribunals and the Court of Appeal (as well as other courts) can be accessed at: www.bailii.org.

Three newspapers also publish case reports (summaries) online. These are:

The Times	(www.timesonline.co.uk)
The Guardian	(www.guardian.co.uk)
The Independent	(www.independent.co.uk).

Another useful source, covering all developments in employment law, not just case law, is the Daniel Barnett website. You can register, free of charge, for regular email updates on recent rulings and developments in employment law: www.danielbarnett.co.uk.

A further useful source, which has a comprehensive collection of employment links, is www.venables.co.uk.

STATUTE

If you want to read the full details of any Acts of the UK Parliament, those from 1988 onwards are accessible at www.opsi.gov.uk/legislation/uk.htm.

EXPLORING A TOPIC

If you want to know more in general about a particular topic, there are a number of options available to you:

- www.cipd.co.uk (Chartered Institute of Personnel and Development)

  Some of the sources on this website are restricted to member access. However, there is a lot of useful information about all aspects of HR that is accessible to anyone.

- www.acas.org.uk (Advisory, Conciliation and Arbitration Service)

  On this website you can access a wide range of material including the Acas annual report, various research and policy documents, Acas publications (including Codes of Practice) and general advice about employment matters.

- www.berr.gov.uk (Department for Business, Enterprise and Regulatory Reform)

  The former Department of Trade and Industry is now part of this department, and this is the department that is responsible for employment issues. On this website you will find updates on any new legislation, consultation documents on employment matters, and information about any legal changes that have recently happened, or are due soon.

- www.ets.gov.uk (Employment Tribunals Service)

  This website gives information about the process of the employment tribunals, as well as having the ETS annual statistics.

- www.statistics.gov.uk (Office for National Statistics)

  This is a government website where statistics on a wide range of topics can be found.

- www.cbi.org.uk (Confederation of British Industry)

  The CBI is a lobbying organisation for businesses in the UK, on national and international issues. On this website you will find its comment on a range of issues, including employment matters.

- www.tuc.org.uk (Trades Union Congress)

  The TUC is the body that represents most trade unions in the UK. The website contains information about a lot of employment matters, and includes comments on developments in employment law.

ASSIGNMENTS

Many employment law courses require students, as part of the assessment process, to write assignments. In this section we look at some of the specific challenges that students face when writing law assignments.

Writing good HR or business advice

When writing about employment law there are two important objectives to achieve:

- to give accurate and clear legal advice
- to apply the law to the given situation.

However, many students forget to do both. Some students write a very good legal explanation but do not apply it to the situation. Imagine you were talking to a manager who knew very little about the issue. It is important that he/she understands the law, but also that he/she understands how it can be practically applied in the organisation.

Some students go to the other extreme and write very good practical advice but forget to explain the law. An employment law assignment that does not reference any law is very unlikely to achieve a pass standard.

Being specific

When giving legal advice it is important to concentrate on the specific points that are relevant to the case. Start by identifying the key point in the question, and then focus your answer on that point. For example, consider Question 3 at the end of Chapter 9:

> **Following collective consultation regarding redundancies you have now identified the individuals who are at risk of redundancy. You have written to all of these employees asking them to come to individual meetings to discuss the situation. One employee has written back immediately stating that he does not want to 'waste his time at such a meeting – management won't change their mind'. How should you react?**

This question clearly relates to the issue of redundancy. An example of the start of an answer that is not specific is:

There are six potentially fair reasons for dismissal – conduct, capability, statutory ban, some other substantial reason, redundancy and retirement. To make a claim for unfair dismissal, an employee must have at least one continuous year's service, unless the reason is one of the automatically unfair reasons that do not require a qualifying period.

Although there is nothing incorrect with the start of the answer, it is not relevant to this specific question! The immediate impression is therefore that the student does not understand the issues.

Using case law effectively

It is very important to use case law to support and illustrate the points that you are making. However, it is important to *use* it, and not just list it. For example, let us assume that we are answering Question 1 of Chapter 3:

> **Joan works as a keep-fit instructor. She teaches at a number of Adult Education classes. Each term she is asked which classes she wants to teach at, and they are advertised in the college literature. If there are enough enrolments, the classes go ahead. If there are insufficient enrolments, the class is cancelled. If she is unable to teach one week, she tells the college that she is not available and they arrange for someone else to take the class. Apply a relevant employment test and determine whether she is an employee.**

Now suppose as part of the answer a student writes:

> …an important test is whether there is mutuality of obligation (*Carmichael v National Power* (2000)).

This is certainly a useful case to refer to – but there is no explanation of why it is relevant to this particular situation. It has not added any value to the answer. There is no requirement to write out the full details of the case, but there is a requirement to use the case to help us answer the question. So a better answer would be:

> …an important test is whether there is mutuality of obligation. In the case of *Carmichael v National Power* (2000) it was ruled that Carmichael was not an employee because she was not obliged to do any work that was offered to her. In this case Joan is not required to carry out any work that is offered to her because she can tell the college she is not available. This would suggest that there is no mutuality of obligation.

In the second answer the student has actually *used* the case to illustrate the point that is being made.

Using up-to-date judgments

It is very important to ensure that you are using the most recent judgment in a case. For example, look at the case of *Dacas v Brook Street Bureau (UK) Ltd and another* (2004) in Chapter 4. Here we see a good example of a case going through the various stages of appeal, and different rulings being given at the different stages. Using an out-of-date judgment (ie the EAT ruling instead of the Court of Appeal ruling) could totally change the logic of your argument.

This case is also a good example of how later cases result in further changes. In this chapter you see how cases that have come after *Dacas* have changed the approach that courts take to the employment status of agency workers. It is very important that you use up-to-date material.

Note also that the age of a case does not necessarily determine its importance. Some cases (eg *Delaney v Staples* (1992) in Chapter 5) contain important rulings that no later case has yet overturned.

Referencing materials correctly

It is strongly recommended that you check with your tutor or lecturer whether there are any particular preferences relating to referencing (eg using footnotes or not). However, there are some general rules to apply.

When citing a case in an assignment you should give the names of both parties and the date of the case (in brackets after the name of the parties). For example:

> *Walker v Northumberland County Council* (1995)

Unless there is a specific requirement from your tutor, there is no need to give the reference data in the actual assignment (for example, for the Walker case, IRLR 35). However, in the list of references at the end of the assignment you should give the full reference:

> *Walker v Northumberland County Council* (1995) IRLR 35

If you have read about a case in a textbook, it is not appropriate to use the name of the textbook instead of the case. However, if you are writing about comments that the author of the textbook has written about a case, you would reference *both* sources. For example:

> Daniels (2008) states that the question of the employment status of agency workers has

been the subject of a number of cases in recent years. In the case of *James v Greenwich Council* (2006) the EAT set out the following guidelines: ...

When citing a piece of statute, on first reference to it you should write out the full name with the date (the date does not go in brackets). If you are referring to it on a number of occasions, you can later use an abbreviation – as long as you link it to the full reference. For example:

The Trade Union and Labour Relations (Consolidation) Act (TULRCA) 1992 defines a trade union. In addition, at section 5 of TULRCA there is a definition of the independence of a trade union.

At the end of the assignment you should have a full reference section. This should be in three parts, all listed alphabetically:

● cases

● statute

● other sources (eg textbooks).

EXAMINATIONS

The purpose of an exam is to:

● test your knowledge

● test your understanding

● test your ability to apply your knowledge to specific situations.

Although it is very important to have a thorough knowledge, it is most important to use that knowledge correctly. You are unlikely to pass an exam just by writing down everything you know about a particular topic, with no application of the material.

What can be taken into the exam?

It is important to find out from your tutor/lecturer or exam board whether any books or other materials can be taken into the examination. For example, the CIPD allows students to take an unmarked copy of a Statute Book into their exams.

Many institutions do allow some reference material to be taken into the exam because they do not want the exam to become little more than a memory test. They would prefer students to have the reference material to hand so that they can be tested on the application of the law, rather than on what they have managed to remember.

If you are allowed to take something into the exam, it is strongly recommended that you do so. Examiners will judge the standard of the work that they mark on the basis of what has been expected of students.

What case law do I need to remember?

The answer to this question depends on whether the exam is closed-book (you are not allowed to have any reference material with you), restricted-book (you can have specified reference material only) or open-book (you can take any reference material with you).

- *Closed-book*

  In this situation you are clearly going to have to remember some cases. Start by asking your tutor/lecturer for a recommended list of cases to learn. If there is no such list, then write down all the key topics that you have covered in the course – for example:

  > Dismissal
  >
  > Employment status
  >
  > Sex discrimination
  >
  > Race discrimination

  Then, for each of these topic areas, identify one to three cases that are really important in addressing potential questions. Try to remember these cases. If you can remember more, that is brilliant – but be sure that you are learning cases from across the syllabus and not just the areas you found most interesting!

  If you get to the exam and find that you have forgotten the name of a case but it is crucial to your answer, then still use it. If you can remember part of the reference, then put that – it is better than nothing. For example:

  > In the case of —— *v A E Dalton* (1987), …

  It is possible that you will remember the name later in the exam and can go back and fill in the gap.

  If you cannot remember any of the name of the case, you could still describe the key points – but you will obviously get more marks if you can reference it correctly.

- *Restricted-book*

  Find out before the exam if you are allowed to have any marks or indexing of sections in a book you are allowed to use. For example, you might be allowed to:

  - write notes on a book
  - highlight key passages
  - use sticky notes with section headings to help you find material quickly.

  Be very sure that you have got the correct instructions. You do not want to get to the exam and find that your book is taken from you because you have not followed the instructions correctly.

  Some students make the big mistake of not revising thoroughly when they are allowed to take material into an exam because they assume they can just look up the key points when they are in the exam. This is a bad error. In employment law you have to be able to apply the law as well as quote it – and you should concentrate your revision on this. Also, there is rarely surplus time in an exam and you cannot waste that time reading a book trying to find relevant information.

- *Open-book*

  Again, it is important to determine exactly what you can take into the exam, and whether there are any restrictions on what you can have written on that material.

  Additionally, it is very important that you still revise carefully. If the examiner knows that the student has had access to a significant amount of reference material, it is likely that the examiner will simply expect a higher standard of answer!

HOW TO REVISE

Students often ask me which is the best approach to revision. The simple answer is that there is no best approach – you have to find out what works best for you. Some of the techniques that I have seen work well are:

- writing out key cases and statutes on index cards – using different colours for different categories of cases; students can then use these key points as memory triggers

- writing out diagrams linking cases to particular topics; this particularly helps those who have a visual memory

- copying out key points again and again until you have remembered them

- making a tape recording of key points and playing it in the car as you drive (although this can be annoying for passengers) – if you do this, please make sure that your main focus is on driving safely.

Another useful approach during revision is to practise using past papers. This allows you to test your ability to write answers in the time required, to test your knowledge, and also to become familiar with the structure of the exam that you are to take (assuming that it has not changed).

HOW TO ANSWER THE QUESTIONS

When looking at a question start by thinking about exactly what it is asking. Make a quick note of:

- the key issue

- the relevant statute

- key cases that could be used.

Check whether the question is asking you to do anything particular – for example, are you being asked to give recommendations, give advice, use recent research, draw on recent case law? Whatever you are asked to do, ensure that you *do* it!

Finally, be sure that your answer addresses the specific question and that you do not write everything you know about the topic. Remember the point that has already been made about the need to be very specific in answering law questions.

EXAM TECHNIQUES

The aim of this chapter is to consider specific issues relating to the study of employment law, and not general study techniques. However, it is worth emphasising the following points:

- Ensure that you allocate your time carefully in the exam. I have seen many students fail an exam because they spent too long on one question, and then ran out of time and were unable to answer the full paper. If there are different sections in the exam paper, work out how long you have for each section, and move on when your allotted time runs out. You can always go back and write more in a section if you have time at the end.

- Read the instructions carefully. Check to see if all the questions are compulsory or if you have to answer a specific number of questions in one section.

- Read the questions carefully. Answer the question that has been set – and not the one you would have liked to answer!

- Do not waste time repeating the facts that have already been given in the question.

- Write legibly.

Employment law is a fascinating area of study. I hope that you enjoy learning about it, and I wish you every success with your studies.

Index

Acas arbitration scheme 26
Access to Medical Records Act 1998 193
Acquired Rights Directive 161
Act 11
Additional Paternity Leave 83
Adoption Leave 83
Advisory, Conciliation and Arbitration Service
    (Acas) 6, 9
Age discrimination 119
Agency workers 51
Analytical job evaluation 102
Annual leave 69
Ante-natal care 79
Appellant 11
Arbitration 10
Assignment writing 216
Asylum and Immigration Act 1996 63
Asylum seekers 63
Atypical contracts 50
Automatically unfair reasons for
    dismissal 141

Bargaining units 170
Basic award 142
Breach of contract 173

Capability 129
Case law 6, 215
Case Management Discussion 20
Casual workers 57
Central Arbitration Committee 10, 170
Certification Officer 168
Civil law 4, 178
Civil Partnership Act 2004 115
Claimant 11
Closed book 219
Closed shops 117
Codes of practice 6
Collective agreements 38
Collective bargaining 104, 171
Commission for Racial Equality 10
Common law 6

Compensation 4, 22, 142
Compensatory award 143
Compromise agreements 21
Conciliation 9, 21, 29
Conduct 131
Confidential Information 196
Conspiracy 175
Constructive Dismissal 139, 209
Consultation 154, 179, 181, 211
Continuity of employment 46
Contract for services 31
Contract law 4
Contract of service 31
Contracts of employment 36
Control test 32
Control of Substances Hazardous to Health
    Regulations (Amendment) 2002 202
Controller of Patents 195
Copyright 194
Corporate Manslaughter and Corporate
    Homicide Act 2007 3, 209
Costs (employment tribunals) 16
COT3 21
County courts 5
Court of Appeal 3, 5, 7
Criminal law 3, 178, 209
Crown Court 3
Custom and practice 39

Data Protection Act 1984 190
Data Protection Act 1998 3, 43, 190
Data Protection Registrar 192
Decisions 7
Deductions from pay 73
Dependant's time off 84
Deposits (employment tribunals) 29
Derecognition (trade unions) 169
Detriment 91
Direct discrimination 88
Directives 7
Disability Discrimination 109
Disability Discrimination Act 1995 87

Disability Discrimination Act 2005 110
Disability Rights Commission 10
Disability - definition 110
Disciplinary warnings 139
Disclosure of Information 172
Dismissal 126
    definition 127
    eligibility to make a claim 129
    potentially fair reasons 129
    right to be accompanied 139
Divisional Court 3
Donovan Report 14

Employees duties 45
Employee status 31
Employers duties 41
Employment Appeals Tribunal 5, 7, 23
Employment Equality (Age) Regulations
    2006 88, 119
Employment Equality (Religion or Belief)
    Regulations 2003 88, 116
Employment Equality (Sexual Orientation)
    Regulations 2003 88, 115
Employment Judge 17
Employment Relations Act 2004 170
Employment Tribunals (Constitution and
    Rules of Procedure) Regulations 2001 28
Employment Tribunals (Constitution
    and Rules of Procedure) Regulations
    2004 19, 28
Equality and Human Rights Commission 10
Equal Opportunities Commission 10
Equal Pay Act 1970 87, 100
Equal Pay (Amendment) Regulations
    1983 102
Equal Pay Directive 100
Equal Pay questionnaires 102
ET1 17
ET3 19
ETO Defence 163
European Commission 8
European Community 7
European Convention on Human Rights 8
European Court of Human Rights 8
European Court of Justice 8
European Parliament 8
European Works Council 179

Examinations 219
Ex parte 11
Ex-offenders 63
Express incorporation 38
Express terms 36

Family friendly policies 2, 5
Fidelity 46
Fixed term contracts 57
Fixed Term Employees (Prevention of Less
    Favourable Treatment) Regulations
    2002 57
Flexible working 58
Flexible Working (Eligibility, Complaints and
    Remedies) Regulations 2001 58
Flexible Working (Procedural Requirements)
    Regulations 2002 58
Frustration of contract 127

Garden leave 42
Gender re-assignment 114
Genuine occupational qualifications and
    requirements 94
Gibbons Report 25, 29, 138
Golden formula 174
Green Paper 5
Gross misconduct 131
Guarantee payments 74

Harassment 96
Health Act 204
Health and Safety at Work Act 1974 3, 201
Health and Safety Commission 211
Health and Safety (Display Screen Equipment)
    Regulations 1992 202
Health and Safety Executive 211
Health and Safety Information for Employees
    (modifications and repeals) Regulations
    1995 205
High Court 5
Holidays 69
House of Commons 5
House of Lords 3, 5, 7
HR1 155
Human Rights Act 1998 9, 184

Immigration and Asylum Act 1999 63

Implied incorporation 38
Implied terms 36
Improvement Notices 211
Indirect discrimination 90
Industrial action 173
Industrial Training Act 1964 14
Information and Consultation of Employees
        Regulations 2004 180
Information sources 214
Injunction 177
Injury to feelings 143, 150
Intimidation 174
Inventions 4, 194
Itemised pay statement 72

Keeping in touch days 81

Law Reform (Contributory Negligence) Act
        1945 209
LIFO (last in, first out) 157
Lock out 179

Magistrates Courts 3
Management of Health and Safety at Work
        Regulations 1999 202
Manual Handling Operations Regulations
        1998 202
Marital status 108
Maternity 78
    additional leave 80
    compulsory leave 80
    dismissal 78
    ordinary leave 80
    pay 82
    protection 78
    returning to work 81
Maternity and Parental Leave Regulations
        1999 83
Maximum working week 70
Medical suspension 78
Mental impairment 110
Misconduct 131
Mistaken belief 134
Mitigation 145
Multiple test 34
Mutual agreement to termination 127
Mutual obligations test 33

National insurance contributions 73
National Minimum Wage Act 1998 1, 75
Negligence 4, 208
Night work 71
Non-analytical schemes (job evaluation) 102

Officious bystander test 40
Open book 219
Opted out shop workers 188
Ordinary adoption leave 83
Ordinary person test 32
Organisation test 32

Parental leave 83
Part-time workers 54
Part-time Workers Regulations 2000 55
Patents Act 1977 194
Paternity leave 82
Pay 72
    deductions 73
    definition 74
    statements 72
Personal Protective Equipment at Work
        Regulations 1992 201
Picketing 178
Plaintiff 11
Political influences 1, 2
Polkey rule 138, 145
Positive action 95
Pre-hearing review 20
Pregnancy see Maternity
Prohibition Notices 211
Property law 4
Protection from Harassment Act 1997 99
Protective awards 156
Provision and Use of Work Equipment
        Regulations 1998 202
Public Disclosure Act 1998 197
Public duties 84
Public holidays 69
Public interest disclosures 197

Race discrimination 109
Race Relations Act 1976 87
Race Relations Act 1976 (amendment)
        Regulations 2003 109
Racial and Religious Hatred Act 2006 3

Range of reasonable responses 131
Re-engagement 22, 142
Recognition (trade union) 169
Red circling 104
Redundancy 153
   consultation 154
   selection 156
   statutory redundancy payment 159
   suitable alternative employment 159
References 42
Referencing material 218
Regulations 7
Regulation of Investigatory Powers Act
      2000 186
Rehabilitation of Offenders Act 1974 63
Reinstatement 22, 142
Religious discrimination 116
Remedies 22, 93, 142
Remuneration see Pay
Reorganisation 134
Repetitive Strain Injury 204
Reporting of Injuries, Diseases and Dangerous
      Occurrences Regulations 1995 202
Resignation 127
Respondent 11
Rest breaks 72
Restricted book 219
Restrictive covenants 195
Retirement 121, 135
Revision 221
Right to Time Off for Study or Training
      Regulations 2001 85
Royal assent 5

Safety committees 210
Safety representatives 210
Settlement prior to hearing 20
Sex Discrimination Act 1975 87
Sex Discrimination (Gender Reassignment)
      Regulations 1999 88, 114
Sexual orientation 115
Sickness absence 130
Smoking 204
Social Chapter 1957 (Treaty of Rome) 1, 7
Social Charter 1, 7
Some other substantial reason 133
Statute 5, 39, 215

Statutory Ban 132
Statutory Dismissals and Disciplinary
      Procedure 18, 135
Statutory Grievance Procedure 137
Statutory Maternity Pay 82
Statutory Paternity Leave 82
Statutory Redundancy Payments 159
Statutory Sick Pay 78
Stress 206
Strike out (tribunal claims) 29
Summary dismissal 131, 151
Sunday Trading Act 1994 188
Sunday working 188
Surveillance 185

Telecommunications Regulations 2000 186
Temporary Workers 57
Time off 84
Torts 4
Trade Union and Labour Relations
      (Consolidation) Act 1992 2, 167
Trade Unions 167
   definition 167
   derecognition 169
   disclosure of information 172
   dismissal of members 119, 179
   independence 168
   industrial conflict 173
   membership 117
   picketing 178
   recognition 169
   safety representatives 210
   time off 171
Transfer of Undertakings 160
   consultation 164
   definition of a transfer 161
   ETO reason 163
   exchange of information 164
   protection 163
Transfer of Undertakings (Protection of
      Employment) Regulations 1981 160
Transfer of Undertakings (Protection of
      Employment) Regulations 2006 160
Transnational Information and Consultation
      of Employees Regulations 1999 179
Treaties 7
Treaty of Rome 7

Trust and Confidence 44

Varying a contract of employment 62
Vicarious liability 99
Victiminisation 95
Volenti non fit injuria 209

Wages 41, 74
Websites 216
White Paper 5
Wild cat strikes 177
Withdrawal of tribunal claim 21
Worker 31, 68
Work permits 64

Work related stress 206
Work rules 41
Working Time Regulations 1998 67
Working Time (Amendment) Regulations
    2003 68
Workplace (Health, Safety and Welfare)
    Regulations 1992 201
Written statement of initial employment
    particulars 36
Written statements - health and safety 210
Wrongful dismissal 148

Young Workers Directive 67